ALWAYS UNDER SIEGE

ALWAYS UNDER SIEGE

OLGA FREIDENBERG'S
DIARY-THEORY AND
THE EVERYDAY TERROR
OF STALINISM

IRINA PAPERNO

CORNELL UNIVERSITY PRESS
Ithaca and London

English-language edition copyright © Irina Paperno, 2026.

Original Russian-language edition, *"Osada cheloveka": zapiski Ol'gi Freidenberg kak mifopoliticheskaia teoriia stalinizma*, by Irina Paperno, © Novoe literaturnoe obozrenie, 2023.

All rights reserved. Except for brief quotations in a review, this book, or parts thereof, must not be reproduced in any form without permission in writing from the publisher. For information, address Cornell University Press, Sage House, 512 East State Street, Ithaca, New York 14850. Visit our website at cornellpress.cornell.edu.

First published 2026 by Cornell University Press

Librarians: A CIP catalog record for this book is available from the Library of Congress.

ISBN 9781501785825 (hardcover)
ISBN 9781501785832 (paperback)
ISBN 9781501785849 (pdf)
ISBN 9781501785856 (epub)

GPSR EU contact: Sam Thornton, Mare Nostrum Group B.V., Mauritskade 21D, 1091 GC, Amsterdam, NL, gpsr@mare-nostrum.co.uk.

Contents

Acknowledgments vii

Introduction 1

1. **"Overture" (1890–1917)** 18

2. **Blockade (1941–1945)** 25

   How Freidenberg Wrote—"Famine and the Total Abolition of Civilization"—"The Soviet Tiamat"—"Dependence, Hunger—and an Unbearable Lifelong Obligation!"—"Stalin's Blood-Soaked Regime and My Mother's Blindness Have Destroyed My Life the Way a Prison Does"—"Our Drama Was That We Were Locked Up and Crammed into a Common Crypt"—"Only a Catastrophe Could Get Us Out of This Underworld"

3. **After the War (1945–1950)** 48

   "A Second Birth into the World as a Corpse"—"Who Can Describe the Soviet Everyday?"—"This Is an Ordinary Soviet Day"—"Departmental Squabbles"—"Public Humiliation Was Revived"—"I Tear the Fabric of Time to Finish the Tale of My Last Love"—"The Archive Initiated Me into the Brotherhood of Universal Man"—"My Life Is Over. This Is Where I End Its Manuscript"—"Apparently, I Cannot Do Without These Notes"—"The University Has Been Ravaged"

4. **"To Fill in the Lacuna": From the University to the Last War (1918–1941)** 92

   "I Entered Petersburg University"—Petrograd Under Siege—"Entry into Scholarship"—"Entry into Academia"—"The Housing Question"—"I Lived Through Khona"—Tristan and Isolde—"My Department"—"Looking Back, You See"—"Your Book Has Been

Confiscated"—"I Don't Know How Historians Will Describe 1937"—"I Wrote My Autobiography for Him"

5. **The Mythopolitical Theory of Olga Freidenberg in the Context of the Political Thought of Her Time**   125

   The New Form of Government—Everyday Terror—The Biopolitics of the Everyday—Surveillance and Ideology—The Great Terror—The War of All Against All—The New Leviathan—Leadership: The Führer Principle and Political Religion—Concentration Camp or *L'état de Siège*—The Philosophy of History—Stalinism Introduced Many New Things—The Testimony of Lazarus

6. **"Conclusion" (1950)**   149

Appendix: The Russian Original of Major Quotations   153

Chronology of Olga Freidenberg's Life and Times   215

Notes   221

Index   241

Acknowledgments

This is a revised and amended English translation of the following Russian-language edition: Irina Paperno, *"Osada cheloveka": Zapiski Ol'gi Freidenberg kak mifopoliticheskaia teoriia stalinizma*. Moscow: Novoe literaturnoe obozrenie, 2023. Translated from Russian by the author.

This book is based on the autobiographical document ("notes," *zapiski*, as she called it) of the Russian scholar Olga Freidenberg (1890–1955). Throughout the book, Freidenberg's notes are quoted from the typewritten copies in the Hoover Institution, Stanford, California: Olga Freidenberg, *Memoirs, Holograph and Typescript* (Books 1–34). Box/Folder 155–159. Pasternak Family Papers. Key quotations are verified from the handwritten notebooks. Most citations include the notebook number (in Roman numerals), chapter number (after a colon), and page number (after a comma). In some notebooks, chapters are not numbered; in such cases, the notebook number is followed by a page number, after a comma. Deviations from this pattern of citation are explained in the endnotes.

Citations to other sources follow the standard practice: in endnotes, complete bibliographical information on each source is given in full the first time it appears in a given chapter.

A note on language: Throughout the main text of the book, the Russian text and Russian proper names are given in the Library of Congress transliteration system, adopting the traditional *–sky* and *–oy* endings (e.g., Frank-Kamenetsky, Dostoevsky, Tolstoy). The bibliographic references in the notes use solely the Library of Congress transliteration (e.g., Frank-Kamenetskii). In some cases, the names of the key figures contain the given name, the patronymic, and the family name with the Russian gender ending (e.g., Anna Osipovna Pasternak, Leonid Osipovich Pasternak, Iosif Moiseevich Tronsky, and Maria Lazarevna Tronskaia). The appendix provides key quotes in the original Russian, using Cyrillic script.

I wish to express my deep appreciation to all those who so generously helped me work on this book. I am profoundly grateful to Ann Pasternak

Slater, Elena Vladimirovna Pasternak, and other members of the Pasternak family for giving me the opportunity to work with the original manuscripts and photocopies before they were placed in the Hoover Institution (beginning in 2003).

The English text of this book benefitted greatly from extensive editorial suggestions offered by Caryl Emerson, Laura Engelstein, and Trevor Perri. I am grateful to Thomas Campbell and Chloë Kitzinger for their expert help in creating the English equivalents of the quotes from Freidenberg's notes. Alice Stone Nakhimovsky left her mark on every page with her masterful revisions. I am immensely indebted to her acumen, stylistic empathy, and extraordinary generosity.

I would like to express my gratitude to colleagues and friends whose critical and discriminating advice has been invaluable in forming and formulating this book's conception. Caryl Emerson, Laura Engelstein, Stefan-Ludwig Hoffmann, Anna Muza, Alice Stone Nakhimovsky, and Harsha Ram are among them.

I have benefitted from discussion that followed my oral presentations of some of this book's material at the international conference "Narrating the Siege: the Blockade of Leningrad and Its Transmedial Narratives" (Ludwig-Maximilians-Universität München, June 2015), the international conference "Poetry and Politics in the Twentieth Century: Boris Pasternak, His Family, and His Novel *Doctor Zhivago*" (Stanford University, September 2015), and invited lectures at Princeton University (March 2016); Humboldt Universität, Berlin (June 2016); Indiana University, Bloomington (October 2019); and University of California, Berkeley (June 2020).

Like many authors and readers across the world, I owe an enormous debt to the publishing house Novoe literaturnoe obozrenie and its editor-in-chief Irina Prokhorova for everything they have done over more than two decades to create a space for free intellectual exchange and international encounter.

I thank Novoe literaturnoe obozrenie for granting permission to include materials in this book that were previously published in two articles—Irina Paperno, "'Osada cheloveka': Blokadnye zapiski Ol'gi Freidenberg v antropologicheskoi perspektive" [The siege of human being: Ol'ga Freidenberg's notes from the Leningrad blockade in an anthropological perspective"], *Novoe literaturnoe obozrenie* 139 (2016): 184–204; reprinted in *Blokadnye narrativy: Sbornik statei*, ed. P. Barskova and R. Nicolosi (Moscow: NLO, 2017), and Irina Paperno, "'Eto dazhe ne blokada i ne osada. Eto prostoi, obydennyi sovetskii den': Poslevoennye zapiski Ol'gi Freidenberg kak mifopoliticheskaia teoriia" [This is not even the blockade or a siege, this is an ordinary

Soviet day: Ol'ga Freidenberg's postwar notes as a mythopolitcal theory], *Novoe literaturnoe obozrenie* 178 (2022): 7–27.

I am very grateful to the editors at Cornell University Press for their trust and judicious revisions.

And I owe a very special debt to Johanna Renate Döring, without whom this book would have not been possible and whose support I treasure deeply.

I.P.

ALWAYS UNDER SIEGE

Introduction

I

"From the first days of childhood, as soon as consciousness awakened in me . . . I had the feeling that nothing within me or outside of me was simply itself, but that everything had a meaning" (I–II, 1).[1] The Russian scholar Olga Freidenberg (1890–1955) wrote these words in 1947 on the opening page of her autobiographical chronicle—a story of her life and times. Freidenberg ultimately settled on a title, *The Race of Life* (*Probeg zhizni*), but as she wrote, she referred to her unfolding text as "notes"—*zapiski*, a traditional Russian designation for a versatile autobiographical genre.[2] Freidenberg then remarked that, under different circumstances, she might have become religious, but growing up in a secular family of Russian Jews, she followed another path in pursuit of life's meaning: literature. Unlike her first cousin, Boris Pasternak, with whom she was close, Olga Freidenberg had no artistic talent. She became a philologist: a scholar of language, myth, and literature.

The idea of life's meaning embedded in literature was one that Freidenberg shared with many in her cohort of scholars. Rooted in the philosophical thought that shaped the humanities at the turn of the century, it was formulated by Wilhelm Dilthey as a part of his conception of the "human sciences" and his hermeneutic method. In 1945, Hannah Arendt summarized Dilthey's ideas this way: life, or, rather, "lived experience" (*das Erlebnis*), is embedded in history and expressed in forms of art and in autobiography. Accordingly, one finds the highest type of man in the artist, who alone is truly "alive." And what if the gods have refused a person the necessary poetic talent? Then, your best option is to interpret artistic expression. The scholar becomes a kind of artist secondhand, and in this capacity a model human being, endowed with understanding.[3]

Looking from the vantage point of 1945, Arendt, a Jew born in Germany, was not inclined to adopt Dilthey's optimistic vision of humanity or history, hence her irony. Living in New York, where she had taken refuge at the beginning of World War II, Arendt was preparing her analysis of the political systems of Nazism and Stalinism, which she called totalitarian. But when, at about the same time, Freidenberg wrote about her enduring belief that everything has a meaning, her words were devoid of irony. She was nearing the end of a long academic career, much of it as a professor of classical philology at Leningrad University. Freidenberg was acutely aware that while she had physically survived Hitler's siege of Leningrad, it was by no means certain that she would survive a new wave of Stalinist repressions that was aimed at isolating the country from the West.

For Freidenberg, who kept her notes so as "to convey to paper and ink an account of the Stalinist days" (XXI: 6, 11), the assumption that life has meaning, the idea of history, and the hermeneutic method were equipment for living in a world assaulted by a "double barbarism, Hitler's and Stalin's" (XVIII: 138, 10). She sometimes addressed a bewildered future historian: "The historian will not understand" (XXXII: IV, 77). But more than addressing any particular reader, Freidenberg was writing for history—"an objective suprahuman process ... in which a single human life forms a part" (XXVI: 75, 57).

Since the 1970s, Olga Freidenberg, who gained little recognition in her lifetime, has been hailed as one of the most remarkable cultural figures of her age. As a theorist, she has been compared to such authorities as Mikhail Bakhtin and Yuri Lotman.[4] As a classical philologist, she has found both enthusiasts and critics.[5] Her lifelong correspondence with Boris Pasternak, first published in 1981 in New York, was translated into a number of languages, attracting considerable attention. Scholars commented on the paradoxes of Freidenberg's posthumous reputation—on the belated recognition that turned her innovative ideas into harbingers of the discoveries of others; on the difficulty of criticizing a scholar who had such a tragic life; and on the clash between her admirers and detractors.[6]

It is also known that Freidenberg left a gigantic autobiographical document, preserved in secrecy, which, unlike her scholarship, has remained largely unpublished and unknown. Written over a decade, from 1939 to 1950, in several installments, Freidenberg's notes are at times an autobiography or memoir, at times a diary or quasi diary. They cover almost the whole of the author's life and half of the twentieth century. Handwritten in thirty-four notebooks, the notes amount to about two and a half thousand pages in typescript. The account of her early life, from 1890 to 1917, written in the winter of 1939–1940 in the form of an "autobiography" (her definition), fills two notebooks sewn into one (later numbered I–II, this text comes to 180 typewritten pages). The notes that cover two crucial periods—the blockade of Leningrad in 1941–1944 (notebooks XII-bis to XX, or 572 typewritten pages) and the postwar repressions in 1946–1950 (notebooks XXI to XXXIV, or 635 typewritten pages)—were written as a diary or retrospective diary. This is a record composed several weeks or months after the events, in part on the basis of loose notes made at the time. In one period, the winter of 1948–1949, Freidenberg simultaneously wrote two accounts. In one set of notebooks, she recorded current events; in another, she wrote her "biography" (her word), covering the years 1918–1941 (notebooks III–XII, or more than a thousand typewritten pages).

Without a doubt, at the center of the chronicle stand the notes from the Leningrad siege (or blockade of Leningrad). When Freidenberg brought her writing to an end in December 1950, she saw her whole life as divided between "before the blockade" and "after the blockade." She gave the nine notebooks the subtitle "The Siege of the Human Being" (*Osada cheloveka*).[a] The image of siege acquired a symbolic meaning: life under siege, which she explicitly equated with confinement in a concentration camp, became a field experience for understanding the condition of unfreedom in the Soviet Union. "In Russia," she wrote, "whether there is a blockade or not . . . a person is always under siege. . . ." (XIII: 59, 88).

Pursuing life's meaning, Freidenberg applied a special "method" (she often used this word). In her personal writings, she not only relied on general hermeneutic principles but self-consciously used specific techniques drawn from the methodology she had developed and employed as a scholar (she called it "genetic semantics").[7] Thus, Freidenberg saw mythological plots and patterns in her life story (she once wrote that her biography followed the archetype of dying-and-rising gods) and relied on metaphor to reveal meaning in routine daily experiences. Attentive to genesis (her word for the origin and evolution of literary forms), she often saw the present as a return

---

[a] In her title, Freidenberg uses the gender-neutral Russian word *chelovek*, which denotes a human being. In this book, I sometimes translate *chelovek* as "man" and sometimes, following current conventions, as "human being" or "person."

of the past and the past as a prototype of the present. She consistently used the strategies of ethnographer and autoethnographer. And she offered theoretical conclusions about her life and about life in general. Once, during the blockade, reflecting on her life and work as she lay in bed on a bitterly cold but air raid–free night, she concluded, "I have never been able to make barriers between scientific theory and the immediate apprehension of life; one has been the expression of the other" (XVI: 122, 17). Equipped with the tools of a humanist's trade, she attempted to extract meaning from her tangled life. And first and foremost, she focused on the horrors of war and terror that seemed to exceed the power of understanding and representation.

Committed to her overall idea of meaning and to hermeneutics, Freidenberg used not only different generic frames—autobiography, diary, memoir—but, as her vision of the world changed, also different strategies of meaning-making, or interpretation.

The "autobiography" of her early years, intended for a specific reader, a man with whom she was in love, presents her childhood, adolescence, and youth as life submerged in an ocean of family love, which made her anticipate other kinds of love yet to come. And she theorized "love" as a "special Weltanschauung" that endowed even trivial experiences with the "deepest symbolism" (XI: 91, 201).

The blockade notebooks are similar to the field diary of an ethnographer, a participant-observer. This is a record of life under catastrophic conditions, when the smallest routines became significant in the struggle for survival. Blaming the desperate situation of the city inhabitants on both Hitler and Stalin, Freidenberg wrote that, given the state system of food rationing in the besieged Leningrad, one was forced to "swallow and defecate under coercion" (XIII: 37, 15). The siege also distorted relationships between family members who shared meager and unequal food rations, turning intimacy, as Freidenberg made clear, into a pernicious bond of mutual dependency. In the notes from the siege, everything that took place is not only semioticized ("everything has a meaning") but also politicized: Freidenberg sees the workings of power in every aspect of daily life. This experience proved to be definitive, both in its traumatic impact on her subsequent life and in its influence on her vision of the world. From then on, Freidenberg viewed everything that happened to her, in public or private, as political.

The notebooks from the postwar years also include elements of ethnographic description, from accounts of everyday hardships to analysis of relationships between family members, friends, lovers, neighbors, and colleagues caught in repressions. After the war, Freidenberg decided that the state deliberately maintained a system of "difficulties" that amounted to "everyday terror" (*terror bytovoi*) (XXVIII: 19, 84). She also carefully describes the unfolding of ideological campaigns against "cosmopolitanism" launched after the war. Her focus is on what she experienced daily in her work at Leningrad University, where repressions targeted departments of humanities. Freidenberg concludes that the ideological attacks on methodologies accepted within the humanities and the administrative "purges" of academic personnel generated petty "squabbles" (*skloki*) between colleagues, as a result of which nobody could live in peace or "breathe freely" (XXV: 63, 9). Hoping to aid a future historian, she offers a detailed documentation of repressive measures, like protocols of meetings and official memoranda. She believes that "what happened at the university ... was no different from what went on in any Soviet institution" (XXX: 12, 57). With this in mind, she makes carefully formulated generalizations about the workings of the Stalinist regime in daily life, at home and at work. Moving into the postwar years, the image of the siege turns into a metaphor used to describe life in the Stalinist state: *l'état de siège*.

Freidenberg's reflections on the ascent of Stalin and generalizations about the workings of the Stalinist system also pervade her "biography," or, rather, the memoir about her life between 1918 and 1941, written simultaneously with the chronicle of the year 1948–1949, the peak of the repressions. The dual vision throws a retrospective light on her earlier life and on the first decades of Soviet power, which she now sees as a prelude of the future tyranny.

In this book, I contend that Freidenberg's autobiographical chronicle contains a systematic, though not always explicit, political theory of life under conditions of unfreedom. Her conclusion is that "Hitler and Stalin, two tyrants, created a new system of government, unknown to Aristotle" (XXVIII: 7, 47). Seeking to describe and analyze the working of this system, she subjected the seemingly trivial course of her daily life to anthropological and political analysis. Freidenberg's notes, I argue, dissolve the distinction between the recording of lived experience and theoretical reflection, be it a semiotic theory of life's meaning or a political theory of the new system of government. Her notes constitute a record of daily life infused with theory. I call this fusion a diary-theory.

How does theory emerge from a diary (or similar record)? For one thing, Freidenberg consistently describes everyday life in language that relies on analytical categories and conceptual metaphors of the kind used by political philosophers, from Plato and Aristotle to Machiavelli and Hobbes to Arendt and Agamben. The notion of the body politic (*corpus politicum*) serves as her organizing metaphor. In describing Stalinist society, she makes imaginative use of the mythological image of the monstrous body of Leviathan as well as the concept of war of all against all, which she modifies to fit the new system. In this sense, I call her theory mythopolitical. And in drawing analogies between the society and the human body, she locates the workings of power in physiological life, offering analysis we now call biopolitical.

Remarkably, one can see parallels between some of Freidenberg's private thoughts about the new form of government and categories, concepts, and conclusions advanced (in a much more developed and disciplined form) by Western political thinkers of her time, like Carl Schmitt, Walter Benjamin, Leo Strauss, Karl Löwith, and Hannah Arendt, as different as these theorists are from each other. Writing in Stalinist Russia, under conditions of strictly enforced cultural isolation, Freidenberg could hardly have read any of these authors, which makes these strange echoes all the more significant.

The parallels between the thinking of Freidenberg and Arendt are especially striking. Like Freidenberg, Arendt, in *The Origins of Totalitarianism*, written in the 1940s, was convinced that Germany under Hitler and Russia under Stalin had introduced a political system that "differs essentially from other forms of political oppression known to us."[8] For Arendt, who, like Freidenberg, was trained as a classicist, the concept of politics was also rooted in Plato and Aristotle, and she measured the new form of government in relation to this standard. Arendt, like other theorists of her time, used Thomas Hobbes, in whom she saw a theoretician of totalitarianism *avant la lettre*. So did Freidenberg. Both Arendt and Freidenberg understood concentration camps—Hitler's and Stalin's—as laboratories of total domination. Arendt and Freidenberg, each from her own perspective, saw Nazi Germany and Stalinist Russia as two versions of the same model of government. And both of them approached the new regime as generating a new kind of historical experience, providing—in very different forms—an anthropology of historical experience of sorts.[9] Using the same analytical categories, images, and methodological moves, drawn from common sources, Arendt and Freidenberg also relied on their own experiences. And while they came to many similar conclusions, in some respects, they thought differently. The differences are as striking as the similarities. For one thing, after World War II, the veneration of history as a teleological process with redemptive power, a view to which Freidenberg fully subscribed, became alien to Arendt as well as to other Western political thinkers.

Freidenberg created her political theory from inside a totalitarian regime, writing from within the beast, so to speak, and in the only form that was available to her: a private chronicle. In her notes, she accumulates the experience of the Stalinist everyday: persistent food shortages; forced housing in communal apartments in which several families, each locked in a single room, share a kitchen and toilet; mutual surveillance in homes and in the workplace; and all-embracing ideological control. All of this, she argues, distorts human relations in families, homes, and offices. Freidenberg thus locates the new form of government within the ordering of everyday life. But the daily experience of totalitarianism was largely unknown to Arendt, who had never lived in a communal apartment or worked in a Soviet university. What is more, Arendt wrote from a distance, and, for Hitler's regime, after the fact. By contrast, Freidenberg self-consciously wrote her analysis as a participant observer, immersed in unfolding events. In this respect, Freidenberg's analysis—theory from the inside—differs from, and supplements, that of her contemporary in the West as well as other students of historical experience.[10]

Needless to say, in her private notes, Freidenberg could not possibly do what Arendt, a professional political theorist and public intellectual, accomplished in her treatise. But in her own way, Freidenberg also wrote for the benefit of the public. Fully aware of the danger involved in keeping her notes, she wrote for the future reader and for "history": "And though I do not know whether [these notes] will see the light of day (who will hide them? where?), I do not want to give up what I consider my duty to history. . . . It's better to risk one's life and write in secret" (XXXII: I, 45).

Freidenberg was also aware of her limitations, and she found it necessary to comment (in parenthesis) on the shortcomings of the notes, which she valued more than her life: "(my notes are free from coercion, incoherent, inconsistent, and written in poor language, reflecting an exhausted and impoverished brain)" (XXVII, 83, 12–13).

Indeed, although a powerful writer, a master of theoretical formulations, Freidenberg did not always write well. There are relentless repetitions, which may seem obsessive, as well as inconsistencies and verbosity; there are passages and pages written in awkward or sloppy language. She usually wrote rapidly and always without a draft.[11] (The reader will not necessarily see these flaws: admittedly, I mostly cite examples of masterful writing.)

Freidenberg also knew that writing was a matter of psychological necessity, an instrument of survival. There is an emotional poignancy to what she wrote. Like many diarists, she used her notes to express and master painful emotions. The notes are infused with anger, grief, despair, disdain, and, occasionally, resentment. And some of Freidenberg's political judgments and opinions about other people who were caught, alongside her, in the tangle of repressions show self-delusion and prejudice. The text reflects the conditions of its writing, and, as Freidenberg wanted the reader to know, in its very form, it testifies to the damage done to the author, body and psyche.

Writing in private—as far as we know, nobody saw her notes in her lifetime—Freidenberg defies certain rules of propriety. Her chronicle offers a merciless vision of herself and others, complete with ugly and disgusting details that are excluded even from most blockade diaries. In part, this can be explained by Freidenberg's position as an ethnographer. Thus, describing the blockade, she provides a record of the workings of the starving body, including the circumstances of digestion and elimination, as well as a picture of a home and a city covered in excrement. In her tormented mind, she feels that there are ways in which the Soviet regime reached each person, "in his bed and his toilet" (XXIX: 3, 12). Chronicling the postwar purges in Leningrad University, she reports not only on the actions of the administration and party leadership but also on the squabbles among her immediate colleagues. Resorting to metaphor, she calls these ugly dealings "the discharges of Soviet academic sewage" (XXV: 71, 43). Freidenberg renders harsh judgments of her colleagues' and students' behavior and does not shy away from showing a person "with his pants down," in both the direct and metaphoric sense (XXVIII: 17, 78).

For Freidenberg, such acts of exposure served political analysis. Thus, she came to see "squabbles," extending from "petty, trivial animosity" to "informing, slandering, and spying," as the "alpha and omega of Stalin's politics" and his "methodology" (XXXIV, 150). Under her pen, the everyday—including the disgusting—acquired an interpretation that turned an account of quotidian experience into ethnography and political theory. In her wartime and postwar notes, Freidenberg provides a self-conscious analysis of such practices from the position of both an observer and a participant, and there is little wonder that at times her own image may seem unappealing. In some ways, she shows herself, too, with her pants down.

We, distant readers, cannot question either Freidenberg's view of life in Soviet society, however unattractive the resulting picture may seem, or the high pathos of history and theory that underlies these records, created under the threat of arrest and annihilation. But the duties of a reader-researcher involve subjecting personal documents to analysis.

In *The Human Condition*, Hannah Arendt wrote about spaces within which "the greatest forces of intimate life" are "transformed, de-privatized and deindividualized, as it were, into a shape fit for public appearance." She saw this in art—in the "artistic transposition of individual experiences." But, Arendt added, we do not need "the form of the artist" to show such transfiguration. In fact, "each time we talk about things that can be experienced only in privacy or intimacy," we bring them out into the public sphere, and thus into the domain of the political.[12] In her private notes, Freidenberg did even more. She explicitly spoke about the forces of intimate life as political phenomena that embodied a new form of government, "the Stalinist system," and prepared her secret chronicle for a possible public appearance sometime after her death.

The story of Freidenberg's archive is a testimony to the times in which she lived and to our own times, and it deserves a comment. After her death in 1955, most of Freidenberg's personal papers and her unpublished scholarship were stored in a large iron chest, bequeathed to a trusted friend, Rusudan Orbeli. They seem to have remained in that chest, unopened, until the early 1970s.[13] Yuri Lotman may have been one of the first people to look inside.[14] In 1973, he published some of Freidenberg's unknown articles in the Tartu edition of *Semiotice*, complete with an introductory essay in which he claimed Freidenberg as a predecessor of the semiotic method he advanced and propagated.[15] At about the same time, the classicist Nina Braginskaia, who became actively involved in publishing Freidenberg's scholarly manuscripts, found a bundle of Boris Pasternak's letters at the bottom of the chest. Thirty-four notebooks containing Freidenberg's private chronicle of her life, the existence of which was unknown to family and friends, also came to light.[16] In the mid-1970s, the notebooks and letters were passed on to Boris Pasternak's family in Moscow. Four copies of the notes were typed up in secret, and then the originals and one typescript were smuggled out of the Soviet Union, most likely through diplomatic channels, and deposited in the Pasternak Trust in Oxford (established by the family of the painter Leonid Pasternak, Boris's father, who left Soviet Russia in 1921).[17] In the fall of 2015, the notebooks, along with many other documents from the Pasternak family archive, were handed over to the Hoover Institution at Stanford, where they are now accessible to researchers.

When the Pasternak–Freidenberg correspondence appeared in print in New York in 1981, prepared for publication by Pasternak's son Evgeny Borisovich Pasternak and his wife, Elena Vladimirovna Pasternak, some extracts from Freidenberg's notes appeared between the letters. At that time, the correspondence, politically subversive by Soviet standards, could not be published in the Soviet Union. To protect E. B. and E. V. Pasternak, their names were not listed in the American edition. Only after 1988 did several editions of the correspondence, complete with the extracts from the notes, appear in Russia.[18] Two longer excerpts were published, in Russian, in 1986 and 1987 in the Paris émigré press. One, entitled "The Siege of the Human Being," dealt with the Leningrad blockade; another, "Will There Be a Moscow Nuremberg?," focused on the repressions of the late 1940s. The editor, under the pen name Nevel'skii, was the Moscow classical scholar Iudif' Matveevna Kagan, daughter of the philosopher Matvei Kagan, a member of Bakhtin's "Nevel circle."[19] These excerpts made a strong impression on the few readers they reached.

In 2013, long after the end of the Soviet regime, Freidenberg's still unpublished notes became the subject of impassioned debate after the historian Petr Druzhinin used extracts in his monumental documentary history of the postwar repressions at Leningrad University, *Ideology and Philology*, published in 2012.[20] The historical veracity of Freidenberg's chronicle, and her character, too, came under attack, in part due to her harsh treatment of fellow scholars. Irina Levinskaia, a classicist from St. Petersburg, was moved to defend the reputations of her teachers. She claimed that Freidenberg, whose work as a classical philologist she did not respect, had described colleagues who were her critics and rivals in scholarship as secret informants given to devious scheming. A retort came from Nina Braginskaia, who said that Freidenberg was "one of the purest persons I've ever known, and nobody can throw a stone at her." She also admitted that she had refrained from publishing Freidenberg's notebooks for several decades. While, for obvious reasons, the notebooks could not have been published under the Soviet regime, Braginskaia attributed later delays to other problems: the sheer magnitude of the text, the need for the careful preparation of a scholarly edition, and also the fear of hostile reactions like Levinskaia's. She then claimed that a fully digitized version of the notebooks is locked under a password on the Freidenberg Electronic Archive website and "can be opened in one click."[21]

While touching on intellectual issues like what constitutes historical evidence in a diary or memoir, this exchange shows the considerable emotional investment the Russian academic community had placed in personal documents of the Soviet experience, even two generations down the line. And for whatever the reason, to this day, more than ten years later, the notes have remained unpublished.

Unlike some of my Russian colleagues, I do not feel that Freidenberg's image as a scholar and person is tainted by her engagement with the ugly reactions of the human body and psyche to tyranny, be it her painfully frank descriptions of how she eats and defecates under duress or her minute records of the departmental squabbles in which she herself participated. There is no doubt that Freidenberg wrote to be read by posterity. And she was aware that, like many of her contemporaries, she had not emerged from her trials intact or unscathed. For me, the fact that, in its very form and tone, the notes show us a damaged life and tormented mind makes this document doubly precious.

What is more, I believe that Freidenberg's notes—an intimate record of life coinciding with the Russian Revolution, two world wars, and several waves of Stalinist terror, written as it was by a philologist and cultural theorist skilled in the use of narrative, metaphor, genre, and the conceptual apparatus of cultural theories—are very special, if not unique. Many diaries and memoirs of the Soviet experience have reached us.[22] Among them, Freidenberg's notes are exceptional in scope, form, and insight, as well as in their self-conscious aspiration to theorize.

An important comparison can be made with Victor Klemperer's gigantic private chronicle of life in Nazi Germany and in the German Democratic Republic, also composed and preserved at great peril. Klemperer, a philologist by training, offered remarkable insights into everyday life under Hitler, though, unlike Freidenberg, he did not offer theoretical reflections on the Nazi regime. And while Klemperer's remarkable diaries, which are not free from self-delusions and the petty complaints of a frustrated academic, have been admired by readers across the world, Freidenberg's notes from Stalinist Russia have remained in an archive.[23]

There is one other personal document from this era in which the author drew theoretical conclusions about the existential and political meaning of daily life under siege—the "notes" (she also used this word) about the Leningrad blockade written by Lidiia Ginzburg (1902–1990), a specialist in Russian literature. Like Freidenberg, though not as consistently, Ginzburg perceived the situation in the besieged city as similar to the condition of camp inmates; she spoke about "well organized hunger" and commented on the enmity that ruled among the starving people. And she also used Hobbesian metaphors and drew analogies between the dystrophic bodies of citizens and the body politic that contained them.[24] Freidenberg and Ginzburg most likely did not know about each other's efforts, even though, by a strange coincidence, they lived within 350 meters of each other, on opposite sides of the Griboedov Canal.[25] In the chapters that follow, I briefly mark some of the similarities between the two accounts. In doing this, I want to suggest that not only was Freidenberg's experience of the Leningrad siege and Stalinist terror shared by other people, but, unbeknownst to her, her very special way of understanding this experience was also silently shared.

Totalitarian regimes, as Arendt claimed, created conditions of "organized loneliness,"[26] and this certainly rings true for the Soviet situation. And yet, as we see from Freidenberg's example, cultural isolation and organized loneliness notwithstanding, people remained connected by a common language and common ideas, whether they lived across the street in a besieged city or on different sides of the world divided by an iron curtain.

The primary task of this book is to bring Olga Freidenberg's notes to light, specifically to readers in the West. Freidenberg wondered, "Do they know [about us] abroad?" And the hope that people abroad might find out how people were living in the Soviet Union gave her "the strength to die in peace" (XXV: 72, 49). In the chapters that follow, I try to both introduce the Western reader to this remarkable text, still unpublished, and provide its interpretation as a very special form of diary-theory.

How does one make sense of more than two thousand pages of a loosely organized personal document? Freidenberg's notes move among several modes, fusing them together. We see a harrowing account of physical, social, and moral suffering, especially during the siege of Leningrad in World War II and the internal repressions of the postwar years. We follow the attempts on the part of a scholar—a philologist and cultural theorist—to make the traumatic experience meaningful by using the methods and instruments of her profession, such as ethnographic description, mythological metaphors, and more. And finally, we face a highly original attempt to articulate a theory of politics and society under Stalin's rule on the basis of the description of daily life. To capture the workings of this multifaceted text, I use different interpretive lenses, focusing on the workings of Freidenberg's autoethnography, her expert use of myth and metaphor, and her theorizing. I use the concept of diary-theory and the notion of mythopolitical theory to integrate the multiple descriptive modes and analytical approaches employed in this work. Freidenberg's text is central to this study, and I offer long quotes. The appendix lists the key quotes in the Russian original.

Because my primary goal is to present Freidenberg's notes as a source that offers theorized insights into key moments of twentieth-century history, rather than provide a biography of their author, I have chosen to present the notes in the order in which they were written and not in the order that follows the chronology of the author's life. Thus, chapter 1 presents the account of Freidenberg's early years, from the beginning to 1917, written in 1939–1940. Chapter 2 presents the notes made during the Leningrad blockade in 1941–1944, which she wrote next. Chapter 3 follows with Freidenberg's chronicle of the years 1945–1950, dominated by Stalinist repressions. In chapter 4, the reader is exposed to the chronicle of Freidenberg's earlier life, between 1918 and 1941, which she wrote in 1948–1949, and here we see the workings of retrospective understanding: the history of Freidenberg's earlier life shows how the author's present casts a distinct shadow on the past. I hope that the brief outline of Freidenberg's biography that follows and the chronology of her life and times at the end of the book will help the reader's orientation.

As one of the aims of the book is to reveal the mythopolitical theory of Stalinism that underlies Freidenberg's chronicle, I pay special attention to the parts that document the Leningrad blockade and the postwar repressions, in which political analysis is of paramount importance. The brief early autobiography and the long memoir of Freidenberg's middle years are present in my book, even though they receive less attention. A separate chapter contextualizes Freidenberg's conception of Stalinism in the political thought of her time, with some excursions into our time, and I put Freidenberg in dialogue with theorists like Hannah Arendt and Giorgio Agamben. This form of presentation entails repetition. Repetition, which is inherent in the diary form, is especially important to Freidenberg as she shows the accumulation of experience that leads to her theoretical conclusions, and my book follows her in this strategy. Throughout the book, I aim to highlight the methods and strategies by which this unique diary-theory was created and to demonstrate that the diary form had implications for the shape of the conceptions embedded in it. This approach involves attention to Freidenberg's writing process, and at several points, I try to reconstruct, step by step, how Freidenberg reached her conclusions in the act of writing. Freidenberg's contributions to scholarship come up inasmuch as her scholarly methodology and conceptions overlap with her life writing, and I rely on existing research on Freidenberg as a student of culture.

First and foremost, this book presents a remarkable document of human life in dark times, an account of historical experience that shows us strategies of physical and moral survival that are inextricable from acts of self-understanding and from the process of writing.

Historians of the Soviet Union, World War II, and the Cold War have assembled considerable evidence of their own, guided by their own methodological principles. They have occasionally attempted to deal with the Stalinist everyday, in different ways.[27] And historians, along with social theorists, have addressed the highly controversial issue of comparing Nazism and Stalinism.[28] But Freidenberg's contemporaneous account may nonetheless prove illuminating. Intellectual historians may be drawn to the way this document presents the clash between the humanistic ideals of meaning-making and life writing, advanced at the turn of the twentieth century, and the dark political visions and political theories formed in the interim between the two world wars, after World War II, and beyond.

Freidenberg's notes have a special significance for today's Russian readers, who are again pondering how to live when power seems to penetrate into one's bed, into one's toilet, into one's body, and into one's deepest self, turning one into an accomplice. It is a familiar picture of a life steeped in daily compromises and self-delusions. But it is not only Russian readers who may benefit from this extraordinary record of living in a state of siege, with its keen vision of a disintegrating society and its merciless picture of institutional life torn by petty enmities between colleagues who are involved in what today we might call "culture wars." With these caveats, I offer this story to English-language readers, most of whom have so far lived under very different circumstances than the Soviet scholar Olga Freidenberg.

II

Readers about to be confronted with the story of Olga Freidenberg's life as she recorded it might find a brief biographical summary useful. Additionally, at the end of the book, there is a detailed chronology that puts the outline of Freidenberg's life and works into the context of Soviet history.[29]

Olga Mikhailovna Freidenberg was born on March 15, 1890, in Odessa, a major seaport on the Black Sea in the southern part of the Russian Empire, today's Ukraine. Odessa's motley, multiethnic population included a large number of Jews, who were unusually cosmopolitan. Freidenberg was born and raised in a secular, assimilated Jewish family and spoke Russian as her first and main language. She had two older brothers: Alexander, born in 1884, who looms large in her notes, and Evgeny, born in 1887, who died in 1901. Both her parents came from traditional Jewish families of moderate income. Her mother, Anna Osipovna Pasternak (1862–1944), married Mikhail Filippovich Freidenberg (1858–1920) against the wishes of her parents. A man of many talents and occupations, including actor and journalist, Mikhail Freidenberg became a self-taught inventor who patented several devices in image projection, book printing, and telephone communications, none of which were put to commercial use. The parents' marriage was stormy and the family's income uneven. The Freidenbergs kept in close contact with the family of Anna Osipovna's brother, the painter Leonid Osipovich Pasternak, and Olga was particularly close to her first cousin Boris, the future poet, born the same year as she was.

Both families left Odessa for major cities that presented greater opportunities: Leonid Pasternak in 1889 for Moscow; the Freidenbergs in 1903 (by some accounts, 1901) for St. Petersburg. The two families continued to spend summers together. In 1904, in St. Petersburg, Olga, whose home tutoring had included instruction in several European languages, began studies at the well-known private gymnasium of E. M. Gedda. She graduated in 1908. As higher education was restricted for both women and Jews, Olga led a private life for some years. She read voraciously, regularly attended theater performances, and traveled extensively, mostly alone, through Switzerland, Germany, Italy, and Sweden. At that time, the family enjoyed relative prosperity, supported by the sale of the patent for her father's major invention, a telephone exchange.

In 1910, a grown-up friendship began between Olga Freidenberg and her cousin Boris Pasternak. This friendship, conducted in rare meetings and intense correspondence, lasted until her death—though after 1936, the cousins did not see each other.

In August 1914, when World War I broke out, Freidenberg returned to Russia from a sojourn in Sweden. During World War I, she worked as a volunteer in the city hospitals, assisting the wounded. After the war, she had no further opportunities to leave the country. She left the city (known after 1914 as Petrograd, later Leningrad) only twice, for short trips to Moscow, in 1929 and 1936.

After the Russian Revolution of 1917 abolished restrictions on university study for women and Jews, Freidenberg enrolled in Petrograd University, first as an auditor, and then, after 1919, as a regular student, specializing in classical philology. Already a mature student, she was well read in Russian, French, English, and German.

In the winter of 1919–1920, during the Russian Civil War, when Petrograd was under siege, Freidenberg's father died of disease and starvation, and Freidenberg herself fell gravely ill. It was then that, still a student, she started working on her first serious work of scholarship, a study of the early Greek-language Apocryphal text "The Acts of Paul and Thecla."

In 1921, Leonid Pasternak left Soviet Russia with his wife and daughters and settled in Berlin. His sons, Boris and Alexander, stayed behind in Moscow.

Freidenberg's graduation from the university in 1923 was followed by difficult years of unemployment and underemployment. And for years, she largely supported herself and her mother by selling the family's prerevolutionary possessions at a flea market. In 1924, Freidenberg defended a dissertation, "The Origins of the Greek Novel," based on her study of "The Acts of Paul and Thecla." The dissertation featured an innovative conception of the origins of the novel, which Freidenberg traced to Christian hagiography and, through that, back to myth. In spite of all her efforts to bring this pioneering work to the attention of scholars in Soviet Russia and abroad, it remained largely unknown. Later, a Western scholar, unaware of her discovery, advanced a similar conception, which has been widely accepted in classical philology.

Freidenberg encountered considerable difficulties in her attempts to enter academia. That she even defended her dissertation was due to the patronage of the influential scholar Nikolai Marr (1865–1934), who found her idiosyncratic approach to the "genesis" (origin and evolution) of literary forms congenial. Marr held a privileged status in the Soviet academic establishment that lasted well beyond his death (his ideas would fall into disfavor with Stalin in 1950). Beginning in 1925, Freidenberg obtained part-time positions and unpaid affiliations with several research institutions, including, after 1926, with the so-called Japhetic Institute, controlled by Marr. In the institute's section for the study of mythology, she began collaborating with Israel ("Khona") Frank-Kamenetsky, a biblical scholar and student of mythology. She was soon linked to this married colleague by deep bonds of friendship and love.

Beginning in 1927, several of Freidenberg's scholarly works appeared in print. In 1931, a study of the myth of Tristan and Isolde, coedited with Frank-Kamenetsky, was published (with Marr's name as the editor). Her dissertation on the origins of the Greek novel remained unpublished, save for a fragment that appeared in 1930 in the journal *Atheist*, for lack of other venues. Over her lifetime, Freidenberg would publish twenty research articles, one monograph, and a number of short abstracts. More than a hundred publications appeared posthumously, beginning in the early 1970s.

In 1929–1930, Freidenberg, her mother, and her brother Alexander were threatened with the loss of the apartment they had inhabited from before the revolution, and the family's struggle to limit the assault on their space, which she described in her notes, was, for a time, all-consuming.

In 1930–1932, after years of marginal professional existence, Freidenberg was given responsible research and administrative tasks in Soviet academia. In 1932, she was appointed chair of the Department of Classical Philology at Leningrad University. The department had reopened after a hiatus dating from the postrevolutionary years; it was now rebuilt, with her active participation.

In the autobiographical notes written in 1948–1949, Freidenberg described herself in the early 1930s as a "Soviet person" intent on "building new things" (VII: 56, 247). She linked her gradual disillusionment with Soviet power to the ascent of Stalinism, beginning with the public purges and arrests that started after the assassination of Sergei Kirov in 1934. In 1935, she defended her second dissertation, published the following year under the title "The Poetics of Plot and Genre." Shortly after publication, the book was sharply criticized in a major government newspaper and withdrawn from circulation. This event, like the struggle over the apartment, received detailed description and documentation in her notes.

In the Great Terror of 1937–1938, Freidenberg's brother Alexander and his wife were arrested; the family never found out that he had been executed in Leningrad on January 9, 1938. Another tragedy of 1937 was the death of her beloved friend and collaborator, Khona Frank-Kamenetsky, in a traffic accident. That same year, her correspondence with Leonid Pasternak's family, still in Berlin (the Pasternaks moved to Oxford in 1938), was interrupted because of the danger of maintaining connections with the West.

In 1939, Freidenberg fell in love with another married colleague, who appears in her notes as B. (there is no need to identify him). That winter, she wrote an autobiography focused on her early years that was addressed to him; it would later become the first section of her extended autobiographical chronicle. Those were the years of the Soviet annexation of parts of Poland (1939) and other areas in the western borderlands in the wake of the Molotov–Ribbentrop Pact (1939) and the war with Finland (1939–1940). Judging by her notes, some made at the time, Freidenberg followed these events with horror and shame. She watched with horror the unfolding of World War II in Europe, especially the fall of Poland, for which she blamed both Hitler and Stalin.

After the start of the Nazi–Soviet War on June 22, 1941, Freidenberg remained in Leningrad; she survived the blockade, but her mother did not. She started keeping regular notes on May 3, 1942, to document what was happening. The notes were interrupted after her mother's death on April 9, 1944, and resume in June 1945, after the end of the war. During the blockade, in spite of the catastrophic conditions, she wrote several works of scholarship, all of which remained unpublished.

At the war's end, Freidenberg resumed her position as professor at Leningrad University and chair of the Department of Classical Philology. Stalin's repressive campaigns targeting "the pernicious influence of the West" and "cosmopolitanism" started in 1946. In her notes, Freidenberg carefully documented how those campaigns unfolded at the university. After the war, her love for B. continued, occupying a large part of her notes. She kept her notes until December 1950. In the postwar years, she continued working on her scholarship, completing several book-length studies, but was able to publish only short abstracts. Under pressure, she stepped down from her position as department chair in 1949 and retired in 1951. For the next three or four years, she worked on a major study, *Image and Concept*, which remained unpublished in her lifetime.

Freidenberg died of cancer on July 6, 1955.

Chapter 1

"Overture" (1890–1917)

When Freidenberg started writing her "autobiography," as she called it, in the winter of 1939–1940 for the object of her love, a man she refers to as B., her early years—from her birth in 1890 up to the 1917 Russian Revolution—appeared to her as an "introduction," or "overture," to her life, in which she traced the motifs that developed in the future. Self-conscious about her task, she also reflected on the idea of autobiography. When, years later, in 1947, Freidenberg assembled her unfolding "notes" into a single whole, she made this story, written in two notebooks (I–II), its first part.[1]

In these notebooks, Freidenberg speaks of herself as a sickly, pensive child immersed in an ocean of all-encompassing, boundless love—first and foremost, maternal love (I–II, 5a). And from her earliest years, she was immersed in literature and art. On the first page, Freidenberg describes her mother telling her the love story of Tatiana and Onegin (from Alexander Pushkin's *Evgeny Onegin*). She remembers "that day, hour, and the setting," and now, recalling that scene, she understands its significance: this was "the appearance of another, second, world"—the world of art (I–II, 1). Her experience back then was "a sense of the greatest revelation of life's meaning." Art, she elaborates, "generalized, penetrated, built a second plan that made the living me into a creator of life" (I–II, 3). This first revelatory encounter with literature created a feeling that Freidenberg described on the opening page of her assembled notes as a sense that "nothing within me or outside of me was simply itself, but that everything had a meaning" (I–II, 1).

The story of Freidenberg's earliest years does not follow a chronology and does not relate external circumstances. The opening chapters convey moments—images, scenes, feelings—drawn from scattered childhood memories. Analyzing such moments, she makes generalizations about their significance: these early experiences are prototypes of the life to come.

Later, as befits an autobiography, Freidenberg describes her family, highlighting their difficulties and idiosyncrasies. Her devoted mother, "proud, self-willed, impulsive," kept the house and made demands on the family (I–II, 24, 36). Her father, a "self-taught man" who became "an outstanding European inventor," was subject to sinful passions, and he struggled to feed the family (I–II, 26–27). Her talented and impulsive brother "Sashka" (Alexander) did not conform to any social norms and conventions, causing the family much grief. The painful death of her other brother, Evgeny, who died of appendicitis when she was eleven, plays an important role in her story. And she presents her first awareness of her body as an encounter with illness and pain. She also speaks of an early awakening of sexual passions. Freidenberg carefully introduces the family of her revered uncle, her mother's older brother, the painter Leonid Osipovich Pasternak. His son "Borya"— Boris, the future poet—born the same year as Freidenberg (she calls him her "brother," her "twin")—occupies a very special place in her life.

The autobiography does not deal with many things one might expect. Odessa, the city of her birth, is barely mentioned. Freidenberg's story is centered in Petersburg, where the family moved when she was about twelve years old. Of the family's Jewishness, Freidenberg says very little, but she makes clear that it was unimportant. In a sweeping dismissal, she describes her family as free from all kinds of "prejudice," be it religion, ethnicity, or "caste" (I–II, 1).[a]

What Freidenberg focuses on are the first books she read (not children's books, but Russian classics, Pushkin, Mikhail Lermontov, Nikolai Gogol); the paintings she saw (mostly in reproductions); her first, breathtaking encounter with cinematography (*The Temptation of St. Anthony*, which her father brought from a trip to London and projected on a home screen); and her first opera (*Lohengrin*, seen on a family trip to Paris). These images, she claims, remain as memorable and familiar as scenes from her own life.

---

[a] Such an attitude was not at all unusual for her milieu and generation. In her autobiographical writings, Lidiia Ginzburg, whose background was in many ways similar to Freidenberg's, was also emphatic about ignoring her Jewish origin.

Describing her entry into the social world, when, at age fourteen—after years of home schooling—she enrolled in a private gymnasium, Freidenberg takes a different tone. Becoming a "social person" led to painful difficulties, a conflict between her "inner life" and "social conventions" (I–II, 56). From then on—and she writes this at a moment when she is facing problems at the university—her life in the social world would always be accompanied by "persecutions and slander" (I–II, 55).

Of specific people outside her family, one of the most important is her gymnasium teacher of Russian language and literature, Olga Vladimirovna Nikol'skaia (later Orbeli), with whose family she would remain in contact for the rest of her life. (Orbeli's daughter would become Freidenberg's executor and the keeper of her archive.) Freidenberg describes her intense friendship with Elena Lifshits, a classmate. The connection with Elena, her "sister-friend," her "twin," which often burdened her, would also last for the rest of her life.[2]

Freidenberg writes about trips abroad, undertaken in part to improve her health, which was threatened by tuberculosis; she describes the mastering of languages, encounters with art, and the inexpressible "feeling of freedom" experienced in Europe. (It is worth noting that when she was writing this in the winter of 1939–1940, life in the Soviet Union had reached a peak of isolation and unfreedom.) She writes about Switzerland; about Germany, which she did not love; about "beautiful Italy"; and about how she "fell in love with countries and people" (I–II, 110). She describes her passions and romances. Her meeting with Boris Pasternak, then a student of philosophy in Marburg University, in the summer of 1912 in Frankfurt (which figures in Pasternak's early novella *Safe Conduct*) plays a significant role. War, as she presents it, interrupted this romantic period. At the outbreak of World War I, Freidenberg was in Sweden, where she fell in love with a pastor whom she contemplated marrying. But in August 1914, she made the difficult journey back to Petersburg. One thing she does not mention is that after 1914, she would never leave the country again. In November 1914, "a new life began": she became a volunteer nurse, a "sister of mercy" (*sestra miloserdiia*), working with the war wounded in the Petrograd hospitals (I–II, 145).

The autobiography ends with a brief description of the 1917 revolution. The war ended; the work in the infirmary was over. The Russian Revolution opened access to higher education for women, and devastated by her recent experiences, Freidenberg entered the university, enrolling (first as an auditor) in the 1917–1918 academic year (I–II, 179). Her autobiographical narrative ends here, with the date on which she finished writing: February 11, 1940.

Much of Freidenberg's autobiography, especially its early parts, is written in a lyrical style reminiscent of Boris Pasternak's early prose, like his story of a girl's childhood, *The Childhood of Luvers* (*Detstvo Luvers*, 1918), or the autobiographical *Safe Conduct* (*Okhrannaia gramota*, 1931). Several principles link her first writings to Pasternak's: the depiction of the intense inner world of a child; the notion of a second plane of being, the world of "images" or art; and the idea of childhood as a prototype for the life to come, with the catastrophic future transparently present in seemingly trivial early experiences.[3] It is safe to assume that Pasternak's powerful prose influenced Freidenberg's writing, but this is not all: Freidenberg's writing is rooted in the shared world of their childhood, adolescence, and early youth.

Emphasizing their shared inheritance, Freidenberg provides long quotes from Pasternak's effusive letters to her, in one of which, from July 23, 1910, he relates their conversations: "I spoke to you about the childhood of one's inner world, which bound us together. And not even spoke, but maybe listened to your recollections of it. But gradually this romanticism of the spiritual world, which distinguishes childhood and culminates at the age of fifteen or sixteen, takes on the external world, which up to that point we had merely observed, grasped its characteristic features, and imitated it, whether able or unable to give expression to it" (I–II, 76).

This conception of childhood as the domain of inner life—the spiritual life that eventually catches up with the outer world, which is hard to grasp—seems to inform much of the story of Freidenberg's early years.

What is also reinforced with Pasternak's letters copied into the notebook is the theme of love. Freidenberg writes suggestively about her cousin's letter: "Twenty-one pages! It was a letter full of a young, strong feeling that dare not speak its name" (I–II, 78). She was twenty years old, she then explains, when Borya's visit to the Baltic resort of Merrekühl (Meriküla), where the Freidenberg family was spending the summer of 1910, turned into something very special (I–II, 69). What followed, in 1910, was an intense period in their lives when the cousins exchanged philosophical letters imbued with "spiritual passion" (I–II, 80). And, as she makes clear, both of them remembered the meeting in Merrekühl, the train journey to Petersburg, the walks through the city, their conversations, and their passion for the rest of their lives.

Pasternak in his letter and Freidenberg in her notes, which incorporate this letter, speak about a shared world they then created, in which one could speak for the other. The young Pasternak, the future poet, played the main role in this world as its primary voice: "I did not yet know that Borya would be a poet, and that it was given to him to speak lyrically for everyone. In this letter he expressed all of himself, but also all of me" (I–II, 78). And at the time she wrote this, Freidenberg still held on to the idea that poetry, and the poet, can speak for "everyone."

As the cousins took long walks through the streets of Petersburg, they engaged in somewhat one-sided philosophical conversations:

> He talked, usually for hours, and I walked in silence. I must admit that I understood almost nothing of what he said. I was immeasurably behind Borya in development, and his vocabulary was incomprehensible to me. But I was enraptured and fascinated by the vastness that his deep, thoughtful, and somehow new words opened up. A new world was being erected, incomprehensible, but fascinating. I was not at all striving to know the exact weight and meaning of each phrase. I could love the incomprehensible; what was new, vast, rhythmically and spiritually close to me led me away from the ordinary to the edge of the world. (I–II, 72)

She makes clear that Pasternak, her brother and teacher, who resembled "no other earthly being" (I–II, 72) and whose mesmerizing, albeit incomprehensible words led her to the other world, played a most important role in her life story. But she also implies that as time went on and she matured, the "brother" and "sister" came to represent two different ways of observing and expressing the world: the artist's way and the (literary) scholar's way.

And as she writes about this view of life some thirty years later, Freidenberg is also speaking in her own mature voice, that of the scholar. She describes her way of thinking using literary analysis: "From an early age, there smoldered in me an interest in the forms that life took, in its metamorphosis and transformations. . . ." (I–II, 117). Now, in her middle years, her life as viewed through the prism of literary theory appears to her as a chain of such metamorphoses, which transformed her early experiences and her early artistic impressions in ever new guises: new forms of love, new forms of the conflict between the inner world and social conventions, new attempts to find expression for the inexpressible. And it follows that her scholarship, focused on literary forms and their evolution, is well suited for the description of an individual's life. Having come to this conclusion, Freidenberg advances an important thesis, claiming that literary scholarship, like art, services double duty as autobiography: "And after all, scholarship, like all creative work, is autobiography. And when I later began to develop the theory of literary forms, the semantics of meaning that gave birth to form; when I strived to encompass the diversity and variety of forms within the unity of semantics reincarnated in them—I did nothing but speak about the life of my soul and my body" (I–II, 117).

To understand what this means in a larger intellectual context, we may recall Dilthey again, even though Freidenberg does not mention his name. In his blueprints for the "human sciences," including literary scholarship,

Dilthey viewed autobiography as the "highest and most instructive form of understanding life," in which "the path of life" (an external manifestation of its inner essence) is captured in a narrative representation of one's experiences, shaped by literary forms. In the twentieth century, many a literary theorist followed this line of thought, some affirming, others challenging that life can be expressed in that way.[4] As a scholar, Freidenberg developed her own strategies of linking "life" and "form." Thus, in accordance with the principles of her scholarly method ("genetic semantics"), she envisioned the course of human life—and therefore the narrative form of autobiography—as the transformation of meaning shaped and reshaped by a multiplicity of forms. And as she worked on her theory of literary forms in her professional practice, she came to understand the shape and meaning of her own inner and outer life. (As her notes progressed, Freidenberg continued to unfold this fanciful conception of autobiography, and we will continue to trace her ideas.)

Concluding the story of her early life, Freidenberg describes her first experiences as an "introduction and an overture"—to the life to come: "I did not know that this was the beginning of my life at its major turning point. That everything I had experienced was only an introduction and an overture.... And that only now my infatuations and passion would begin, along with true love...." (I–II, 179). As for the idea of the future "true love," let us recall that this was addressed to her beloved, for whom she wrote these notes.

Ten years later, in 1949, when she was recounting the story of her life between 1917 and 1941, Freidenberg described how she worked on this autobiography during the cold and miserable winter of 1939–1940, after the beginning of World War II. She kept her life going by writing the autobiography of her early years "for him" (XI: 92, 208). The two notebooks were essentially a declaration of love at the time of war. B. read her notebooks with intense attention (or so it seemed to her), and he was impressed by Freidenberg's kinship with Pasternak: "He is your brother not only by blood!" (XI: 90, 192). But the reading did not bring Freidenberg and B. any closer, and this threw her into despair. Her feelings persisted, and throughout the notes, Freidenberg continued to describe everything related to her unrequited love for B. as deeply significant, even though she realized that he was an insignificant man and not necessarily even a decent one.

In 1949, looking back at her first autobiography, Freidenberg formulated her conception of love: "Love is a special Weltanschauung. Time stops. There is no duration in it. Everything that has been, remains living in all its details . . . if it's connected 'with him.' Every trifle receives a special significance. Nothing perishes or disappears. Everything requires interpretation, everything is full of the deepest symbolism" (XI: 91, 201).

According to this conception, love is one of the mechanisms of meaning-making, which stops time and preserves the experience forever in images or symbols that require interpretation. In part, this idea prefigures what, much later, Roland Barthes wrote in a work that fused autobiography with semiotic theory, *A Lover's Discourse* (*Fragments d'un discours amoureux*, 1977). Reflecting on the painful experience of love (and, in his life story, love for his mother stood side-by-side with erotic love, often unfulfilled), Barthes spoke about the "signifying economy of the amorous subject." As he put it, love creates meaning out of nothing, and in this sense, love is "a kind of festival not of feelings but of meaning."[5]

Viewed in the context of her notes, Freidenberg's first autobiography can indeed be viewed as an "overture" to the story of her whole life. As we see in the chapters that follow, the themes and motifs of this introduction—her mother's love, the second world of art, the discrepancy between the inner and the outer, the social world, the ailing body, and institutional conflicts and slander—are repeated and developed throughout the notes. So is her theory of meaning and her conception of autobiography. But with the invasion of Hitler's army into the Soviet Union in June 1941, a new force entered Freidenberg's life and her notes. Without abandoning the pathos of love and meaning that informs her early autobiographical writing, she employed another strategy of understanding: the political hermeneutics of catastrophic experience.

CHAPTER 2

Blockade (1941–1945)

Historians have written about the devastating nature of the war between Nazi Germany and the Soviet Union during World War II—fought, on both sides, with extreme, unrestrained violence. For military historians, it was a war characterized by the "barbarization" of warfare. The Third Reich invaded the Soviet Union with overwhelming force, aiming at extermination by any means. The murder of Jews in the occupied territories is the most horrifying example of the Nazi policy of total extermination. Overall, Soviet losses and sacrifices were horrendous, and the Soviet response became increasingly brutal. Another complication noted by historians is that both sides were pursuing a war against external enemies as well as internal enemies among its own population.[1] With everything we know about World War II, it would not be an exaggeration to say, as many historians have done, that the siege of Leningrad (*blokada Leningrada*) between 1941 and 1944—when, by some estimates, between eight hundred thousand and one million people, or roughly half the city's prewar population, died from starvation and enemy fire—was a campaign in which the cruelty of the war manifested itself with particular force, resulting in urban catastrophe.[2]

Many people wrote diaries and memoirs about the Leningrad blockade.[3] And in Russia today, the history of the Nazi–Soviet War (in Soviet historical terminology, the Great Patriotic War) has acquired strong political resonance. The memory of the Leningrad siege has become a subject of sharp controversy among politicians, historians, and ordinary citizens.[4]

How Freidenberg Wrote

Freidenberg opened a notebook to write about her war experiences on May 3, 1942, beginning with what had happened since the war began on June 22, 1941, almost a year earlier. Like other blockade diarists, she describes the conditions in the besieged city: the brutal bombardment and artillery fire, the severe food shortages and starvation under a state system of food distribution, the collapse of city services like water supply and sewage disposal, the bitter cold in unheated buildings, and the deteriorating relationships among family members, neighbors, and friends. But in other ways, she writes differently. This chapter begins by outlining Freidenberg's strategies.

First and foremost, Freidenberg's vision is intensely political. Her aim is to systematically document the unfolding catastrophe, focusing on what, on the very first page, she identifies as a double evil—"war with Hitler" and "our politics" (XII-bis: 1, 1).[5] When she speaks about air raids or artillery fire, she assigns the blame to both "the Germans," who "killed Leningraders with inhuman cruelty" (XII-bis: 17, 40), and the city authorities, who failed to protect the civilian population (XII-bis: 17, 44). When she writes about food shortages, she focuses on the state system of food distribution, which, in her desperation, she presents as a total failure: "Day after day, week after week, a human being was given nothing to eat. The state, having taken upon itself the task of feeding people and forbidding them to trade, procure, and exchange, provided absolutely nothing" (XII-bis: 29, 80).

Freidenberg's observations of the situation in the city as a whole and its political causes are interspersed with descriptions of how she and her mother lived. We learn that, for some time, they had been supplementing their rations with supplies they had collected in 1937 after the arrest of Freidenberg's brother. At the time, there had been no opportunity to send him care packages. But these supplies were coming to an end. Sharing meager food rations, and confined to one room heated by a makeshift stove, Freidenberg and her mother were locked in a condition of mutual dependency she calls "tyranny," and family life was increasingly dominated by petty feuds and quarrels. Freidenberg meticulously describes their situation.

Describing the everyday routines of life under siege—"how we lived"—with the methodical thoroughness and merciless objectivity of a field ethnographer, Freidenberg also does something else: from the very first page of her notes, she speaks about the "theoretical significance of the events"

(XII-bis: 1, 1). And she soon comes to the conclusion that the blockade is a situation of complete unfreedom: "No one had any choice in anything, no opportunity for freedom or escape" (XII-bis: 23, 62).

About three weeks after she started to write, on May 27, 1942, Freidenberg's story reached "today," and for a while, her account became a diary: "May 27, 1942. There was an air raid at night. Mother could not sleep. . . ." That same day, Freidenberg describes the condition of her emaciated body, speaking in terms of bodily structure: "Today I donned my childhood coat. . . . I am practically no more. My body has wasted away while I am alive. I have the structure of an eight-year-old." She speaks about the catastrophe and ponders the future: "It's time to face this catastrophe. What could one wait for, hope for?" (XIII: 59, 90).

On that day, she decided that life under siege felt like prison confinement: "This is how an inmate of a concentration camp must feel. . . ." (XIII: 59, 89–91). On another occasion, resorting to metaphor, she calls the siege "a domestic concentration camp" (XV: 108, 5). Later, she explains the similarity: "A person is placed, as in a concentration camp, in a hopeless situation" (XVII: 127, 12). She also uses other symbolic frames, describing the siege as life in the underworld, where she and her mother have been forced by "a bloodthirsty serpent." She is clear that by the serpent—the ruler of the underworld, like the monstrous Leviathan—she means Stalin (XIX: 163, 71).

The winter of 1942–1943 was extremely cold, exacerbating the situation. As the winter cold set in and ink froze solid, Freidenberg stopped writing. She resumed her notes in the spring of 1943, again reconstructing the events and experiences of the preceding months. For the most part, the blockade notes are a "retrospective diary."[6]

Freidenberg's chronicle follows a calendar cycle. After the horrors of the first blockade winter came the "resurrection" and "transfiguration" experienced of the spring of 1942: post and telegraph resumed working, and the relaunch of the streetcars was "a great symbolic event" and "a true Christian transfiguration" (XIII: 53, 70–72). Here, as elsewhere, Freidenberg resorts to the mythological symbolism of death and rebirth. She describes seasonal holidays (New Year's Day) and birthday celebrations. Special food was saved for those days, but after these feasts, she and her mother became ill because their starving bodies could not digest rich food. The respite was followed by a second horrible winter (1942–1943) and then another spring. The actions of the city administration repeated themselves: "the same holidays, handouts of food, shameful delays of rations, starvation" (XVII: 127, 11; April 1943). The third winter (1943–1944) brought new torments. Freidenberg did not see much relief in the Soviet offensive that broke the line of encirclement, announced on January 27, 1944 (XV: 111, 11–13). The third winter was overshadowed by the serious illness of Freidenberg's mother, which she describes in minute, harrowing detail.

Sometimes, she recalls specific days: on "16 January [1943]," it was bitterly cold, and there was no food in the house; "we were perishing," she writes. Crying in her cold bed late at night, Freidenberg appealed to "life" for "mercy." And the very next day, life sent them a gift: her student Nina suddenly appeared on their doorstep, bringing bread, butter, and sugar (XVII: 128, 13). Freidenberg would recall this day more than once. She remembered other times: January 26, 1944, was "a day when all winter miseries were at an apogee." The temperature dropped to minus thirty degrees Celsius. Cold wind penetrated the entire apartment though windows shattered by enemy fire. The last crumbs of the food rations were eaten. The wood stove emitted acrid smoke. There was a fierce air raid at night. Then, an artillery attack lasted the whole day (XV: 112, 15). Commenting on this day, Freidenberg switches to political language: "Where could a person hide from the enemy-aggressors who besieged him, from the state, from the tyranny of friends and foes, from this enormous and powerful system of violence, in which freedom was disregarded?" (XV: 112, 15). Here, as elsewhere, she sees enemies everywhere. An all-embracing system of oppression comes from both the enemy and one's own state, from both strangers and friends, leaving a person "besieged" from all sides. Here, Freidenberg uses the siege as a metaphor for the human condition under tyranny.

Still describing that January day, Freidenberg moves to a philosophical meditation on life and its variability: "Yes, this day, like many others, was experienced and lived through. But life, even life in the USSR, in Russia, cannot remain monochromatic, even in a besieged city among besieged people" (XV: 112, 15–16).

Elsewhere, "life" appears as a mythological category: "Life protected me and carefully led me on a difficult path over an abyss." And on this occasion, Freidenberg comments on her strategy: "Generalizing and symbolizing, as always, life's manifestations . . . I saw in this unexpected fact . . . the deep essence of mother-life" (XIV: 96, 72–73).

Referring to herself and her mother, she asks: "How have we lived? How have we lived through these years?" (XVIII: 154, 79). And she answers her own question: "[We lived] like everybody else: not looking ahead to the future and not thinking about tomorrow. People, perishing, have all learned implicitly to live two inches at a time. Time has cramped, shriveled up, and frozen" (XVIII: 154, 79–80).

In Freidenberg's chronicle, the question "how have we lived?" reaches far beyond the description of the everyday, eliciting both philosophical and political reflections. Describing a peculiar sense of time that added to an overwhelming feeling of isolation, Freidenberg also thinks about the political aspects of the situation, surmising that nobody outside the besieged city knew what life was like there, especially people abroad, because they were offered only the falsified "official" version. And so, the people locked in Leningrad—"people living without water and sewage, targeted by day by shrapnel shells, bombarded from the air by night"—perished in obscurity (XVII: 129, 15). She bitterly laments that official propaganda created a fictitious world that has nothing to do with real life or social reality: "Life is horrible. It is replete with torments, and it consists in its social essence solely of fictions" (XVII: 133, 33). As Freidenberg notes on more than one occasion, even worse for the inhabitants of Leningrad was that the horrible conditions of everyday life under the siege passed for "normal life": "Life in its humiliating downfall went on as normal" (XVIII: 157, 87).

On another occasion, lamenting that people outside Russia "did not know," she once again equates the siege to the situation of concentration camp inmates, unfolding this metaphor: "International public opinion did not know, did not suspect that the besieged city languished in a domestic concentration camp, where human beings were subjected to violence, death, all the horrors of starvation and struggle with physical nature, all the deprivations suffered by beings cast off and exploited by the state" (XV: 108, 5).

In her desperation, Freidenberg sees the Leningrad blockade as a double assault in which two tyrannies joined forces. In her view, the shelling of the city that lasted for hours, day after day, in all neighborhoods, was "a double barbarism, Hitler's and Stalin's" (XVIII: 138, 10). Further, she explains that while "the Germans" targeted peaceful citizens, women, and crowds of civilians (XVIII: 142, 25), "Soviet power" demanded that people show up for work exactly on time, and consequently, people would find themselves on the streets, rather than in bomb shelters, during the attacks (XVIII: 138, 9). She concludes, "This was a double barbarism. . . ." (XVIII: 142, 25). And then she describes the desperate situation in one sentence with two subjects, "the Germans" and "our tyrant": "The Germans pounded the streetcar stops and all the places where the public congregated, the peaceful unarmed public that our tyrant forced to live and work on the front line. The streetcars turned into a bloody mess" (XVIII: 155, 80). Here as elsewhere, Freidenberg's account seems to be motivated by her desire to preserve "how we lived" and to break through official "fictions."

And amid all this horror, Freidenberg experienced "rare but sublime hours" alone with her scholarship (XVII: 133, 33). She describes one such moment: on February 25, 1943, in the dead of night, after yet another quarrel with her mother, she lay in bed reflecting on the problem of form and content, which had long been an object of her philological studies, and was able to imagine those categories extending far beyond their original sphere to the mysteries of the universe: "The problem of form and content is the problem of life and fate, of nonbeing and divinity, of cosmos in the physical and spiritual sense. Living and suffering, working as a scholar on texts and books, I nurtured this one passionate question, posed to the silent universe" (XVI: 122, 17). In the dead of a cold night during the blockade, while nurturing a problem that other scholars in a similar situation might consider an academic matter, Freidenberg formulated her life strategy: "I could never set up barriers between scientific theory and the immediate apprehension of life; one was the expression of the other" (XVI: 122, 17). Alone, "in the darkness of the night," without friends and students, "without books," "without rights," tormented by life, she felt that the theoretical question about the relationship of form and content and, along with it, "quite profound philosophical conclusions about myself and about life in general" might be revealed to her (XVI: 122, 18). Even under these circumstances, she thought—and wrote—about life in general and about her own life in the theoretical terms that had originated in her scholarship. Later on, the nine blockade notebooks (XII-bis–XX), collected under the title "The Siege of the Human Being" (*Osada cheloveka*), would form the central part of Freidenberg's extended life chronicle.

In many ways, the picture that emerges from this chronicle corresponds to what we know from other personal accounts. Like others caught in the blockade, Freidenberg took upon herself the task of documenting the living conditions, focusing on her own situation. Like them, she wrote in the consciousness of the historic significance of everyday life under blockade. But this is not all she did. Detailed ethnographic observations aimed at creating a faithful account of the peculiar blockade everyday stand side by side with conclusions that are formulated in terms of philosophical anthropology and political philosophy. Viewed from this perspective, the blockade figures as a laboratory of sorts for the investigation of the human condition, focused on the condition of extreme isolation and complete unfreedom created by what she sees as Hitler's and Stalin's two-pronged assault on humanity. And she put the methodological instruments of the contemporary humanities to use in analyzing this situation.

In the remainder of this chapter, I present several moments from Freidenberg's extensive blockade notes. The presentation is divided into sections focused on distinct themes or stories, and while following thematic lines, I try to proceed in chronological order.

"Famine and the Total Abolition of Civilization"

Using, as we have seen, the forms of "diary" and "retrospective diary," Freidenberg's record is written from the position of a participant-observer, as defined and practiced by the anthropologist Bronislaw Malinowski (whom she does not mention but whose work she knew).[7] Freidenberg uses anthropological categories: people ate what they could, she reports, "getting used to the raw rather than the cooked" (XVIII: 139, 12). She compares emaciated women with bloated stomachs, who fed on raw food, to members of a primitive tribe—"myself included," she adds (XVIII: 139, 12). She describes how, sitting by the fire of a primitive stove installed in the kitchen, "in her soul," she prayed to the god of fire to whom "all ancient mankind prayed" (XIV: 99, 81). She explicitly speaks of society's enforced regression to a primitive stage of "famine and the total abolition of civilization" (XVII: 134, 45). Now, the country "was living in the Stone Age" (XVIII: 138, 11). (And Freidenberg was not alone in making this observation.)[a] The society in which she lived resembled the type described by anthropologists—and for Freidenberg, a student of myth and ancient cultures, the similarity may have been an additional justification for assuming the position of an ethnographer and autoethnographer.

From this perspective, she describes every physical and social aspect of the "eating process" (XIV: 89, 45): the quantity and quality of food items, ways of cooking, manners of eating, quarrels over food (in the bread line and in her family kitchen), and digestion and excretion. She describes the "structure" of the bread they ate and the structure of the excrement: "The bread was so horrible that it came out in the feces as undigested particles . . . as whole heaps of the same structure it had before digestion . . . as if this were bread, not excrement" (XII-bis: 29, 81). There are things that are usually trivial, but now, under siege, they are often dramatic and always significant.

As Freidenberg documents the collapse of the institutions of urban civilization, it occurs to her that the residents of Leningrad have been "handed over to the power of nature": "We were no longer protected by everything that civilization had developed over many centuries. We had no houses, no dwellings, no fuel, no warm clothing, no running water or toilets, no sewage disposal to carry off human waste, no food, no light, no protection of the law" (XV: 111, 13).

---

[a] Lidiia Ginzburg also commented on the "the secondary barbarism" in the blockade, and she also located the reasons for this in the conditions of the everyday: "With the collapse of everyday routines [*byt*], man acquires caveman ways, a caveman's attitude to fire, to food, to clothing." Lidiia Ginzburg, *Zapisnye knizhki. Vospominaniia. Esse* (St. Peterburg: Iskusstvo, 2002), 727.

On second thought, she sees things differently. Deprived of modern conveniences, people were not turned over to the power of nature but to the coercive power of a state equipped with modern institutions and technology: "The whole day was spent in overcoming unfortunate everyday obstacles that human civilization had long forgotten; these obstacles were intensified by the fact that they did not unfold in nature, but through complex machinery of state violence and the most complicated twists and turns of an advanced technology aimed at destroying and torturing people. Neither Robinson [Crusoe], nor Paleo-Asiatic peoples knew taxes, ration cards, airplanes, or artillery fire. . . ." (XV: 113, 17).

True to this idea, throughout the blockade notebooks, Freidenberg carefully follows the workings of social institutions that organize everyday life in besieged Leningrad—the system of food distribution, new forms of exchange and gift giving (invaluable gifts of food and fuel received from friends and students), the changing relationships within the family, and more.

Throughout her account, Freidenberg is preoccupied with the mechanisms of power, big and small. She pays special attention to the system of privileges in food distribution: "There were different categories of people, different categories of rations. . . . It was not permitted to talk about them" (XIII: 37, 15). She comments on the consequences: "Some people died with blue lips, suffering from diarrhea, while others strode home carrying proteins, fats, and carbohydrates in their backpacks" (XIII: 37, 15). And she comes to the powerful conclusion, masterfully formulated: "[Man] was forced to eat and defecate under coercion" (XIII: 37, 15). Describing a dynamic that contemporary scholars would call biopolitical, she sees basic physiological processes like eating and defecating as objects of coercion by state power.

From the position of an ethnographer who is attentive to the workings of political power, Freidenberg makes observations about her own body: "My God, how emaciated and ugly I was. . . . Hips, breasts have disappeared. Full-breasted since I was a girl, I found myself castrated, as if this were not the structure of my body" (XIII: 52, 67–68). While speaking in professional terms ("the structure of my body"), she is imbued with horror, and her observations are highly personal; she is afraid that, even if she were to meet B. in the future, she would no longer be a woman. Intensely political in her vision, even in this intimate moment, Freidenberg blames power—that of Hitler and Stalin: "One winter with Hitler-Popkov, and the woman in me is finished!" (XIII: 52, 68). (Popkov was the head of the Leningrad municipal administration.)

Freidenberg then makes generalizations. Observing her own body and her mother's, she claims that "certain functions and features of human organs have changed" (XIII: 52, 69). She speaks about herself and about all blockade women as a new anthropological type: "And we all became like this. Women without hips, without breasts, without bellies, women with male structure" (XIII: 52, 68). She mentions that women stopped menstruating; there were no pregnant women. She generalizes that during the first blockade winter, both "women and men lost their natural characteristics." She notes that changes in the structure of the facial bones were in evidence as well. She was especially struck by the changes in the shape of the scull and forehead. How horrifying, she remarks, "when in front of your eyes human nature changes. . . ." (XIII: 52, 68–69).

Focusing on the changes in the functioning of human bodies, Freidenberg pays close attention to a topic that other chronicles of the blockade tend to avoid: the products of bodily waste. She notes that "there was no person or family, no apartment without acute diarrhea, sometimes up to nineteen–twenty times per day" (XIII: 34, 3). She describes the condition of the houses and city spaces: "The yards, the floors, the streets, the snow, and the squares were all flooded with a stinking yellow sludge" (XII-bis: 31, 86). She relates the condition of her own home in technical detail, with figures: "The communal apartment above us flooded us with excrement. I took out up to seven pails of feces every day, waiting for the moment when the excrement was hot and fresh, otherwise it would freeze in ten to fifteen minutes, creating an impossible situation" (XII-bis: 31, 86).

As she describes what is disgusting in the human body and human behavior, including her own, Freidenberg does not hesitate to transgress the generally accepted rules of propriety. At the center of a painstaking description of how she and her mother try to evacuate from the city on a train filled with university faculty stands the shame and embarrassment of academic colleagues forced to defecate in public. Breaking off an intellectual conversation, they relieve themselves near or under the stalled train, often in view of each other and always within reach of each other's senses. She does not spare details of the sounds and smells and she gives the names of those involved. This situation played a major role in her desperate decision to return home while the university proceeded to evacuate to Saratov (this decision would have grave administrative consequences for her). Merciless to herself, Freidenberg describes how, upon returning home, she lost control over her bodily functions at the apartment's threshold: "The hot liquid rushes out and floods my legs, my dress" (XIV: 77–78, 12–21).

When fragments from Freidenberg's blockade notes appeared in print, such descriptions, related to her own everyday under the siege and that of others, shocked some readers. A comparison with Bronislaw Malinowski's *Diary in the Strict Sense* comes to mind. In this personal diary of ethnographic observation, Malinowski recorded his disgust at the everyday hygienic conditions in which he had to live in the field, detailing his bodily ailments along with his often-unflattering opinions about the "natives." Malinowski's diary was published in 1967, many years after his death, and caused a scandal in the academic community. Here is how the anthropologist Clifford Geertz described the "squabbles" (his word) among the readers scandalized by the publication: "Much of the shock seems to have arisen from the mere discovery that Malinowski was not, to put it delicately, an unmitigated nice guy. He had rude things to say about the natives he was living with, and rude words to say it in."[8] So did Freidenberg.

"The Soviet Tiamat"

In one of the most remarkable episodes of her notes, Freidenberg, the participant-observer, deploys the mythological image of the chthonic goddess Tiamat to encapsulate the fall of civilization. The calamity that calls this symbol forth seemed to her worse than all previous trials: it was a flood of sewage that backed up in her bathroom. Trying to describe this catastrophe, she thinks of what she had experienced already: flooding from above (through the ceiling), overflowing sinks, bulging toilets. Her initial metaphor may be biblical: "Once upon a time, suffering consisted in 'drinking the cup to the bottom': that was how ancient man metaphorized misfortune. But in Soviet life, the metaphor for misfortune was a cup running over. . . ." (XV: 115, 25–26). Here, Freidenberg makes her method clear: she "metaphorizes" (to use her term) the sinks and toilets overflowing with sewage to create a new symbolic image: a cup of excrement running over. She may, indeed, be making ironic use of the biblical line "My cup runneth over" (Psalms 23:5; Russian Orthodox Bible 22:5).

As she proceeds, metaphors reflecting the calamity stand side by side with an ethnographically precise description, complete with technical terms (the type of bathtub plug) and numbers (thirty to fifty pails of excrement). Then, unfolding metaphors into whole mythological plots, Freidenberg personifies the backup of sewage as an intrusion of primordial chaos:

> I heard the momentary gurgle of pipes in the corridor, and it filled me with an inexpressible horror. I glanced into the toilet—the bowl was full to the brim with crap again, but my instinct told me that that was not yet the whole story. I opened the bathroom door with a sinking heart and saw that the bathtub was filled to the very brim with a black

stinking liquid, covered over with lard. This terrible sight cannot be compared with anything else. It is more terrible than aerial bombardments and heavy artillery fire. There is something eerie, almost mystical, in this influx not from above, but from below, when the plug (stopper) is closed. The huge receptacle with the black, dirty water watches frightfully, banefully, threateningly. It is infinite and ungovernable, this elemental force made of pressure and liquid welling up from below, this Soviet Tiamat, primordial chaos and filth. I could hardly carry out and lift, with difficulty, our few daily dirty pails. But could I scoop out and carry the thirty to fifty pails of our enormous bathtub? Its black, frightful contents looked at me with fathomless eyes; this filling-up right to the brim struck me with horror and the sense of a never-before-experienced calamity. One moment more—and this stinking black liquid would flood us, our house, our rooms, and it would rise up and push out, and it would overflow, and this would be a flood from below, from the unknown and ungovernable deep that is beyond the scope of our sight. And I am alone, and weak, and it is evening, and it is winter. Shall I run for help? Where to? To whom? How can I leave a helpless old woman here? (XV: 115, 26)

The image of Tiamat comes from the legend of creation of the world in the Babylonian epic Enuma Elish. A chthonic monster embodying primordial chaos, Tiamat must be vanquished and subjugated by the higher gods to create world order, but she is not conquered entirely, and her subliminal presence continues to represent a threat.[9] (This is a shared mythology: the image of the ever-threatening Tiamat also impressed some of Freidenberg's contemporaries who lived under Soviet and Nazi terror.[10]) As a native of that mythic world, Freidenberg sees—and experiences—the excremental mass in her bathroom as an intrusion of the threatening underworld. But this is a new myth: a myth about *Soviet* Tiamat.

The calamitous excrement flood occurred on February 15, 1943 (Freidenberg is precise in dating), at a time when she was unable to write. When she describes the event later, she comments on how the situation unfolded: "I am writing this in April, and the bathtub is still full, dark, and threatening" (XV: 116, 27). Now she goes further, analyzing the changes in her body and psyche. In her analysis, mythological metaphors stand side by side with references to political background. Freidenberg sees the conditions of life under blockade as a product of two tyrannical regimes, and on this occasion, as on many others, she equates her situation and that of the whole city with prison confinement:

> This state of siege, created by tyranny, has kept the city, me, my body, and psyche, in special, ultra-prison-like mode. I have grown accustomed to reckoning only with the edges of the filled bathtub and looking solely at its rim. Had the level risen? Would it overflow today, or not?—Nothing else interested me. . . . The cause of these phenomena and the elimination of these calamities—these had vanished like a chimera. Only the rim! Only the semantics of the thin top edge that serves as the boundary between life and death, the symbol that reflects my present day. (XV: 115, 27)

Engaged in self-reflection, Freidenberg understands that, living in a special prison mode, she no longer thinks in categories like cause and effect and does not contemplate practical actions. Looking at the situation from a position of a "native," an "ancient man," she experiences the flood in the bathroom as an appearance of Tiamat. Looking from the position of an anthropologist, she speaks in terms of "symbol" and "semantics."

Bronislaw Malinowski famously described the workings of myth in "primitive societies" in his book *Myth in Primitive Psychology* (1926): "Myth as it exists in a savage community, that is, in its living primitive form, is not merely a story told but a reality lived."[11] Ernst Cassirer voiced similar conclusions on the power of mythic thinking in primitive society in his *Language and Myth* (1925) and *Philosophy of Symbolic Forms* (1925–1929). And in her study *Poetics of Plot and Genre* (1936), Freidenberg, who listed Malinowski's work, as well as Cassirer's, in her bibliography, presented "primitive psychology" in a similar way. In that book, she writes about the "metaphorization" of life processes in images of eating, excreting, birth, and death and about the personification of natural forces in the images of gods. She analyzes mythological metaphors rooted in everyday experience and in bodily processes. Both in her scholarship and in her blockade notes, Freidenberg, like other scholars of her time, treats myths and mythological metaphors, like the Soviet Tiamat, not as tropes but as forms of experience.[12] Unlike other scholars, whose position remained purely theoretical, she treats myths as a "reality" that she not only analyzed but also experienced in her daily life.

"Dependence, Hunger—and an Unbearable Lifelong Obligation!"

Attentive to the workings of power in state institutions, homes, and human bodies, Freidenberg also traces the changing dynamics in intimate relationships under the siege. One day, a former lover of her brother, Antonina, showed up at their doorstep: "She had the chance to tie us hand and foot with her favors. These were morally and physically difficult days. Antonina was killing us by bringing us bread every other day" (XIII: 43, 33). Freidenberg explains her strong reaction as an inability to tolerate dependency: "Dependence, hunger—and an unbearable lifelong obligation!" (XIII: 43, 34). Judging by her language ("killed . . . bringing bread"), she was aware of the tragic paradox in her assessment of this situation.

Another story of dependency, concerning her student Nina, unfolds over two years. Mobilized for hospital work, Nina ("a Komsomol member") received a "military ration." One day in the summer of 1942 she encountered Freidenberg on a city street and was shocked by the physical change in her teacher. Soon she started to drop by with small gifts of food (XIV: 78, 20). Freidenberg mused about the difficulty of giving and accepting such gifts: "She did the hard work of charity naively and purely, not understanding how difficult it was, and how difficult my mother and I were. . . . We suffered from wounded pride" (XV: 107, 2). For weeks, Nina brought precious food from her military rations. And then she stopped coming. Freidenberg notes that her sense of the situation (what it "seems") had changed: "What I had taken for lofty, heartfelt feeling now seemed to me a passing superficial fancy. . . ." She elaborates, "She broke me, conquered me. Then she lost interest. . . ." (XVIII: 155, 82). Now she is thinking that Nina's charity was motivated entirely by a will to power. When the "frolicking Nina" came again, bearing gifts, Freidenberg was so distraught that she could hardly stand the young woman's presence (XVIII: 155, 82). But then, in the winter of 1944, came a new and formidable challenge: her mother's illness. Freidenberg writes that "only Nina could help me now." Nina promised to bring medicine—and once again disappeared. "My soul at last recoiled from her," writes Freidenberg, "and I could never forget or forgive her" (XIX: 164, 75).

But what about the "unbearable lifelong obligation"? Nina is mentioned in the postwar notes: when she returned to the university, Freidenberg did everything she could to help Nina get her diploma, even as she understood that her academic achievements were below standard. Freidenberg could not forget what those blockade gifts of bread meant for her mother (XXIV: 56, 50–53).

A similar drama swirled around a friend of the family, Elena Lifshits. In this case, too, it was a burden to Freidenberg to accept the help that Lifshits insisted on offering (XV: 110, 9). There came a moment when the intrusive friend was literally refused entry into the house. But during her mother's catastrophic illness, Freidenberg wrote her a letter, and Lifshits came: "I had forgotten all the petty things." It seems that Lifshits also forgot the offense: she offered "to help with everything," and she did. "A human being is complex. . . ."

decided Freidenberg (XIX: 171, 89). After the war, when her relationship with Lifshits again came to a crisis, she wrote, "Romances and dramas don't happen in love alone. They also happen in friendship and in thought" (XXVIII, 89–90).

On this occasion, Freidenberg makes an important admission. She decides that her judgments about people, as expressed in her notes, are flawed: "Characterizations of a person are usually false. . . . Whether I am talking about Mama, about Tamara, about Raisa, about Lifshits, I am lying, denigrating, or praising" (XVI: 119, 8). (Tamara, Raisa, and Lifshits were close friends.) And she suggests that "only art can characterize a person" (XVI: 119, 8). Even now, analyzing the unbearable moral burdens of living under siege, Freidenberg thinks of a hermeneutic problem that she had posed in her first autobiography, comparing art and scholarship as two ways of approaching life's meaning.

"Stalin's Blood-Soaked Regime and My Mother's Blindness Have Destroyed My Life the Way a Prison Does"

It is with special intensity that Freidenberg speaks about the central drama of life under siege: the intimate relationships within the family. She explores the workings of power in both the official and the intimate sphere, aware of the paradoxes inherent in this parallelism. And she sees two powers working in tandem against her: "Stalin's blood-soaked regime and my mother's blindness have destroyed my life the way a prison does" (XIII: 59, 90).

As Freidenberg records it, her mother was becoming positively childish: blind to the true causes of their circumstances, she blamed her daughter for everything. Freidenberg herself was growing ever more irritable (XII bis: 24, 65). She singled out hunger, misery, and shared rations as the cause of the irritation, bitterness, and resentment that ruled every family and home (XII-bis: 24, 66). Day after day, she pondered her family situation: "My thought was constantly focused on my relationship with my mother. I thought about this day and night, on the street and in lines, during any kind of work, during breaks. . . ." (XV: 118, 35). She understood that reflection did not bring relief: "My bitterness was in direct proportion to the analysis I performed day and night on my mother and our relationship" (XIV: 80, 25). And she found herself resorting to ancient solutions rather than analysis: "I called upon the god of patience. But where is he? What is his name? There was no such god" (XIV: 80, 25).

Documenting how they lived, day after day, Freidenberg notes deterioration in both mother and daughter: "Mother was losing her mental equilibrium. Her irritability was becoming pathological. She tormented me. . . ." (XIII: 44, 37–38). But she does not spare herself: "I was no longer my former self. My quiet disposition and my patience were lost. Sickly, spiteful, my cheeks saggy, without breasts or hips, I was bitter and irritable" (XIV: 80, 25). Desperate and bitter, she is attentive to the complex dynamic of the power relationship. She comes to the conclusion that, paradoxically, her mother's helplessness and dependency were the weapon of her dominance (XIV: 80, 24–25). She observes herself blaming her mother for her own ugly feelings in regard to her (XIV: 80, 25). And yet she records that there were other moments: "Then we would open our souls to each other, and one found her own feelings in the other, and we felt horror and grieved together" (XIV: 80, 25). Through her blockade notes, Freidenberg follows this dialectic of resentment and remorse.

Scenes, quarrels, reproaches, accusations, insults, and wounded feelings play an enormous role in Freidenberg's painful record, and she understands both the trivial nature of each separate incident and the enormous significance of these events. Mother and daughter quarreled over three potatoes (whether to fry them in the leftovers of linseed oil to create a second course or add to the thin soup); about drinking tea, often reduced to hot water (the daughter thought they should limit liquids); and about the advantages and disadvantages of potatoes over bread ("mother craved bread") (XVIII: 152, 70). There came a moment—a trivial quarrel in the kitchen that started with an argument about the size of a pea ration—when Freidenberg experienced "raw affect" that frightened her in its intensity: "It seemed to me that this could not end well: 'Either I will kill her—or she will kill me'" (XIV: 93, 61). To get her emotions under control, she seized a piece of paper and made a record "for these notes" (XIV: 93, 61).

She knew that murder was not beyond the realm of possibility: elsewhere in her notes, Freidenberg related a story of a close friend, Raisa, who had killed her mother and herself. In an uncontrollable emotional state (Freidenberg used a legal formula), Raisa had tied her mother to a chair and set the apartment on fire; both died. Before this, Raisa, a single mother, had taken her small daughter to a children's shelter. Freidenberg and a friend spared no effort to find the child, but when they located the shelter, they were told that the little girl had died from measles (XIII: 39, 19; XIII: 58, 86–87; 64, 105–107). Later, when beset by "unhealthy thoughts and feelings" about her mother, Freidenberg would recall "this shattering family drama" (XVI: 119, 8–9).

Freidenberg was fully aware that the situation in which she found herself was both inescapable and morally intolerable. In this context, she coined the metaphor that would become the title of her blockade notes: "the siege of the human being," or "the siege of man" (*osada cheloveka*): "I found it impossible for two close people to live together in an atmosphere of quarrels, silence, strikes, and spiteful acts. This spiritual squalor and siege within the family was intolerable to me. But the siege held firm even there, penetrating even further, into the very heart of a man, suffocating and haunting man everywhere, even alone, even at night, even in his deepest self" (XIV: 106, 109). Writing this passionate admission, Freidenberg employs and develops the Aristotelian metaphor identifying city and person.

Thinking about power dynamics in the family, Freidenberg turns to family history. Analyzing herself, she sees the roots of her resentment in the past, suggesting that unconsciously ("in the depth that is inaccessible to consciousness"), she had blamed her mother for interfering with her life: "She intruded into my love. . . . She intruded into my friendships and militantly positioned herself between me and my friends. She undercut my scholarship, making me into a house servant" (XV: 118, 35). This behavior, to Freidenberg, constitutes "tyranny": "I could not forgive her for her tyranny. . . ." (XV: 18, 35). Recall that earlier she used that word in reference to political power: "the state of siege created by tyranny" (XV: 115, 27). State and the family had worked in tandem to destroy her life.

Freidenberg understood that retrospective judgments like these did not improve her situation; she was also aware that these unhealthy emotions had entirely overpowered her: "This retrospective view of a life that had been wasted for no reason, consumed by another soul with nothing in return, burned me day and night. I couldn't hide from it anywhere. It overtook me in the street, in bed, at the table, and while reading, it grew in me like a cancerous tumor and filled me with bitterness" (XV: 118, 36).

Turning to her mother's condition, the daughter sees her as a constant threat: "My mother, meanwhile, was in a constant state of intense and bitter irritation. I had to live in this atmosphere. She blamed me for everything. If I was feeling peaceful, I was always making excuses for something . . . for the lack of sewage disposal, for bad pasta, for the war" (XV: 118, 36). Here, as elsewhere, we see that she felt herself under attack.

But then Freidenberg changes her position. Her resentment, or ressentiment, is replaced with empathy. She starts to "leave herself" and enter into her mother's situation, which she defines through the administrative term "dependent" (*izhdivenka*): "Then I would relent and be overcome with pity. My plea was now for one thing: to forget and forgive; to conquer the dragon in my soul with light. I began to transform into my mother and abandon my own self. I felt weak, old, infirm. A dependent—that is what I was . . . a burden and torment to me, my only living child. I trembled with compassion. . . ."

(XVI: 118, 1–2). Note that in this remarkable passage, "I" and "me" mean both "I, the daughter," and "I, the mother."

The analysis continues: "When I got food, I would divide it equally between us, so she could eat and drink as much as and whenever she wanted to" (XVI: 118, 1–2). The comment on sharing the food ration goes to the very heart of the matter, highlighting the peculiar conditions created by the state system of food distribution. Mother and daughter found themselves in a situation familiar to many families in the blockade. Freidenberg had a Category One ration card, the so-called "worker's card" (*rabochaia kartochka*). Her mother was classified as a "dependent" (*izhdivenka*, the same word we saw earlier). This category for housewives, children, and the elderly provided so little that people relegated to it could survive only through the sacrifices of family members with a "worker's card." In one of the ironies of the Soviet system, the "worker's card," originally meant for people doing physical labor, was extended to other privileged groups, including high-ranking academics with advanced degrees. Freidenberg carefully describes the resulting emotional dynamics: "Observing her from the outside (especially later on, in the winter), I was comforted by the fact that her survival over two terrible winters spoke quite objectively in my favor. I had shared half of my life with her, half of my breath. With the worker's card and rations I could have lived perfectly well, without going hungry. . . ." (XIV: 90, 50–51).

If Freidenberg allowed herself some moral satisfaction in her conduct toward her mother, as she notes, her mother denied her "even this consolation": "Once she told me: 'Don't think I owe it to you that I am alive at a time like this, that you are the one who looked after me and fed me so well. I was given a healthy nature, and that's not your doing. I only owe my parents'" (XIV: 90, 50–51). Unable to accept her daughter's sacrifice, to feel indebted, her mother insisted on the absolute preeminence of parental authority. Freidenberg sees this as the emotional dynamic created by two overlapping power regimes: that of the state, which has taken upon itself all control over food distribution, and that of the family, in which mother, dependent on her child for survival, claims the absolute authority of parents over children.

But the power of the state was capricious. The worker's card could not be taken for granted. One day—days blurred into one other, but this date, August 31, 1942, was firmly imprinted in her mind—Freidenberg was told that she would lose her privileged ration. This was a catastrophe. Divided with her mother, that ration was barely enough to feed them; a lesser handout would mean death for both of them. In painstaking detail, Freidenberg describes her efforts, spread over five days, to furnish documentary proof of her rank and status as a professor—and, with it, her "right to bread" (XIV: 92, 53–67).

This crisis would repeat itself more than once. Freidenberg's position was precarious: since she had not evacuated with the university, she lost her stable employment, and ration cards were issued at the workplace. To maintain a ration card, for most of the war years, she held a succession of temporary academic positions. Dozens of pages in the blockade notebooks are devoted to descriptions of her desperate efforts to retain the Category One card to which her academic rank entitled her and obtain an additional "academic ration" through the organization that provided support to scientists and scholars (Dom uchenykh). She carefully describes procedures—making applications, obtaining certification, gaining access to the offices of the bureaucrats in charge—and records the hours spent in the waiting rooms of important people who, she felt, had power over life and death. Humiliating dependency on people in power—important officials as well as their secretaries—occupies a huge part of these painfully detailed stories.

A lot of attention is given to secretaries.[b] A secretary is the first step on the road to an important official, and that secretary's power, however infinitesimal, could prove fatal to a person reduced to struggling for her right to bread. Freidenberg gives many examples of such interactions (XVIII: 136, 3–4, 6, 29, 31, 35). On one occasion, a lament following a humiliating confrontation leads her to a statement about the machinery of the Stalinist state: "Humiliation at the hands of a typist, humiliation at the hands of a secretary with her hair loose.... Oh, that horrible Stalinist machine! Oh, those wheels of folders, resolutions, dry hearts, hair let loose and short skirts, malicious glances, inhuman callousness" (XVIII: 144, 38). In this painful vision, the secretaries of important officials (whose frivolous appearance evokes particular scorn) play as much of a role as bureaucratic procedures enshrined in personnel folders and official judgments on personal petitions.

One may wonder about Freidenberg's understanding of her own role in this corrupt power game. Was she aware that, in her struggle for survival, her insistence on her (small) privileges made her a participant? She does not address the issue directly. But once, describing one of her many efforts (in September and October 1942) to maintain the privileged rations that barely sustained mother and daughter, she refers to an all-pervading "consciousness

---

[b] Secretaries of influential officials and their uncanny power also preoccupied Lidiia Ginzburg in her blockade notes, and the scholar Irina Sandomirskaia made a far-reaching interpretation of such observations: when a man threatened with starvation goes to the proper authorities for ration cards, "the new Leviathan meets him in the guise of a secretary." Ginzburg, *Zapisnye knizhki. Vospominaniia. Esse*, 725–726. Irina Sandomirskaia, *Blokada v slove: Ocherki kriticheskoi teorii i biopolitiki iazyka* (Moscow: Novoe literaturnoe obozrenie, 2013), 255–256.

of one's own villainy" and mentions "compromises, quarrels, and insulting people one loves." She concludes this oblique admission of complicity with a remarkable image meant to capture the condition of living under siege: "O yes, the soul was already stained, its purity lost. Life has hardened, tearing the veils away from what was forbidden and shameful, revealing a dirty, skinny butt" (XIV: 93, 60). As a scholar of myth, folklore, and literature, Freidenberg knew that the symbolic image of the lower strata of the body—the "butt" (*zad*) that produced degrading material (feces)—was associated with moral and social degradation.[13]

"Our Drama Was That We Were Locked Up and Crammed into a Common Crypt"

In one remarkable passage that concerns her relationship with her mother, Freidenberg speculates about the underlying causes of their moral degradation, focusing on the theme of eating and defecating in a situation of forced cohabitation: "Our drama was that we were locked up and crammed into a common crypt. Civilization understood the individual characteristics of each person and created houses, apartments, and rooms. . . . It realized that man is not cattle, and even close relatives need autonomy and privacy. Cohabitation, living in a heap, was invented as a form of state punishment for a crime. Only in prison are people crowded together; if they spend the day and sleep in the same room and defecate right where they eat, it is a prison. The tyranny normalized this into everyday routine" (XVI: 119, 6). Here, she comes to a significant theoretical conclusion: the situation in which she and her mother, as well as other people, found themselves during the siege was tantamount to imprisonment. And under tyranny, prison conditions become the everyday norm.

Freidenberg returns more than once to the idea of the normalization of catastrophic conditions. At the beginning of the catastrophe, the "Bolsheviks"—her sarcastic usage—were taken by surprise. But they soon recovered and "declared the unendurable, exceptional situation to be the norm" (XVI: 89, 47). She explains further: "It was as if it had been decreed that the situation was 'on the whole, satisfactory' and involved only isolated 'malfunctions,' 'difficulties,' and 'deprivations.' In this way, the method of temporary torture was given permanence and legitimacy as one of the components of life. Human nature was cancelled. One did not have to eat. Starvation was accepted as a normative condition" (XVI: 89, 47).

Elsewhere, Freidenberg applies the idea of normalization to artillery fire aimed at civilian populations. Such barbaric attacks "continued now day after day, for hours on end, simultaneously in all city neighborhoods." She concludes, "History had known sieges and catastrophes. But never before had human disasters been conceived as a normative everyday occurrence" (XVIII: 138, 10).

Earlier in her notes, she remarked that "a Russian," having experienced the terror of the 1930s, became indifferent to death and died in a different way than "a European" (XII-bis: 23, 62). Returning to this idea, she draws an analogy between death in German artillery attacks and death in Soviet prisons and camps: "[The Russian] submitted to the shelling and silently died in the prime of life and health, just as he had died in the cells of Cheka [secret police], in the exhaustion of the concentration camps" (XVIII: 138, 10–11).

Freidenberg's analysis of her "Russian" (Stalinist) subject does not end with this generality. The same person who meekly submits to power, even the "insignificant power" of "arrogant store clerks, store managers, arrogant building superintendents," assumes a different attitude toward equals: "But when the Russian comes face to face not with power, but with [another] person, the person becomes a beast" (XVIII: 138, 11). She describes the extraordinary rudeness, malice, and aggression, up to physical violence, deployed by people, including women, who found themselves in store lines, at the market, on a streetcar, or at a public water faucet (XVIII: 138, 11). Anyone who protested against power, even in microscopic measure, provoked passionate, malicious hatred (XVIII: 138, 11). Freidenberg concludes that this atmosphere of submission to state authority combined with the enmity of all against all is the direct result of living under tyrannical power, "the power [that] tortured these morally empty, exhausted people without mercy" (XVIII: 138, 11).

Freidenberg understands that human frailty is universal. But in the Stalinist state, enmity and aggression are normalized: "There are bad people everywhere, in all countries. There is envy, slander, intrigues in all nations of the world, just as all milords and miladies have bowel movements. This is true, but nowhere has this spiritual filth ever turned, as it did under Stalin, into an organized social system. Here the human being is poisoned, oppressed, suffocated, and persecuted in an official, legalized manner, by the entire state apparatus in all its terrible power" (XVII: 129, 19). Freidenberg's conclusion is unequivocal: "The Stalinist system was such that it was a breeding ground for the worst human bacteria—venality, betrayal, lies, greed, meanness that found nutrient medium in it" (XVII: 129, 20).

As experiences inevitably repeat themselves, she again and again sees the penetration of the Stalinist state into everyday life. She sees Stalin in every recess of her own life, her own body, and her own mind. In November

1943, on the anniversary of the 1917 revolution, incessant repetitions of the leader's name on the radio led her to this tirade: "It was Stalin to and Stalin fro, Stalin here and Stalin there. People's entire lives, all their everyday routines, the whole of their leisure time were stuffed like sausage with Stalin. You couldn't go to the kitchen, sit down on a chamber pot, have lunch, or walk out onto the street without Stalin turning up behind you. He got into your guts and into your soul, broke into your brain, plugged up every hole and gap, chased a person down, rang his bell, got into his bed under his blanket, haunted his memories and dreams" (XVIII: 156, 85). And Freidenberg self-consciously used these details of everyday life as material for large-scale political and historical generalizations: "One does not have to describe battles and bloodshed, great travails or deeds. To illuminate the epoch, it is enough to show ordinary everyday life in its average, most usual manifestations" (XVIII: 152, 72).

"Only a Catastrophe Could Get Us Out of This Underworld"

On November 25, 1943, Freidenberg's mother suffered a stroke, and this new catastrophe released them from their moral "fall," or, as Freidenberg put it, the "underworld":

> Only a catastrophe could get us out of this underworld from which we could not, no matter how much we suffered, break free on our own. Everything was now clear, both historically and biographically. I was unable to endure the agonizing memories and pangs of a guilty conscience. Mother arose in all the glory of her spiritual image, in her terrible suffering, in her deepest love, devotion, and pity for me. I remembered her hunger, her craving for bread, how I did not buy it and did not believe her, how I wondered about her function in my life and why she was a parasite on my life. I burned with pain. All things suddenly acquired their proper meaning. The fall of man, my own fall, my blindness—I could almost feel these things, I could touch them. (XIX: 159, 66)

Now, in the face of death, Freidenberg's understanding of their past life as family tyranny, carefully developed in the notes of the preceding months, strikes her as a mental aberration and an instance of moral degradation. And she sees her mother as returning to what she had been: "Moments of clear logical consciousness emerged through the delirium. Mama was returning to life. But she rose from the dead not as the person she was during the blockade, but as her former self, a mother who was tender, gentle, and infinitely good and dear" (XIX: 163, 71). Both mother and daughter return from the other world, morally reborn.

The image of the underworld has a prominent role in Freidenberg's scholarship. There also, it is a mythic domain of death into which one enters, or falls, and from which one returns, or rises. As she wrote in her lectures on the theory of folklore of classical antiquity, the hero of the chthonic myth "walks in and out of the underworld."[14] She worked on these lectures during the blockade.

Developing her own mythology, Freidenberg evokes the image of Stalin as a chthonic monster who captured mother and daughter in the underworld, the domain of death and degeneration, from which they now rise to a new life. She reiterates, "What could have released us from the underworld where man was driven by the bloodthirsty serpent?—Only a catastrophe. Only complete rebirth. And we went through it" (XIX: 163, 71). In these fanciful images, the classical mythology of the underworld is merged with the Christian mythology of life after death, with both systems affirming a cycle of death and resurrection. In their new life, mother and daughter live in a state of unblemished harmony: "We have experienced the total bliss of meeting again" (XIX: 163, 71). Their reconciliation is imagined as the literal merging of bodies and souls into one: "Our hearts melted with love. Head-to-head, nestling against each other, catching each other's breath, we reveled in the feeling of boundless closeness and complete spiritual and biological unity" (XIX: 163, 71). As these formulas suggest, mother and daughter have been granted the otherworldly experience of total redemption.

In this new life, the roles are reversed: the daughter attends to her mother's inert—partially paralyzed—body as one would care for a child: "I combed her hair, washed her, kept her clean and dry. I braided her hair around her head" (XIX: 163, 71). The daughter spoon-fed her mother porridge every two hours; she washed diapers, as many as thirty a day, and twice a day cleaned her mother's soiled body with warm water (XX: 179, 103).

This picture of life in an inverted world comes to a climax in an astounding episode in which Freidenberg witnesses her own birth: "On the night of March 28, the very night when, fifty-four years earlier, my mother, in great pain, had given birth to me, I was again present at the terrible labor pains of an eighty-four-year-old woman. Once, she called out to me and said:—Let the child out of my belly! I was going through the only suffering inaccessible to a person. That night I saw my own birth" (XX: 176, 99). The reality behind this is that Freidenberg's mother was suffering from persistent stomach pains. In delirium, on her daughter's birthday, she imagined herself giving birth.

In the last weeks of her life, Freidenberg's mother screamed from pain almost constantly, as Freidenberg herself, by necessity, ate, drank, washed, and cleaned. Freidenberg felt that she was losing her mind (XX: 178, 100). Yet even then she continued to work.[15] Her job at the Herzen Pedagogical Institute was essential to keep her ration card. During these horrible days, she was lecturing on the *Iliad*—so it comes as no surprise that, amid all the suffering, she saw her mother's death in mythological images.

In her 1936 study, *Poetics of Plot and Genre*, Freidenberg had claimed that, in mythological thinking, "such biological facts as satiation of hunger, the birth of a child, or the death of a person are apprehended apart from their real essence" (56). And in another place, she stated that "eating, as conceived in primitive society, merges with the acts of birth and death. . . . To put it in our language, eating is death and resurrection, as well as a reproductive act." (67). These associations are connected, she suggested, with the symbolic meanings of "mother earth": "death in the consciousness of primitive society is a generative element, the earth—and the underworld is the earth—is the mother from which not only plants, but also animals and people are born" (63). And such thinking culminates in an image of "life-giving death," the maternal body that both consumes and gives forth life (63). She concluded, "Our three concepts—'death,' 'life,' 'death again'—are, for the primitive mind, a single, mutually pervasive image" (64).[16] Describing the moments of her mother's illness and death in her blockade notes, Freidenberg reached for mythological notions familiar from her professional work, like the cycle of death and rebirth and the image of the mother as life-giving death. As she endured catastrophe, these concepts and images guided her apprehension of her own experience.[c]

Freidenberg's mother died on April 9, 1944. On May 1, her daughter completed her harrowing account of this slow death and brought her blockade notes to a close. It seemed to her that her life, too, had come to an end.

---

[c] A mythological understanding was not available to Freidenberg's contemporary Lidiia Ginzburg. In her blockade writings, Ginzburg also described—albeit in fictional form—her deteriorating relationship with her mother, with whom she shared her privileged food rations. Like Freidenberg, Ginzburg focused on the dialectic of what she called "pity and cruelty." Ginzburg's autobiographical character is similarly tormented by pangs of conscience when the hero's "aunt" dies from starvation, but for both fictional hero and the author, there was no reprieve. Unlike Freidenberg, Ginzburg—a rationalist—had no recourse to the psychological or rhetorical resources of mythological thinking. Death was ultimate and final, without a second chance for reconciliation. See Lidiia Ginzburg, *Prokhodiashchie kharaktery: Proza voennnykh let. Zapiski blokadnogo cheloveka*, eds. Emily Van Buskirk and Andrei Zorin (Moscow: Novoe izdatel'stvo, 2011), 17–59, 557–558.

CHAPTER 3

After the War (1945–1950)

"A Second Birth into the World as a Corpse"

Freidenberg returned to her notes, broken off on May 1, 1944, after her mother's death, to mark the end of the war. On June 26, 1945, alone in the empty apartment, she opened a new notebook. It seemed to her that she, too, had not survived: "I looked biology in the eye. I lived under Stalin. A person cannot survive two such horrors" (XXI: 1, 2). She describes her dead and dying body: "My eyes are shrinking and dimming. My hands have long died. The bones have thickened. . . ." (XXI: 1, 1). She prepared her students Sonya and Beba for their dissertation defense, asking herself, "What are students and scholarship to a heart that has no life in it?" (XXI: 4, 6). But her "dead heart could not be taken to the Volkovo Cemetery," and she faced "a second birth into the world as a corpse" (XXI: 4, 8). She now applied the mythological concept of rebirth, which she used earlier, to the image of the living dead: she is a dead body that acts in the world. This feeling would last throughout the postwar years.

Freidenberg was intent on writing. Writing did not come easily, but it was necessary: "It was hard for me to return to these notes. I associated them with writing about my mother, during the blockade, in the underworld, where our consciences fought against the laws of physiology. But I have returned to them, ready to overcome the bloodiest traumas, just to convey to paper and ink an account of the Stalinist days. This is my protest against the suffocation of the human being" (XXI: 6, 11).

Keeping notes was a self-conscious act with ethical and political significance. And writing brought some psychological relief: "a world of images" opened before her, bringing back her past life. Freidenberg sets out to write as if looking at herself from the outside, and she later calls this part of her notes (beginning with notebook XXI) "Memoirs about My Own Self" (*Vospominaniia o sebe samoi*). She also felt that the notes had a philosophical meaning: it was a "sacred space"—"a metaphysical encounter of the future with the past" (XXI: 6, 11). But despite these weighty goals, she soon stopped writing.

It was only on June 19, 1947, that Freidenberg opened her notebook again: "Two years separate the last lines of these notes from today" (XXI: 9, 18). She feels tormented by the burden of limitless, boundless time: "There is not much left to do: pass through time. . . ." (XXI: 5, 13). She considers various means of self-destruction ("throw myself out of the window or drown. . . .") but realizes that "to perish is as difficult as to survive" (XXI: 9, 19). Having reached "the extreme of emptiness," she returns to her notes as "a single means of salvation" (XXI: 9, 18).

Like her contemporary Walter Benjamin, Freidenberg is acutely interested in the temporal dimension of human historical experience. She has a sense of boundless, empty time: "I want to delimit it by caring for things, fill it in by moving in space, but nothing shortens it. No matter how many things I have to do, time does not shrink" (XXI: 4, 7). Her life, lived in anticipation of death, feels like walking through time: "Time flows, streams. And I walk through its tunnel, waiting for the end of the journey" (XXI: 9, 18). A sense of "empty time" hits her suddenly, interrupting action: "I stop writing. The so-called things-to-do have no significance for me. Here I am, sitting down away from my desk. Here I am, walking. Her I am, standing by the window" (XXII: 16, 14). In front of her is time: "Time. A bottomless wasteland. This vast temporal emptiness is frightening. Bare time. My God, what if I do not die for a while?" (XXII: 16, 15). Freidenberg lives and writes "with a tremendous effort, as if under coercion" (XXII: 16, 14). Life itself has become a form of coercion.

When the day is over and she falls asleep, Freidenberg dreams of her mother and brother. Her dreams, "filled with time duration, associativity, thoughts, causal and temporal connections," remind her of her past (XXIII: 42, 55). Waiting for death, she continues to write, and, while she does not comment on this, narrative creates duration and connections (temporal, associative, causal). Writing conjures images from the past and memories of the dead. In this way, writing creates a sense of meaning otherwise accessible to her only in her dreamworld.

Returning to her notes, Freidenberg once again describes the last months of the war, this time from the perspective of 1947. The university returned from evacuation. She describes meeting with old friends, colleagues, and students. Two of her closest students, Sofia Poliakova ("Sonya") and Berta Galerkina ("Beba"), ill and exhausted, started working on their dissertations under her mentorship. The reunion with B., her unrequited love, seemed ordinary and mundane: "Is this how we imagined this meeting after death?" (XXII: 15,13). She describes prolonged attempts to regain her status as professor at Leningrad University. (Her employment was interrupted when, during the blockade, she had not evacuated from Leningrad with the university.) Reflecting on this humiliating situation, she resorts to body metaphors: "A person who held a certain position with the Bolsheviks yesterday, and today has lost that position, distinctly feels a change in his body. . . . You are suddenly deprived of the qualities of a physical body. You are not seen; your voice is not heard. You become as weightless as mythical angels" (XXI: 10, 22). Feeling diminished by the emptying of her "earthly being," she has to make a physical effort to open the heavy doors of the dean's office (XXI: 10, 22).

Freidenberg's first postwar notebook includes impassioned descriptions of "squabbles" in the Philological Faculty and the Department of Classical Philology. At first, it was unclear who would occupy the position of department chair, which had been Freidenberg's before the war. She learned that the position was offered first to Ivan Ivanovich Tolstoy, her former teacher, and then to Iosif Moiseevich Tronsky, who had acted as temporary chair in evacuation. Freidenberg was outraged. Seeing her colleague Tronsky and his wife, Maria Lazarevna Tronskaia, as enemies, she describes them as heading a military operation: "Maria Lazarevna ran the headquarters, in which everything was instantly known" (XXI: 3, 4). The theme of the struggle for power in the department and the image of the enemy persist to the last page of her postwar notes. Finally offered her old position as department chair, she accepted, despite believing that the university had emerged from the war in a condition of "moral decay" (XXII: 12, 2).

Shortly before the end of the war, Freidenberg was hospitalized with a serious illness, and she compares this "horrible place, a Soviet hospital," to "a Soviet prison" (XXII: 23, 34). In the hospital, she heard about the fall of Berlin: "Soiled, humiliated, having lost everything, I stood face to face with that day" (XXII: 24, 41). At this moment, she embarked on describing the postwar years. She wrote very quickly, combining, as she did during the blockade, the forms of diary and retrospective diary, in which descriptions are recorded some weeks or months after the events.[1]

This chapter presents selected moments from Freidenberg's voluminous postwar records. Some sections focus on major themes and conceptions, among them her conception of the Stalinist everyday and her idea of history, while others follow the plot of her life story, particularly her love for B. Uniting them all is Freidenberg's chronicle of the ideological repressions she experienced at Leningrad University during the postwar years. And in her analysis, the institutional culture and professional behavior within the university are an integral part and a model of the Stalinist system.

"Who Can Describe the Soviet Everyday?"

Just as she did during the blockade, Freidenberg describes her daily routines with the thoroughness of an ethnographer. Her point is to capture the essence of "the Stalinist everyday," which she now sees as a system of repression. Grasping how it works and even describing it is far from easy: "Who can describe the Soviet everyday [byt], the everyday of Stalin era? It will eventually become as unfathomable as a mirage. A deliberate system of 'difficulties' has been created—Sisyphus's rock, which inevitably rolls downhill. These torments are indescribable: now there is no water, now, no electricity; now, the telephone is broken, now the radio is silent" (XXIII: 34, 19). She reiterates, "Everyday life [byt] was indescribable. One often heard: 'Nobody will ever understand this' or 'nobody will ever know about this.' These are the thoughts of prison inmates!" (XXV: 63, 12).

As if imagining a future reader, Freidenberg carefully describes specific procedures and situations: obtaining food (the rationing system persisted long after the war), cooking dinner, getting a pair of reading glasses, dealing with rats and bugs in her apartment. She subjects these situations to a sociopolitical analysis and uses extended metaphors to advance her conclusions. Once, lying in her flea-infested bed and hearing rats under the floorboards, she decided that this is how "the regime reached each person, up into his bed and his toilet" (XXIX: 3, 12).

One of her conclusions is that everyday difficulties were deliberately created. During the war, Freidenberg had described them as exceptional, specific to the siege. Now, after the war, the conditions of daily life, still unbearable, are seen as intentional: "From the outset of Stalin's reign, the state developed a whole system in which a person foundered. A deliberate system of starvation and humiliation did not allow people to think about anything but overcoming harsh conditions. Backbreaking labor for a pittance was exploitation of man not by man, but by the state—a colossal beast-like machine, much more terrible and insurmountable than the individual person. This state exploitation surrounded people from all sides and did not let go of them, neither at home, nor alone with themselves" (XXIII: 34, 19–20). The state is pictured here as a gigantic, animal-like machine. Describing its function, Freidenberg inverts Marxist terms: the exploitation of man by man turns into the exploitation of man by the Soviet state.

Trying to pinpoint the core of the repressive system, she lists several features (forced labor, starvation), focusing her attention on the domestic order: "Forced slave labor at an assigned place without the right to leave or protest. Hunger, and, ultimately, a home in which each room houses an entire family, where a person has to share living space with strangers who are assigned there, where there's a shared kitchen and a shared toilet, where everything is broken—stoves, plumbing, toilet seats, floors, waste pipes. Fights and drunkenness in the apartments, loudspeakers and radios, swearing and women's squabbling, stinking diapers, bedbugs; a person of culture is put in the company of scoundrels and bandits. . . ." (XXIII: 34, 20).

The Soviet communal apartments that she carefully describes here are a preoccupation throughout her notes and an object of anthropological analysis. (Freidenberg herself did not live in a communal apartment.) She sees enforced communal living, which was widespread in the Soviet Union both before and after the war, as an institution of social oppression and control—a place of confinement and a breeding ground of social animosity. Later, she adds that communal apartments were a site of mutual observation and surveillance.

These general descriptions then move to the story of a particular person who lived in her apartment building, Elizaveta Fedorovna (she does not list her last name). Her daughter went missing during the blockade and was presumed dead; a prostitute was installed in the daughter's room. This woman's day, in Freidenberg's retelling, looks like this: "Coming home from the job she had been forced into, located behind the Finland Station freight shed; exhausted by the streetcar commute after a hard and hungry day, she barely has time to eat before night falls. And in her own apartment, her own home, she is subjected to her neighbor's offensive presence" (XXIII: 34, 20).

Freidenberg is striving to be precise, providing her subject's name and patronymic, as well as the time, place, and specific circumstances of her life. What especially interests her is the domestic situation of a "cultured" person under conditions of enforced cohabitation with people who function outside "cultured" behavioral norms. She concludes with a mythological image of Stalinist society as a gigantic body that has been beheaded—that is, deprived of its "intelligentsia": "Having beheaded Russia by killing the whole of the intelligentsia, Stalin made the body alone into a country" (XXIII: 34, 21). Like many among her highly educated contemporaries, she sees the intelligentsia as a spiritual and moral force that has now been destroyed, undermining the integrity of the whole society.

Later, enumerating the key components of the Stalinist system once again, she again mentions hunger and the unbearable conditions of everyday life and then adds something else: the ideological repression that started after the war. She calls this condition "suffocation" (*udush'e*), which reaches beyond the intelligentsia: "no one could breathe any more, not only scientists or artists, but any person" (XXV: 63, 10).

When she describes the workings of postwar food distribution, which operated on principles similar to what she observed during the blockade, she also speaks in terms that suggest the disintegration of the body politic. And the range of repression is broadened to include the whole population:

> People are locked up, but they are not fed. A huge number of people live without bread rations. Many categories of people have been created who do not receive any bread rations at all. Bread is not sold in stores; this is forbidden. . . . Everybody trades on the black market. And it can't be otherwise. Nature itself demands. . . . The inequality is terrible. People in the Academy of Science or the Party enjoy the good life, and they've lost all shame. In one and the same shop, different people receive different food based on their rank. . . . No state has ever known such a hierarchy. (XXV: 63, 10–11)

Freidenberg is describing two different processes here: first, the fractionalization of the social body as people are divided administratively into different categories, and second, the moral decay of individual people, some driven by hunger to black market speculation and others enjoying privilege without shame. Moving to the intimate sphere, she makes the metaphor of the body politic explicit: "Thought is stifled. The human body, deprived of its head, has become promiscuous." Relationships are too easy to form and dissolve: "People get together and split apart—the whole of Russia comes together and splits apart, simply, without drama. . . ." With whole families sharing a single room in a communal apartment, couples copulate in the presence of others: "They live like cattle, in the same room. Here are parents, there are newlyweds. Here are children, there are their fathers lying with their mothers." She concludes, "It's a system, a state system of dishonor" (XXV: 63, 11). The disintegration of the family is a product of housing policy and, in a way, the loss of the intelligentsia. In both cases, the state is responsible.

For the most part, Freidenberg does not seem to doubt her conviction that the state is capable of controlling everything, including sickness and health: "The illnesses in the population are caused by the state" (XXV: 71, 43). During a flu outbreak soon after the war, she writes that the government, if it wanted, "could have eliminated this disaster." And it did not eliminate it "only because this was not in its plans" (XXIII: 38, 35).

The nation is "mortally ill." Like Freidenberg herself, "Russia" as a body politic has not survived the war:

> Russia was made to look like a victorious power. Now, in 1947, it is obvious that Russia did not win the war. But even in 1945 it was clear that the victorious nation was terminally ill. It was saved by numbers and ignorance. No matter how many people died, no matter how many were sick and indigent, it was lost from view. Russia emerged from the war depressed, mentally ill, barely dragging its feet. It was hard to meet a person who did not suffer from heart attacks or hypertension. Brain hemorrhages and strokes had become commonplace, no longer related to age. (XXII: 28, 51)

As she describes the "indescribable" Stalinist everyday—food shortages, ideological suffocation, moral decay, discord—Freidenberg focuses on the role of the state that creates the unbearable conditions for the daily life of its citizens (or so she thinks), and she links the social and the individual body.

"This Is an Ordinary Soviet Day"

Relating her daily routines, accumulating the repeating experiences like all diarists, Freidenberg generalizes her observations, making theoretical conclusions about the workings of the Stalinist system. In this way, she creates her diary-theory. This section traces her method and process on the basis of specific examples.

The entries examined fall between December 1947 and January 1948. Aiming to describe the conditions of life over the preceding fall and winter, Freidenberg starts by looking through the scattered notes made at the time on loose pieces of paper. She cites one such shorthand record of immediate observation: "Torturers! Gas. Light. The queues are deliberate" (XXVIII: 7, 46). Then she adds in the voice of today, "I look above history" (XXVIII: 7, 46). From that perspective, she concludes that "Marxism has failed": the new forms of material "base" have not abolished exploitation. The secret police "suffocates a person outside of his home and in his home, outside of his consciousness and in his consciousness" (XXVIII: 7, 46). Turning to the everyday, she creates a masterful (though difficult to translate) formula: "Everyday life is maintained in a distinctly Stalinist way" (*byt byl vyderzhan po-stalinski*) (XXVIII: 8, 49). She illustrates this principle on the basis of a single typical day: "Over one day, first the telephone malfunctions, then the radio is silent, then there is no water, then then no electricity" (XXVIII: 8, 49). As though observing from above, she generalizes, "But everyday life is not only a matter of these 'temporary difficulties.' It is deliberate ruination" (XXVIII: 8, 49).

Several weeks pass. Freidenberg describes rumors about an impending monetary reform, panic among the citizens, the disappearance of food from stores ("familiar empty shelves once again"). Thinking of her experience during the blockade, she extends the concept of siege: "I told myself that one should always prepare for a siege, always expect it; that under our conditions, the power of the state lies in wait for us everywhere, like an enemy" (XXVIII: 10, 56). (During the siege she had written that "whether there is a blockade or not," in Russia, "a person is always under siege" [XIII: 59, 88].) In these formulations, the word "siege" is a metaphor for the Soviet regime, which besieges its own population.

Having reached the memorable date of December 16, 1947, when food rationing came to an end under a new monetary system, Freidenberg records her impressions of the first day of "free" trade (her quotation marks). She finds chaos (XXVIII: 12, 57). In this new situation, she reiterates her former conclusions about the deliberate nature of all-pervasive everyday hardship, attributing the initiative directly to Stalin, who has turned life into an interminable struggle: "And so, Stalin makes life into the rock of Sisyphus. He takes everything away: there's no hope, no salvation, no peace" (XXVIII: 12, 58).

Freidenberg then shifts her attention to the university, where ideological repressions created impossible conditions. Then, she returns to domestic life. In despair, she reiterates that "no one will ever understand the tortures of everyday Soviet life." Again, she relates the experiences of a day in her life—this time, a concrete day: "Take today. I get up, there is no electricity. . . . It's cold. . . . Shall I write? Read? It's dark. . . ." (XXVIII: 14, 68–69). She again concludes that deprivation is a part of Stalinist terror: "State torture joins forces with domestic torture" (XXVIII: 14, 69). Contrary to her earlier stance of looking "above history," here she ties analysis to personal anger: "I am not a historian, and therefore I would like to speak about my era with indignation" (XXVIII: 15, 70).

Then she returns to life at the university and its oppressive bureaucratic routines. Over the course of a month, she has tried and failed to hire a secretarial assistant. Each step has been stymied by procedural obstacles, while the young woman she was trying to hire, who was not yet eligible for employment-based food rations, was starving. She pauses to ask herself whether her view of the situation was delusional or real and whether the obstacles were deliberate (a form of bullying bordering on torture) or spontaneous (a product of postwar devastation and bureaucratic chaos): "Is it delusion, reality, the executioner's bullying, mental torture, or the devastation and chaos of a thousand folders, 'departments,' supervisors, assistants, and deputies?" (XXVIII: 16, 76). Her head spins.

On this occasion, Freidenberg seems to doubt her idea that the everyday difficulties were deliberately created. The same question arises for us, her readers. Is her insistence on intentionality perhaps a delusion that stemmed from exhaustion, the mental state of someone who barely survived the war and then continued to feel besieged by countless difficulties? Whatever the answer, the idea that everyday difficulties constitute an essential part of Stalinist terror is of primary importance for Freidenberg's developing political theory. And the way she wrote may have influenced her thinking. The diary form is by nature repetitive, and these constantly recurring circumstances confirmed her conviction that the difficulties and hardships were part of a system and call for an explanation.

Soon after posing her unanswered question, Freidenberg starts to describe another day. This time she narrates from her lofty position as professor, with irony and detachment befitting her status:

> Here is my ordinary day—and I am a "professor." I get up—it's freezing. It's snowing. A blizzard. I put the kettle on—there's no electricity. In the dark I set up the stinking old kerosene stove.... Candles, matches, kerosene, stench.
>
> When the morning ceremonies were completed, the light came on. Ah, the joy of Soviet life, how dazzling it is! For a moment all sorrows are forgotten. You forgive the whole world. You carry the pots and kettle, catch the Horatian "moment," turn on all the burners, all the appliances.
>
> I make a soup from boiling water, oil, and cabbage. When it's ready, I hurriedly dress, open the windows to get rid of the kerosene stench, and go outside, soothed and rested, to breathe the frosty air. (XXVIII: 17, 76–77)

But a peaceful walk proves impossible: the courtyard and sidewalk are covered with slippery ice, and the building janitor refuses to sprinkle the treacherous surfaces with sand as she requested. The janitor is consumed by class enmity, Freidenberg thinks. All this amounts to a political phenomenon: "Soviet

AFTER THE WAR (1945–1950)

winter." In this coinage, the political ironically overwrites the natural: "I am returning home. These damned Soviet winters, these impassable yards, these icy slippery streets with their broken bones and concussions! Outraged, frustrated, I get undressed, preparing to return to my chores. I turn on the stove to finish cooking dinner. The electricity is off again!" (XXVIII: 17, 77).

After this difficult day, a "regular day" that feels horrifying in its routineness, Freidenberg stands motionless by the window: "The day is lost. I stand, arrested [*arestovannaia*], by a cold window" (XXVIII: 17, 78). (In English and French, the word *arrested* has the secondary meaning of "immobilized," and Freidenberg seems to play with this meaning, though this is not the case in Russian.) A moment of understanding has come, and she generalizes by drawing a parallel with the blockade:

> I stand and think about the blockade, think new thoughts. It becomes clear to me that the whole blockade was the passport of the Soviet regime. You suddenly open the door and see man in his unadorned natural state. Everything experienced in the blockade was a typical expression of Stalin's deliberate deprivation and repression, his persecution of the human being. But that was the abridged libretto. Before the blockade and after it: the same prison method, played out slowly and protractedly. . . . I write these lines almost in the dark. History shines its light on me. I am freezing. This is not even a blockade and not a siege. This is an ordinary Soviet day. (XXVIII: 17, 78)

This difficult winter day, reminiscent of the siege, is now seen as "ordinary" and a symbol of the Stalinist system and method. Behind the diary-like record of the everyday stands a political theory, expressed in images. The image of man in his natural state recalls her blockade notes about defecating in the presence of others, another emblematic picture. The excerpt examined here is different in that it reaches an important theoretical conclusion: "Until now, there was political terror and religious terror. Stalin introduced the terror of the everyday [*terror bytovoi*]" (XXVIII: 19, 84). And Freidenberg draws a parallel between the ordering of daily life and the workings of the state: "Both in the everyday and in the state, there is the same system of pressure" (XXVIII: 19, 84). But the entry does not conclude there. The diarist Freidenberg, having made her point, seems unable to stop, and she offers yet another piece of evidence with the description of another day: "Here is one more example. . . ." (XXVIII: 19, 84–85).

Conclusions can be drawn about Freidenberg's method and strategy. Like many diaries, Freidenberg's notes represent a day-by-day record of everyday life, and in her case, the notes come close to a field diary of an ethnographer. But this is far from all she does. Freidenberg created a conceptual frame based on the idea that the everyday hardships in the postwar Soviet Union were intentional: it was a new kind of terror, everyday terror. Within this frame, a chronicle of the everyday is transformed into a political theory of the Stalinist regime; she writes a diary-theory.

"Departmental Squabbles"

Like domestic life, the everyday life of the postwar university is a subject of analysis for Freidenberg. With its "hellish cold, untidiness, ruination, deadness, bureaucracy," the university serves as a "mirror" of the Stalinist system (XXVIII: 19, 84).

In the first postwar months, before the start of the full-scale repressive campaigns, Freidenberg's attention is focused on routine bureaucratic procedures and rituals: appointments, programmatic decisions, dissertation defenses, scholarly sessions, department meetings, and celebrations of jubilees and anniversaries. As we see from her language, Freidenbérg chose to view academic procedures in an anthropological mode. Thus, she writes about "rituals": "It was time for the special session. In accordance with the ritual established in the USSR, I had to deliver a solemn report to the Faculty Council. The Rector's directive with its 'expressions of gratitude' marking all personal anniversaries, the end of the academic year, and various dates was to be read aloud. There were to be greetings from the dean and faculty chairs. And, finally, on the last evening, after the traditional exhibition and a scholarly symposium . . . on the last day there would be a potluck banquet" (XXVI: 77, 64).

With the thoroughness of a chronicler, Freidenberg pastes into her diary the printed texts of "directives" and "resolutions" or copies them by hand. She also focuses on what she calls "departmental squabbles" and "the usual academic intrigues" (XXIV: 46, 5, 9). Applying the acumen of an anthropologist and the passion of a participant intimately involved in all proceedings and conflicts, she assumes the additional role of theorist, seeing historical and political significance in everything she observes. The procedures, rituals, and squabbles are all examples of "Soviet bureaucracy" and "Soviet behavior" (XXIII: 31, 8).

Later, after several years of well-organized ideological campaigns and administrative purges, Freidenberg would claim that the "squabbles," which she now defines in a political vein as "informing, slandering, spying," are in fact major instruments of Stalin's state policy (XXXIV, 150–151). But in 1945–1946, she mostly presents the goings-on as a part of the Soviet academic everyday.

Her first observations concern dissertation defenses. Freidenberg believes that, in addition to initiating young scholars into the closely protected Soviet academic community, dissertation defenses have turned into battlefields on which larger political forces play out, and she relates the dramatic events surrounding the dissertation woes of several students. Two, Sonya Poliakova and Beba Galerkina, are her own students; the third, Natalia Moreva, works under the supervision of her enemy, Tronsky. For Freidenberg, the students' difficulties were far from trivial: "Spring 1945 went by for me under the sign of Sonya's defense" (XXII: 26, 43). From notebook to notebook, she recounts with great emotion the obstacles involved in obtaining an advanced degree, from the difficult conditions of working in the postwar city to what she sees as the elaborate machinations by warring members of the academic community and vicious attacks by the officially appointed discussants. Her intention is to show how forces ranging from power struggles among colleagues (the usual academic intrigues) to the repressive structures of the Soviet academic establishment converge to prevent young scholars from entering into the sacred space of academia.[2] One particularly dramatic public defense, Galerkina's, is presented as a military battle: "I stood up. . . . I spoke loudly and sharply, and the air was hushed, [as if] pierced by dropping shells: 'There is a travesty going on here . . . young research workers are being ridiculed and maligned'" (XXIII: 43, 63).

The speeches are over, and the votes are counted: a negative vote signifies defeat. Freidenberg suspects intrigues, believing that her enemy, Tronsky, may have deliberately used her student as a sacrificial victim for the purpose of protecting his own student: "In my presence, he appealed to everyone: 'A sacrifice is called for. Galerkina's case is simply hopeless. We need to save Moreva'" (XXIII: 43, 64). Believing that the attacks on her students were, at least in part, caused by animosity toward her, she thinks that both colleagues and students have been denouncing her to the dean, the rector, and "Moscow." Remarkably, Freidenberg admits that she does not always understand "who is squabbling with whom and against whom" (XXIV: 46, 5), but she sees the situation as a struggle of epic proportions. From notebook to notebook, Freidenberg follows the unfolding of events at higher administrative levels. Her student Galerkina failed her defense but received her degree in the same academic year, 1945–1946, in a decision made by a higher body, the university's Academic Council. Struck by this unexpected development, Freidenberg resorts to the language of myth or ancient tragedy: "It was horrifying: the prospect of getting under Fortuna's feet" (XXIV: 51, 31). But this was not the end of the story. Much later, in January 1949, in the midst of the major repressive campaigns that hit Leningrad University with special force, the decision to grant Galerkina her degree was reversed at the level of the central government by the Expert Commission of the Education Ministry. Galerkina was summoned to Moscow to present her case. Freidenberg solemnly describes this new turn: "While Galerkina is on her way, I inscribe these lines into the notebook of history." Viewing the unfolding situation as a historical battle between "us" and "them," she instructed her student, "Don't lose heart. Remember the historical nature of this moment. In any case, we are the victors, and not them" (XXXII: IV, 70).[3] As we know from her memoir, Galerkina agreed with Freidenberg's take on the situation.[4]

At another point in her narrative about university affairs, Freidenberg finds herself looking over documents in her home archive:

> I have various papers, documents, long scribbled notes, short memos, sometimes newspaper clippings. Oh, these traces of passion and boiling blood, these old papers, almost always labeled "Petition" [*zaiavlenie*]! The graveyards of my hot throbbing heart, my heaving and boiling brain, the curve of my life.
>
> Unsent letters, unfiled petitions, that's what they are. When I die, what will be left is my scholarship, my furniture, my money, and these unfiled petitions and unsent letters.
>
> No one has written lyric poetry about them; no novelist has known about them. But how much is hidden behind them! How much they say about the Soviet era, about the passions of a person who was constantly fighting defensive wars—plotting, shooting, bleeding, and carrying deep psychic wounds. They remind me of the hair shorn by the Germans from the victims of "death factories." Piles of hair. (XXIV: 47, 10)

As Freidenberg writes these lines, she prepares a petition of May 28, 1946, addressed to the rector, in which she asks to be relieved of her position as department chair. The petition was written during the struggle around Galerkina's dissertation defense, and Freidenberg decided that if a graduate student failed, her adviser could not stay on. The resignation letter probably remained unsent. In any case, Freidenberg remained at her post.

It may be surprising to the contemporary reader to see procedural documents described with such pathos, as both traces of a person's most intense feelings and historical evidence of victimization, like the hair shorn from victims' heads in Nazi death camps. But in Freidenberg's eyes, the unsent petitions are the traces of an epic, unequal struggle of a Soviet subject with overwhelming state power. It does not matter that the struggle has unfolded in the sphere of the mundane, academic or domestic. This said, let us not forget that these words were written under circumstances that (as Freidenberg once put it) held her body and psyche as if in a "prison regime." Such passionate descriptions testify to the conditions under which she lived and to the damage that had been wreaked on her exhausted mind—as she was keenly aware.

As Freidenberg knew, documents like these would not become objects of representation in lyrical poems or novels. But her own notes might fill the gap. She writes about academic squabbles in a style that endows bureaucratic routines with symbolic meaning and historical significance, leaving behind the "hot traces" of an individual life that had "coincided with the Soviet epoch" (XXVIII: 13, 59).

"Public Humiliation Was Revived"

Freidenberg was an astute observer of the political scene, and judging by her notes, she soon understood that the "Resolution of the Central Committee of the Communist Party on the Journals *Zvezda* and *Leningrad*," adopted on August 14, 1946, and made public in the newspaper *Pravda* on August 21, signaled the start of a new repressive campaign targeting culture and education. The newspaper publication was preceded by several public speeches delivered in Leningrad by the party secretary A. A. Zhdanov, who, among his other duties, had been put in charge of cultural policy and international relations. Zhdanov, who had fulfilled important administrative functions during the siege, was a familiar figure in Leningrad. (There were rumors that he indulged in gluttony throughout the blockade when residents died from starvation.) The resolution had been explained to the university community at a general meeting at the beginning of academic year 1946–1947. Freidenberg recorded her conclusions about the new turn of events a year later, in the summer or fall of 1947, when the scale of the campaign was clearer to her. As she understood, these developments signaled a decisive change in the political course of the country: a "patriotic turn" toward "the great Russian people" and away from "the pernicious influence of the West." Freidenberg was amused that the change had been demonstrated to the faculty by the appearance of the rector at the meeting not in jacket and tie but in a Russian folk shirt. And the rector lamented that during the war, "many Soviet people were unfortunately abroad," where Western culture had blinded them to true values. A new vigilance was now necessary, meaning a careful selection of academic personnel and careful control over publications (XXIV: 58, 58).

Soon after these events, Freidenberg started documenting the implementation of the new political course at the university. She recorded that "public humiliation was revived"—a reference to the purges of the 1930s. "The first victim," she writes, "was Eikhenbaum." Boris Eikhenbaum was a distinguished specialist in Russian literature. As she recalls, "He behaved . . . with dignity, and for this he was beaten even more painfully" (XXIV: 59, 60).[5] From this point, the political chronicle of repressions became the main focus of Freidenberg's notes.

Freidenberg placed the unfolding situation in a broader historical context. As we now know from historical studies, her observations are quite accurate. In the late fall of 1947, she writes:

> After Zhdanov's speech, the final sprouts of emerging life were strangled. European culture and kowtowing [*nizkopoklonstvo*] were declared synonymous. An artificial cultural isolation was created. The Russian seventeenth century, with its hatred of everything foreign, was resurrected by the secret police. . . .
>
> Ivan the Terrible is our political ideal. Peter the Great has become a traitor because he cut a window to Europe. Police-enforced Pan Slavism has been revived. It's been kept secret, but in the winter [1946–1947] a secret order was issued [to libraries] not to give out any foreign publications to scholars, even old publications. Secret lists were drawn up with the names of people who were allowed to check out foreign studies (for example, scholars of Western literatures, classicists), but those names were carefully "checked out." Then we were secretly "instructed" that foreign scholarship could only be used negatively: to expose, polemicize, etc. Stalin put out a slogan: "surpass foreign scholarship." (XXV: 64, 16–17)

Freidenberg then relates the speech of Alexander Fadeev, the chairman of the Writers' Union, delivered on November 26, 1947. (She calls him "Agent Fadeev," meaning an agent of the state security.) Fadeev's speech heralded a new wave of brutal attacks against intellectuals. Among the victims were the prominent philologists Vladimir Shishmarev, Mark Azadovsky, and Vladimir Propp, her colleagues from the Philological Faculty. Another target was the long-dead theoretician of the comparative study of folklore and literature A. N. Veselovsky (1838–1906), whose work Freidenberg held in high esteem. She felt the familiar pressure and prepared for worse:

> Agent, a.k.a. head of the Writers' Union, Fadeev, recently gave a big speech in which he castigated [*prorabotal*][a] A. N. Veselovsky: "a slave

---

[a] The special verb *prorabotat'*, literally "to work through," referred to brutally castigating specific individuals. It was used in Soviet repressive campaigns as they unfolded in institutions. The related noun *prorabotka* was a public ceremony of castigation. A person who performs this act is *prorabotchik*. Freidenberg usually puts the term into quotation marks. And on one occasion, she describes *prorabotka* as a "medieval ritual in which bodily annihilation has been replaced by moral murder" (XXIV: 47, 12). Here (as Foucault after her), Freidenberg seems to note a progression from the medieval punishment of the body to the modern Soviet punishment of the soul.

of the Romano-Germanic school," a pseudo-scholar, "the founder of kowtowing to foreign countries." Now another wave of public shaming of prominent scholars is upon us. When you know that these are old men with trembling heads, with the urological problems of old age, half-dead people from whom their wives hide "criticism" of that sort—the impression is even worse. Now they have publicly, with street-level vulgarities, shamed old Shishmarev, sick Azadovsky, and the elderly, honest Propp. We await more. From year to year, Stalin keeps up the tension. From year to year comes a new wave of purges, threats, arrests, exiles, harassment. A person is crushed in every possible way, physical and mental. (XXV: 64, 18)

To clarify the historical context, the postwar repressive campaigns in the area of culture and education started in the summer and fall of 1946. Their main theme, as Freidenberg noted, using an official formula, was the "struggle with the pernicious influence of the West" (*bor'ba s tletvornym vliianiem Zapada*) or with "kowtowing to the West" (*s nizkopoklonstvom Zapadu*). Later, in 1948, the term "cosmopolitanism" came into use, and the phrase "anti-cosmopolitan campaigns" is often employed by historians. Historians view these internal campaigns, which they link to the Cold War, as a reaction to the encounter with the West during World War II, when the Soviet Union formed a temporary alliance with capitalist countries. Now these same countries were seen as a major threat—hence the idea of the intensifying conflict between two systems and two ideologies, the Western, bourgeois system and the Soviet, communist (or Marxist-Leninist) one. After the war, official discourse used the rhetoric of struggle or war to describe the situation in the country (the struggle with internal enemies) and in the international arena (the ideational struggle with the capitalist West).[6]

These campaigns, as they unfolded in academic institutions, entailed a radical revision of methodology in the humanities. The overhaul started, as we just saw, with attacks on the influential late nineteenth-century scholar A. N. Veselovsky (1838–1906), a Russian literary theorist who had laid the groundwork for comparative literary studies and used the comparativist method to explain the genesis and historical development of literary forms.[7] The idea that Communist Party administrators paid close attention to approaches in literary studies may seem bizarre. How much subversive power could a method of literary analysis present to the Soviet state? In fact, the Soviet leadership always attached political significance to literature. Veselovsky, in all likelihood, became an ideological enemy because his comparative-historical method viewed Russian literature as part of "world literature" and

Russian literary forms as imported from the West. This was, by definition, "cosmopolitanism"—and a political threat. The concept of "world science" (the Russian language uses one word, *nauka*, for sciences and humanities) was attacked for similar reasons, and scholars in literature departments were criticized for their "antipatriotic" tendency to promote both "world literature" and "world science." The first public "purges" at Leningrad University were conducted under such slogans.

As Freidenberg surmised, this was only the beginning. Crackdowns on other disciplines and on the arts soon followed. The anticosmopolitan campaign increasingly targeted scholars and authors of Jewish decent, becoming, by the beginning of 1949, an antisemitic campaign. And at this time, public shaming and disciplinary measures within academic institutions were accompanied by arrests.

Among the first victims in 1946–1947 were professors in Leningrad University's humanities departments, who were reviled by the administration and ostracized by colleagues and students for methodological (read: ideological) errors. We could say that the new wave of Stalinist terror started with what Western academia today calls "culture wars." But the stakes then were much higher.

These developments had a deep personal meaning for Freidenberg. And the situation at the university deepened her sense of deadness, her alienation from life itself: "I lost the last vestiges of life force in my soul. My face turned heavy, leaden. People who saw this face recoiled. . . . And I myself, looking at myself from the outside, was amazed at this deadening, murderous brokenness, trying to find a term for it. There was none. No, no kind of "distressed" or "depressed" or even "despondent" could convey this cold, stony state. . . . It was all over. I was violently made to live, as people are violently made to die. Does a person have to live? Ha!" (XXV: 66, 23). Freidenberg's thoughts then turn to the destruction of her family, and she adds that she, too, had died: "My brother was exterminated. The mind can't fathom this! . . . Then the siege. No, a living soul can rise up, but the dead cannot rise again" (XXV: 67, 24). Memories of the blockade gave her an idea of how she could end her life: "I thought a lot about death. Suddenly an idea struck me: starvation! After all, I had seen how, lying in bed at home, a person could totally weaken and die. At home, by myself, slowly, with preparation—this fulfilled all my desires. But I needed some time. I have to finish these notes at all costs. I will not die in silence. No, I will finish my work. I hate those who are silent in the face of the tyranny of life" (XXV: 67, 25).

Once again, life is a "tyranny," while her notes keep her alive. The notes, though, must be preserved, and that is another problem: "But what will be

AFTER THE WAR (1945–1950)

the fate of what I've written? To whom do I hand this over?" She had plans to leave the notes to her disciple, Sonya Poliakova, but now she has doubts: "I no longer consider Sonya my heir." Freidenberg does not see Sonya as "combat-ready," and she is discouraged by what she sees as Poliakova's surrender to "academic decorum" (XXV: 67, 26). In the future, she would change her mind about her heir, and about Sonya, more than once.

Freidenberg's animosity toward her colleagues did not decrease as they became the subject of official denunciations. And yet the repressions made her see some of them in a different light. Thus, while she writes that, "in essence," Boris Eikhenbaum "was not a good man," she adds that he was a thinking man, "he was a European" (XXIV: 59, 60). (She is making cosmopolitanism a virtue.)

As she writes, Freidenberg is aware of the unbecoming, petty character of the things she relates: the ugly Soviet ideological attacks, the undignified behavior of this or that unworthy person. To address a nagging sense of unease, she turns to methodological and historical generalizations: "I cannot be hurt by any person or phenomenon that I don't respect—not by harassment, attacks, or Soviet public accusations; not by actions on the part of figures like Meshchaninov or Zhirmunsky, people who are envious, venal, and pathologically vain. They're not what affects me, these discharges of Soviet academic sewage. But life always affects me. My mind makes generalizations out of insignificant phenomena, seeing in them the voice of an entire epoch" (XXV: 71, 43).

Judging by her language, she sees a symbolic analogy between the disgusting social behavior she sees in postwar life and the floods of human waste she described during the blockade with an openness that most other chroniclers shunned. And in her zeal, Freidenberg makes a pair out of the linguist Ivan Meshchaninov and the philologist Viktor Zhirmunsky, scholars who, as she knows, would not be seen as comparable by many of her colleagues.[8] She then explains the problem with Zhirmunsky (a widely respected scholar) as she sees it. He is an "opportunist" who kept changing his methodology in accordance with the political Zeitgeist: "He was a mystic, a formalist, a vulgar sociologist," and during the war, he abandoned the study of German culture, which had been his main field, to turn to "our Uzbeks and Kazakhs"; in a word, he always bowed to power and followed the currently accepted trends (XXV: 71, 43). (Research into the minority cultures of ethnic groups that comprised the Soviet Union was encouraged under Stalin's nationality policies.)

Let us pause to consider an ethical question. Freidenberg's notes are full of derogatory comments and harsh judgments about her colleagues: how should we deal with them? Ignoring this part of her notes would be tantamount to misrepresenting them. But discussing them brings up other problems, as it would be hard not to identify people by name. To discern whether Freidenberg had real grounds for making her moral judgments seems equally inappropriate. My approach is this: the question of whether Tronsky or Eikhenbaum or Zhirmunsky—or, for that matter, Freidenberg herself—was a "bad" person or an "opportunist" is in no way a subject of this book. Instead, this book tries to show how Freidenberg, one of the professors who was publicly shamed and threatened in the course of the Stalinist repressions of academic institutions, reacted to this onerous experience and attempted to make sense of it.

Our story continues with a focus on Freidenberg's reactions. The increasingly vicious public denunciations of scholars and their responses to these attacks made her confront the outcome of her whole life. The period under discussion here is the winter of 1947–1948: "It's not about the Zhirmunskys. . . . It happens like this: you are living your life when suddenly the very thing that you have seen and known for a long time hits you on the head. This winter I began to retch and choke as the outcome of my life rose up in my throat. I no longer believed in salvation. The thought that, after all, I would not publish my work suddenly became a gunshot wound. Love and scholarship! Two catastrophes are too much for one person" (XXV: 72, 46).

In more than one way, the new wave of purges put Freidenberg's whole life under threat. Losing her job was a distinct possibility, and it was still more unlikely than before that she would be able to publish. And, as we will see, disappointment in love was also on her mind.

If there was a source of hope that not everything would be lost, it lay outside Stalin's Russia. More than once, Freidenberg muses about her hopes, shared by her cohort: "Our eternal, common question: 'Do they know [about us] abroad?'! . . . Yes, they do! And this thought gives the strength to die in peace" (XXV: 72, 49). Of living in peace, there was no hope.

There was an additional irony: just as Freidenberg was writing this, McCarthyism was gaining strength in the United States, including in its universities. The practice of publicly accusing individuals of disloyalty and subversive communist activities was in some sense an inverse of what was going on in the Soviet anticosmopolitan campaign, though the forms were different, as were the consequences. Freidenberg remained unaware of McCarthyism.[9]

"I Tear the Fabric of Time to Finish the Tale of My Last Love"

Throughout the postwar years, Freidenberg continued to write about her love for B., even though she had grave doubts about his value as a human being. Once, marveling at his successful career, she considered whether he might be an informer: "What if he is an informer, an agent of the secret service? Who could vouch in this nightmarish life for one's brother, friend, husband, or lover?" (XXIII: 41, 54). And yet, to her own astonishment, her feeling endured.

One joyless day at the end of July 1947, Freidenberg dreamed of B. Waking up in her empty apartment, she asked herself, "Who decided that hell is underground? It is also found in the grieving human heart" (XXIV: 52, 33). She starts writing "about him, about B., about last summer, and about the last love." A year ago, B. had come to see her, happy and tender, after a long absence: "This was amid [department] squabbles, anxieties, strong pulsations of the heart" (XXIV: 52, 33).

But before she turns to his visit, she wonders about the survival of her notes: "Maybe these notebooks will perish?" She wonders what makes her write. The answer is clear to her: nothing but "faith in history" (XXIV: 52, 33). And it is also clear that her love is a part of the historical record.

With this, she proceeds to tell the story of B.'s previous visit, beginning in a solemn, epic mode: "And so, it was summer. It was the second half of July. It was summer. It was Monday" (XXIV: 52, 33). Preparing for B.'s visit, she had decided to go to the market, and she remembered that in 1942, walking along this route, she was almost killed by an exploded shell.[10] This memory—she recalls the circumstances in graphic detail—made her feel faint, and in this condition, she allowed the apartment door to shut behind her, with the keys inside. It seemed to her that she left herself behind (XXIV: 52, 33–34).

At this point, Freidenberg interrupts her story to comment, in parentheses, on her condition at the moment of writing: "(Today is my name day, this is why I am crying so much)" (XXIV: 52, 33). She remembers how, when her mother was still living, July 24 was celebrated in the family. She thinks about her hopeless, late love. Was consummation even possible for an aging woman, "after the blockade, under Stalin?" (XXIV: 52, 39). Speaking of her love, she decides to interrupt the flow of time and the order of storytelling: "I tear the fabric of time to finish the tale of my last love" (XXIV: 54, 46). The thought makes her comment, as she often does, on the nature of time: "Time does not consist of segments. Its flow links past and future, which, in reality, do not exist" (XXIV: 58, 57). She then describes, out of chronological order, several postwar meetings with B.

One of their meetings occurred in August 1946, soon after the publication of the threatening "Resolution of the Central Committee on the Journals *Zvezda* and *Leningrad,*" a document, in Freidenberg's words, "unprecedented in its open cynicism." Alone together, they spoke about the resolution

(XXIV: 58, 58). Whether she wants it or not, love is located in historical time: each time, they met amid the academic squabbling and political catastrophes of Stalin's rule.

Returning to her story several notebooks later, Freidenberg confronts the mystery of her enduring love. She asks herself why, "knowing this dark soul well, evaluating B., in general, negatively, I . . . loved him" (XXIX: 2, 8). To explain the mystery, she attempts a philosophical formulation of love. Earlier in her notes, she had referred to love as "a special Weltanschauung" that endows everything with meaning. Now she sees it as a force that does not depend on either subject or object and does not depend on time: "[Love is] a strong feeling that is beyond will or desire, irresistible, given once and for all, something not becoming, but already 'become,' something almost devoid of subjectivity" (XXIX: 2, 8). Writing this, Freidenberg thinks that she has brought the story of her love to a conclusion, but the future would show otherwise.

In a later notebook, B. comes to see her when she had "almost learned to live without him." This decisive meeting likely took place in summer 1948. Nine years of hopeless love was resolved, now, in a first kiss. Then she records: "Soon he came again, and I gave myself to him" (XXXI: 20, 14). The sexual consummation was an excruciating failure, and she explains it in historical and political terms: "It has turned out that I am unsuitable for a modern Soviet man" (XXXI: 21, 16). The problem lay in the body: "B. rejected me for failing to handle his body" (XXXI: 23, 23).[11] And this is how the tale of her last love came to an end.

"The Archive Initiated Me into the Brotherhood of Universal Man"

One day—she does not specify when—Freidenberg again contemplated ending her life. As we saw in a similar sequence earlier, she chooses starving herself to death, a blockade-related resolution: "One could stop eating! . . . This is so simple, so accessible! In happy excitement, I started thinking this through: at home, in my own bed, having prepared everything in advance, my affairs thoroughly in order; in summer . . . without needing to skip work. . . . I instantly cheered up, calmed down. . . . From now on I had a purpose in life: to live for death! To urgently prepare my archive" (XXVI: 75, 55–56).

Freidenberg is aware of the irony of her situation: having decided to die, she comes to life. "To live for death"—this was a good life. And one thing was essential: to prepare her archive. And an opportunity presented itself: "Precisely during those good days, I got an invitation from the Public Library to turn my archive over to them: manuscripts, letters, jottings, biographical materials, notes and so on. . . . You can imagine how I was uplifted and inspired by this offer!" (XXVI: 75, 56).

Elated, Freidenberg discusses her "idea of archive," behind which stands "the idea of history." She writes on a high-pitched note, endowing "history" with metaphysical pathos:

> The sense of history as an objective process has always spoken in me with great force. Therein lay my certain faith, my absolute worship of an objective supra-human process—my materialism, if you like, in which a single human life formed a part of everything in existence. I'm not talking about historiography, that pitiful science, but about history as a world process. Here nothing is ever discarded or forgotten. It is the absolute life of being and non-being, expressed in eternal variability. The paradise that peoples have dreamed up, immortality, the "other world"—all of this exists, but it is called not heaven, not paradise, not Valhalla, but history. It cannot be deceived, no matter how much documents are falsified, and facts distorted or concealed; only historiography succumbs to falsification. More than once, I've heard from friends: "No one will ever find out about that! All the sources will be forged, all traces of the crime hidden. History will never find out about our life!"
>
> The idea of the archive was the idea of history. The smell of immense time wafted over me. This passion for the supra-individual and supra-epochal was my native element. I had received a letter which told me that I was not alone in the world. The archive initiated me into the brotherhood of universal man.
>
> I became unrecognizable. My face grew soft and bright. This was the joy that had long abandoned me. (XXVI: 75, 56–57)

This idea of history as an objective, supraindividual process, an "absolute" life unfolding in accordance with universal principles, was rooted in Hegelian philosophy, and Freidenberg shared it with many of her contemporaries. The documentation of an individual life was especially significant as a record of this supraindividual process.

With the acumen of a cultural theorist, she understands that this vision of history is a secularized version of immortality. She poses a "sense of history" as the equivalent of a religious feeling—a "faith"—whose material embodiment is the archive. Collecting documents for history, the archive promises transtemporal being even to a materialist. Living under the constant threat of annihilation, she desperately holds onto this faith.

And yet, it soon becomes clear to Freidenberg that she cannot send her personal papers to the Leningrad Public Library. She will not "swallow the bait of the Soviet surveillance system" by turning her highly subversive notes over to a state institution. She starts preparing materials for her own archive: for the iron chest (XXVI: 75, 57). And even so, she sometime loses trust in its efficacy: "The archive! Who is going to lug that chest? To where?" (XXVIII: 19, 86).

"My Life Is Over. This Is Where I End Its Manuscript"

In early August 1947, Freidenberg opened a new notebook to finish her story: "My life is over. This is where I end its manuscript. It may last a short time, or years, but this makes no difference. Its main tour has come full circle, and it can now either repeat itself or vary in detail. Nothing new or vital can happen anymore, nothing from which the soul grows" (XXVII: 83, 6). She imagines how things would repeat, in variations, along the calendar cycle: "In winter, I will turn yellow, heat the stove, wait for death, write scholarly studies and notes for the archive, count down time, dream. In summer I will sunbathe and grow young, I will strive to free myself from shackles on a path to happiness.... I will write about poetry, comedy, prose.... I will lose my friends, outlive them.... There will be inexhaustible domestic torments.... There will be persecution of some kind at the university. Perhaps the newspaper harassment of scholars and writers will intensify" (XXVII: 83, 6–8).

This imaginary picture of future misfortunes feeds on Freidenberg's sense of the current political situation in the country, which she describes as extreme unfreedom:

> We live in complete cultural isolation.... A person is persecuted and slowly, ceaselessly strangled. There is physical and moral pressure. A bunch of opportunists speak on behalf of the downtrodden, depersonalized, tormented masses. The pressure is such that you can't have friends of your own choosing, you can't correspond with loved ones, you can't speak in your own apartment, because it is populated by strangers. There is no freedom anywhere or in anything. Thought patterns are fished out from one's brain, and how Stalin would like to invent a special X-ray to steal into the soul and the liver! This is a period in which spiritual culture has been completely canceled. Art is forbidden by the police. Studies in the humanities are not published. Biology, chemistry, and physics are declared "state secrets not subject to disclosure." Monotony and grayness are everywhere. Everything is frozen and lifeless.
>
> I will not live to see redemption. I will not see a Moscow Nuremberg.... (XXVII: 83, 9)

Freidenberg's idea of a "Moscow Nuremberg," which she brings up at the end—her hope for redemptive judgment in this life—recurs in her postwar notes.

Since she has lost all hope, she decides to bring her notes to an end: "I am discontinuing these notes. Plots, forms, interpretations will invariably repeat themselves" (XXVII: 83, 10). Thinking she is about to conclude, she turns again to the political situation. She evaluates it from a comparative perspective, remembering the humanistic ideas of her youth and thinking about life in Western Europe:

> I no longer believe in freedom and humanity, without which I cannot live. Of course, there are different degrees of imprisonment. We live perfectly well. We shouldn't make comparisons with Europe, but with concentration camps and prisons, with hard labor and death factories. We have the right to work in our profession, to go to the theater, to the cinema, to visit, to walk freely in the street. We have the right to stoke the stove and bask in the sun. We are in the category of people living under the supervision of the secret police in a large city-camp. (XXVII: 83, 10)

This vision of the city as a concentration camp was prompted by a visit she received in the fall of 1947 from an old colleague, A. I. Dovatur, who had served a long prison sentence, followed by exile: "Dovatur unexpectedly returned from 13 years in exile. He seemed to have more life in him than I did. We began to reminisce, to compare. He told me about a distant, gloomy concentration camp where tens of thousands of people languish and die of physical torments.... There is not much difference between their lives and ours. There is no difference in substance. Only the degree is different. We have a freer regime" (XXVII, Afterword 2, 21).[12]

Since the notes do not, in fact, conclude here, it is worth leaping forward to an incident a year later, when she encountered another returnee from the camps. This time—it is November 1948—Freidenberg suddenly received a telegram from Musya, her brother's wife, announcing a visit: "This strange, alien person coming to me! From the realm of death" (XXXII: I, 45). Unable to bear Musya's presence in her home, Freidenberg found a place for her to stay. She tells the story of this visit in the present tense, with dramatic detail. The bell rings. Next to Musya "stands a man in the uniform of the political police." It turns out that this is Musya's new husband, who is also "her boss in the camp." Musya explains that when her prison sentence ended, she found work in a camp and married her boss. Freidenberg states, "She is proud of this" (XXXII: II, 49). And once again, Freidenberg compares two kinds of camps and two kinds of inmates: "How happy she is to be back in Leningrad!

How she laughs, how life is bubbling in her. . . . How dead I was compared to Musya. My camp is more stifling to newly sprouting life than that other one, hers. No, that's not it: she had a goal and a hope in front of her, and that kept her going; but I see nothing ahead of me" (XXXII: II, 49–50).

The encounter evoked contradictory feelings: "Life, life! Everything in it is possible, any paradox. At my table sat a Chekist,[b] and I had warm, brotherly feelings for him. I mentally blessed him for taking Musya in, for loving her and supporting her" (XXXII: II, 50).

Not fully able to grasp this situation, she simply cited Musya's words: "'No, no one, no one can understand my happiness in being here, in being alive, in having overcome everything, everything . . . only a person who lived through the same thing I did, only that person would understand!'" (XXXII: II, 50).

This encounter with people from another world—the underworld—crushed Freidenberg both mentally and physically: "Both of them were from a special, otherworldly place, the world of Soviet reality and the Soviet underground, from Kolyma, the legendary home of slavery and hard labor. I did not put a single question to this long-suffering woman. Terrible things themselves rose chillingly from her boots and coat, from her involuntary words. . . . When they left, I could barely drag my legs to the bed. They, my legs, could not bear the weight of my thoughts and terror" (XXXII: II, 51). Then Musya and her companion disappeared, without coming to say goodbye. (Musya's status was still that of an exile confined to Kolyma.)

But in the summer of 1947, when Freidenberg decided that her manuscript, like her life in the city-camp, was coming to an end, she thinks about the people she encountered in her daily life and recalls B.'s words: "B. used to say to me: 'Don't judge people. Especially Soviet people.' He meant that they had been put in a situation in which they had to resort to any means to save their lives" (XXVII: 83, 10).

But this wisdom does not come easily to her. She reflects at some length on her unfortunate tendency to judge people, which coexists with her willingness to help others. She tells herself that she needs to love (*nuzhno liubit'*) her friends and tolerate their weaknesses; she needs to value the dedication of her students (XXVII: 83, 10). As for her colleagues, she cites a note she made about them on a scrap of paper in a particularly difficult moment: "They are guided by vanity, ego, honors, money. . . ." Still, they leave her free to be herself. To each his own: she has her scholarship (XXVII: 83, 12).

---

[b] Literally, a Chekist is a member of the Cheka, the first in the succession of Soviet secret police agencies. The word was used for agents of the secret police over the whole span of Soviet history.

Freidenberg knows and at times regrets her tendency to judge others. Concluding her record, or so she thinks, she describes how she sometimes uses her notes as a dumping ground for her worst moods and emotions. In this context, she added that her notes, "incoherent, inconsistent, and poorly written," reflect her "exhausted and impoverished brain" (XXVII: 83, 12–13).

With this, she brings (she thinks) her torturous account to an end. A few scattered comments follow. Then, she marks the date: "August 5, 1947" (XXVII: 83, 15). It was probably then that Freidenberg organized her notebooks into a single, serial text, prepared a list of contents, and gave the whole text a title: *The Race of Life* (*Probeg zhizni*).[13]

"Apparently, I Cannot Do Without These Notes"

Not long after the "final" date (August 5, 1947), Freidenberg restarted her notes, writing in the same notebook, number XXVII. On the cover, we find the crossed-out words "conclusion to all the notes" (*okonchanie vsekh zapisok*). Above them is a different phrase: "Prolonged afterword" (*Zatiazhnoe posleslovie*). The word "prolonged" may have been added even later. She continues her chronicle: "It's been a month and a half. I am ill with heart problems and am not seeking treatment in order to hasten my death. I have cleaned out an iron chest, and in this coffin, I am putting my works and my inner world. This will be my archive" (XXVII, Afterword, 15). She is still preparing for death, still thinking about her archive, and still identifying herself and her "inner world" with her notes.

As she writes on, the plots, forms, and interpretations indeed repeat. She hates Stalin, she laments the demise of the university. She berates her colleagues. One of them is "an unbearable nonentity, malicious, resentful, and petty"; another is "a petty and foolish schemer, a pompous, vaudevillian fool." She provides their names (XXVII, Afterword, 16). She lists "honest scholars," who took the beating, and decides, "They are dead men" (XXVII, Afterword, 21). She despises "governors" (*upraviteli*), this "brutal force" of people in administrative power who "organize our daily life" (XXVII, 17). She makes a conclusive judgment about Stalin's rule: "It's no longer a regime. It's confinement" (XXVII, Afterword, 18). And once again, she decides to bring her notes to an end: "Finally, into the iron chest." Then, she assigns a new concluding date: "September 20, 1947" (XXVII, Afterword, 19).

A month later, on October 25, 1947, Freidenberg starts writing again, on the same page: "Apparently, I cannot do without these notes" (XXVII, Afterword, 19). She soon starts another notebook. Looking back at the last few years, she searches for their meaning and thinks of the scholarship she has completed (a study of Roman comedy, Palliata, and a work on Sappho's lyric), still unpublished: "As I look back over the three years in which I did not die, I search in vain for their meaning. What have they given me? Not a single joy. During these years I have created Palliata and Sappho, two children I gave birth to in prison. A bitter motherhood!" (XXVIII: 19, 86).[14] Her time frame here runs backward to her mother's death during the blockade three years earlier.

Now, memories of the blockade hit her suddenly, tearing the veil of time. Freidenberg describes these experiences as flashbacks, traumatic visions from the past. The death of her mother in 1944 merges in her consciousness with the death of her father in 1920 during the Civil War, when Petrograd had also been under siege. She confronts terrible images of human degradation and decay: "And suddenly the image of siege.... I saw my dying father's forehead sloping, like a moron's. I saw myself when, trembling with greed, I hid from my mother and in the kitchen, alone, in the semi-darkness, reverently chewed something, washing it down with swill. I saw how my mother and I, our bodies melting away, competed inwardly, thinking who would live to eat the other's unfinished share. I saw how they dug a hole for my mother and lowered her coffin into the green swamp" (XXVIII: 5, 36). Her one goal is "to make it to the grave somehow.... May I redeem my soul, which has seen Stalin and Hitler, with the sufferings of my final years!" (XXVIII: 5, 36).

In January 1948, at the end of the notebook, she once again thinks of bringing her chronicle, and her life, to a close. Then she writes about her intention to supplement her account with the story of the years that have not been covered by her notes: "A heavy task still awaits me, one that I instinctively shy away from. I must summon my past from the grave to fill in the lacunae in my notes, from my entry into the university to the blockade" (XXVIII: 20, 90).

She must "resurrect" her past, bring the dead to life, and write about her unfulfilled hopes. She feels driven by the "pathos of history" that is stronger than her suffering. And she will speak in the "sacred space" that opened to her "since the first days of consciousness": "there is no louder impulse in me than this self-evaluation of my life, this tête-à-tête with the universe called the notebook" (XXVIII: 20, 90). This task delays the completion of the notes, which in turn delays death.

Yet she revisits the idea of death: "I cannot live any longer." Lying in bed, she turns to the problem of the body: "I lie here and wonder where to put this unburied body. Take it away and dump it? Shove it into the water? Throw it out the window? Stuff it with germs? Poison it?" (XXVIII: 21, 91). Another final date appears at the end of notebook XXVIII: "January 14, 1947." It may have seemed to Freidenberg that time had stopped, for this is clearly a mistake: the year was 1948. And this time, too, Freidenberg continued to write her chronicle of current events.

"The University Has Been Ravaged"

Throughout most of the notebooks she filled in the postwar years, Freidenberg chronicled the course of the repressive campaigns against "the pernicious influence of the West." From year to year, she described the changing cultural climate: the atmosphere of artificial cultural isolation, the suspicion of everything foreign, and the increasingly aggressive attacks in the press at "kowtowing to the West." She became especially alert when the campaign unfolding on the pages of newspapers "spilled over directly into institutions of higher education and research institutes": "Stalin's claws reached the representatives of academia" (XXIX: 7, 29–30). She saw the repression within her own university as a model of what was taking place in the country as a whole: "The university is Russia in miniature" (XXIX: 5, 19).

Trying in vain "to look for logic in these attacks" (XXIX: 5, 16), Freidenberg details what is happening before her eyes in the humanities departments, where comparativist and formalist approaches to literature and folklore came under attack as products of "Western bourgeois ideology." One of the first measures she describes is what she calls a "punitive session" held on April 1, 1948, targeting—not for the first time—her colleagues from literature departments, the scholar of Russian literature Boris Eikhenbaum, the comparativist Viktor Zhirmunsky, and the folklorist Vladimir Propp.[15] All three had been close to the formalist school of literary scholarship in the 1920s but were otherwise quite different. Freidenberg focuses less on the ideology behind the attacks and more on the act of ideological purification and its consequences for those immediately targeted. Being ill—she suffered from chronic sepsis after the war—Freidenberg could absent herself, but she requested and received the minutes of the meeting. Writing several months after the event, she describes the meeting on the basis of these minutes and the accounts of others:

> Finally, a meeting was scheduled to "discuss" the harassment at our Philological Faculty. The day before, a similar "meeting" was held at the Academy [of Sciences], at its Institute of Literature. All the literature professors were publicly shamed. They were forced on pain of political punishment to renounce their views and denounce themselves. Some, like Zhirmunsky, did it "elegantly" and smoothly. Others, like Eikhenbaum, tried to protect themselves from moral nakedness and coura-

geously hid their shame. He was alone, however. Propp, who had been mercilessly tormented for being German, was starting to lose the dignity he had long maintained. The others did what was required of them.

The professors were tortured with the most terrible torture instrument—their scholarly honor. (XXIX: 7, 30)

Here, as earlier with her definition of *prorabotka* as the moral equivalent of medieval bodily torture, Freidenberg develops her idea of the modern punishment of the soul.

Freidenberg analyzes the established order of these ritualized "denunciations": "The structure of the 'session' was as follows: first Dementiev spoke and denounced everyone present, after which the others took turns flagellating themselves" (XXIX: 7, 32). As she knew, A. G. Dementiev (Dement'ev), the head of the Soviet literature program at Leningrad University, also served as the head of the press section at the City Party Committee (that is, the Communist Party Committee for the city of Leningrad). The proceedings at the university were a part of a centralized ideological campaign directed by the city's Communist Party leadership. At this point, Freidenberg's main interest, though, is not the order of the procedure or the chain of power but the psychological and moral state of people compelled to participate in public rituals of confession and repentance. She comments, "All those present at this moral flogging were in a state of severe mental nausea. 'Those who survived this meeting (they said to me) would not be able forget it for the rest of their lives'" (XXIX: 7, 32). Eikhenbaum told her that at the meeting, he felt "incapable" of renouncing Veselovsky, a literary theorist who was important to him and who was currently serving as a symbol of "kowtowing to the West." But later, writes Freidenberg, Eikhenbaum did this in writing (XXIX: 7, 32).

Freidenberg learned from her former students Beba and Sonya (now, junior colleagues), who were present at the meeting, that criticism aimed at her own scholarly methodology was voiced by the party functionary, Dementiev, and her colleagues Natalia Vulikh (née Moreva) and Tronsky. Reflecting on these attacks a few months after the event, she notes a change in her attitude. At the time, she did not fully understand what was happening. Now, it is clear to her that the methodological criticism leveled at her, like "the absence of historicism" and "insufficient attention to questions of class struggle," were quite dangerous "in that acute political moment" (XXIX: 7, 33). In the immediate context of the well-organized campaigns, "every foolish word was a political denunciation" (XXIX: 7, 35). But from the perspective of "history," the "terrible words" were insignificant: "What will remain of them in the history of scholarship?" (XXIX: 7, 35). In the future, as we will see, it would not be easy to maintain this double perspective, distinguishing between "this acute political moment" and "history."

Freidenberg describes the reactions of specific people, beginning with their physical reactions. The distinguished Pushkin scholar Boris Tomashevsky, "a cold man, not yet old," fainted when he stepped out of the auditorium after the "flogging." Mark Azadovsky, who had a heart ailment, fainted during the meeting and was carried out of the room (XXIX: 7, 30–31). After the meeting, Eikhenbaum kept waiting for a "black raven"—a police car—to come for him and others (XXIX: 7, 38). Tronsky, as Freidenberg made sure to record, showed up at her home to make up for his behavior, trying to present his public criticism of her inattention to "the class struggle" as something they could laugh over together; she received him coldly (XXIX: 7, 38). She decided that Tronsky, who, under different circumstances could have been a decent man, "sold his soul to the devil" (XXIX: 7, 40). As for the practical consequences, the account of the meeting that appeared in the newspaper *Pravda*, the central organ of the Communist Party, did not mention Freidenberg's name. This time, the danger passed her by (XXIX: 7, 43).

Soon Freidenberg read a report in the university newspaper on another punitive session, carried out at a meeting of the Communist Party cell of the Philological Faculty. There, the "methodological mistakes of Professor Freidenberg" were criticized by Vulikh, "who also addressed mistakes of her own."[16] Alarmed, Freidenberg took a decisive step: on April 14, 1948, she submitted her resignation from the post of department chair. The administration ignored it (XXX: 9, 44).

What was to be done? Colleagues wrote repentant letters, but Freidenberg "chose another way" (XXX: 9, 45). Rather than making a written statement, she asked for a personal meeting with Dementiev. In her notes, she relates what she said at this meeting, doing her best to present herself as a "Soviet scholar." She has had nothing to do with the notorious comparativist Veselovsky and, on the contrary, has always promoted "national scholarship." She has "fought against formalists." Then, she spoke indignantly about the distortion with which "our formalists" like Tronsky polluted classical philology (XXX: 9, 46). Freidenberg records her words, couched in stilted Soviet idiom, without any comment, but she speaks about the party functionary Dementiev with clear irony: "He was a confessor of a special kind, a priest of the political police" (XXX: 9, 45). He accepted her explanations, admitted "errors" in the accusations aimed at her in the university newspaper, and assured her that she would not be allowed to leave the department that she had created and headed. It seemed to her that her tactical maneuver had succeeded: for a time, the threat had passed her by (XXX: 9, 46). But then she reveals the irony of the situation. Freidenberg makes clear that she is relating this conversation several months after it took place, when she already knows that the reassurance was a delusion. The purges have reached her. Her description of the meeting serves as an illustration of her past naivete.

Freidenberg's account of the events of spring 1948 continues in painfully profuse detail. To mention just the main points, she reports that Vulikh was appointed head of the Communist Party cell in the Department of Classical Philology. This means that her former student had become her "critic, biographer, boss, and [criminal] investigator" (XXX: 11, 53). She believes that in the eyes of the party, Vulikh and Tronsky held the "correct" point of view on all major problems of scholarly methodology, while she, Sonya, and her other students held the "incorrect" one (XXX: 12, 55). With her usual acumen about the larger meaning of events, Freidenberg understood that categories of philological criticism were now politicized and, therefore, potentially criminalized: "Now everything—semantics, theory, genesis, metaphor, image—quickly acquired a criminal quality, and a political one at that, aimed at undermining Soviet scholarship" (XXX: 12, 56). It was no longer possible for people at the university to breathe freely or nurture a free thought. Reaching for a familiar metaphor, Freidenberg compares the university—and with it, any institution in the Soviet society—to a concentration camp: "We worked in a modern, improved prison—a concentration camp. Everywhere the situation, the relations between people, the nature of work was exactly the same, and what happened at the university or conservatory was no different from what went on in any Soviet institution" (XXX: 12, 57). With this in mind, Freidenberg continues her detailed documentation.

As the new Communist Party leader in the department, Vulikh directed Freidenberg to conduct a "session of self-criticism," scheduled for June 1, 1948. Reflecting on the situation in which the department members found themselves, Freidenberg uses the metaphor of defecating in public: "A man goes to the toilet and drops his pants. He can't manage without it." She continues, "But he does not take off his pants in public. Life has two different planes" (XXX: 14, 65). In the postwar world, this principle no longer works. Just as during the blockade, under different circumstances, she and her colleagues would be forced to drop their pants in public.

Freidenberg then compares their situation to what Russian readers knew from Fyodor Dostoevsky's novels, famous for their excruciating scenes of self-laceration. She calls the coerced public repentance of Stalinist subjects "Stalinist Dostoevskyism" (*stalinskaia dostoevshchina*). Such self-exposure has always been abhorrent to her even as a "purely theoretical" possibility (XXX: 14, 68). But what faced her now was not theoretical; it was a horrifying necessity. As department chair, Freidenberg was expected to speak at the mandated session of self-criticism. Preparing for the "battle," she carefully considered her "tactics."

During these tense days, her student Sonya called to game out a possible scenario. It included a threat: "If you allow yourself to say anything about my research topics, I will allow myself to say that you, the department chair, were not familiar with them or interested in them. . . ." Freidenberg is shocked: "Insolence, academic vanity, disrespect for the teacher—and this on the eve of a political proceeding!" She thinks of an unexpected analogy from mythology: this would be equivalent to "Isolde denouncing Tristan" when he faced the ordeal of the red-hot iron. (Freidenberg uses the Latin term for trial by ordeal: *ordalium*.) She replied that when plotting "how to escape the bandits," the conversation should not turn "to substantive issues." Soon Sonya called again "in spasms of remorse." Freidenberg could not stand these "moral roller-coaster rides" (XXX: 14, 67).

Preparing for the ordeal, Freidenberg looked though Tronsky's 1947 textbook, *History of Classical Literature* (*Istoriia antichnoi literatury*), which, for a variety of reasons, she strongly disliked. She particularly disapproved of Tronsky's view of literary history, often deploring in her notes his complete failure to understand the origin and genesis of early literary forms (XXX: 15, 79.) But on this read, she noticed something else: a passage that praised Veselovsky and his comparativist methodology, citing her own book, *Poetics of Plot and Genre*. "So that's the bomb!" she decides (XXX: 14, 69). If she were to mention this passage to bring him down, she would fall alongside him. She believes that Tronsky was counting on her silence. Indeed, "people are now persecuted for the mere mention of Veselovsky." And there was an additional complication: Freidenberg was listed as the head of the editorial board for the textbook. Because of these compromising circumstances, Tronsky thinks that he has her under control. This complex calculation prompted her to consider a tactical move: "I would have to perform self-criticism and then expose Tronsky and Vulikh" (XXX: 14, 69–70).

And so, Freidenberg writes, "the day of my public discreditation" arrived. Her notes give a long and painstaking description of the session: the room, the assembled audience, the speeches (XXX: 15, 70–82). Looking back, she believes that she was able to keep psychological distance: "I did not allow this meeting to touch my inner self and was not present at it, as it were. . . ." (XXX: 15, 79). As department chair, she had to speak first, and she found her own "form" for this "agonizing act," which she describes with obvious irony. Standing near the podium, but not mounting it, leaning against it "in an intimate pose," she talked "slowly and thoughtfully." She made the required overview of her research and administrative work and gently mocked her past methodological errors (XXX: 15, 72–73). Freidenberg believed that her offer of "self-criticism" would forestall the dangerous accusations prepared by her "enemies," Tronsky and Vulikh, whom she would attack first. But as she spoke, she began to feel that to criticize Tronsky and Vulikh, as she planned to do, was beyond her: "I wanted to keep my hands clean, touching nobody, and carrying my own cross on my own shoulders." She discerned a risk: her "enemies" might themselves raise the issue of their "mistakes," thereby enhancing their moral authority. Still, "guided by both moral sense and a fighter's inclination for risk," she gave her speech without attacking her antagonists (XXX: 15, 73). But then Vulikh presented the official "party line," accusing Freidenberg of a number of methodological errors, like a view of the genesis of cultural forms that failed to consider class struggle (XXX: 15, 73). The phrasing seemed to Freidenberg to be Tronsky's. As usual, students were invited to speak out, and many attacked their professors. Freidenberg sat "and calmly listened to the flood of slander, lies, abominations. . . ." (In her notes, she names one student.) She was gratified to see that two students ("former soldiers, simple, rough-looking guys") had the courage to stand up in her defense, and she lists their names (XXX: 15, 74).

Here the narrative shifts to the present tense, as if Freidenberg is broadcasting from the auditorium: "Then, Sonya takes the floor" (suffering from tuberculosis, aggravated by these events, Sonya is "skin and bones"). Ivan Tolstoy speaks: "He maneuvers so as not to say anything bad about me, but not say anything good either." And now Tronsky mounts the podium. She writes, "He takes the formidable tone of a religious authority. Not a peep about himself. . . . He attacks [my view of] genesis and condemns my efforts to promote young scholars." Finally, it was the turn of Dementiev himself. "This is the moment of God's judgment," she comments. Everyone awaits the "verdict" (XXX: 15, 77–78). Listening to his denunciations, she hears phrases she believes were fed to him by Vulikh and Tronsky: "Dementiev delivers a guilty verdict. He classifies me as a follower of Veselovsky. Although, he says, it seemed to me that I was withdrawing from Veselovsky's positions, in fact I was affirming them. The evidence: I studied literary forms (so I am a formalist), and I studied the genesis [of literary forms]. Next, Dementiev repeats what Vulikh whispered to him, using Tronsky's phrases. Not having read my work and having no education, Dementiev freely offers what sound like responsible scholarly evaluations. Several times he emphasizes the correctness of Tronsky's "attitudes" [*ustanovki*] and nods lovingly in his direction" (XXX: 15, 78–79). At this point, the narrative acquires a melodramatic quality, but not without self-irony. Freidenberg rises to criticize Tronsky's views, and she reads out a dangerous quote from his textbook, where he talks about Veselovsky, the outlaw.

I stand up for my final word. I take Tronsky's textbook out of my briefcase. Sonya, who begged me not to ruin my relationship with Tronsky, freezes. My friends catch their breath.

Now I shed my mask and stand chest to chest with the audience. No spring can match the elasticity of my holy indignation. I step into the middle of the room, straighten up, holding my hands behind my back. I stand before them, chest and face raised toward them. In a posture of fearlessness, with angry eyes, I hurl my will and my truth at these executioners. Sternly, threateningly, overcome by inner passion, I say to them firmly: yes, I accept and obey the party line, but you cannot force me, in the name of party discipline, to accept what I have fought against all my life, what I will continue to fight against. What right does Tronsky have to dictate terms to me? Who is he? How did he come to be my teacher?" (XXX: 15, 79–80)

How should we understand this bizarre—theatrical and self-ironic—scene? How did Freidenberg understand the situation and her own role in it? Was she driven by the need "to escape the bandits" at any cost, even if this involved not only subterfuge and role-playing but also attacking her colleagues in the department? Or did she, perhaps without even noticing it, switch to "substantive issues" and express her genuine methodological objections to Tronsky's textbook? Did she realize that she was not, in fact, keeping "her hands clean"? Or was she, at that moment, entirely possessed by a fighting spirit? Was she aware that "at this acute political moment," the kind of methodological criticism she was deploying, however valid, amounted to "a political denunciation" as well as self-denunciation? (The words in quotation marks I use here are phrases Freidenberg employed to describe Tronsky's and Vulikh's attacks on her.)

There is no doubt that we, distant readers of Freidenberg's notes, cannot judge any of the participants in this drama. Nor, I think, can we fully understand their situation. There are reasons to suspect that Freidenberg herself did not fully understand what her words might entail. But if I quote Freidenberg's heroic denunciations of tyranny and perceptive judgments about Stalinism, I must also quote her descriptions of her own damaging tactics.

The notes describe the aftermath of this meeting, including an administrative resolution criticizing both Freidenberg and Tronsky for failing to overcome Veselovsky's bourgeois methodology. Shortly after, Freidenberg again submitted her resignation as the chair of the department, and it was again ignored (XXX: 16, 82, 87). For the sake of the historical record, she transcribes by hand the entire extensive text of the resolution. The section ends in these words: "This document, invisible to history, shows the situation, or rather, the system of internal terror, in which the university lived. The complete suppression of human personality, of initiative, the depressing impossibility of maneuvering a living human thought" (XXX: 17, 96).

Through Freidenberg's efforts to preserve it in her notes, along with her detailed report on the momentous "session of self-criticism," this document is no longer invisible to history. And while the painful contradictions in her own behavior may have remained unclear to Freidenberg, her meticulous and merciless account has made them visible to us, her distant readers.

Freidenberg points out the deterioration in relationships among colleagues and students caught in the net of terror: "Every member of the department watches. . . ." The sentence is interrupted because the notebook came to an end in the middle of a phrase (XXX: 17, 96). It continues in the next notebook: "all the others and can veto them" (XXXI: 17, 1). From this formulation, it follows that everyone has become a potential agent of terror, given the power to "veto"—today we might say "cancel"—another person. Again and again, Freidenberg describes a state that resembles the Hobbesian war of all against all.

The moral situation is especially important to Freidenberg. Attentive to the mirroring of the state terror in the university and in her department, she sees the past and present "squabbles" as a gravely serious issue. Discussing these seemingly trivial conflicts, she comments on "the terrible picture of the moral degradation of all our professors" (XXXI: 18, 3). And she connects the ugly conflicts over routine procedures with the "big repressions," which "skewed" everyone's conceptions of academic conduct (XXXI: 19, 6). On one occasion, commenting on the moral degeneration of faculty and students, she again pictures Leningrad University as an institution that operates like "a concentration camp": "in the concentration-camp university all good things fatally degenerate into bad things" (XXIX: 1, 2).

There were moments when Freidenberg seemed to understand that her own psychological, or moral, condition was far from normal: "All these disturbances, great and small, caused by the general system of inverted morality, have strongly affected me" (XXXI: 19, 8). Whether or not she was aware of all the implications, Freidenberg knew that she and her colleagues were living and working in a situation of damaged or "inverted" morality.

The "atmosphere of slander, gossip, lies" spread through her department (XXXII: I, 28). To describe her feelings, Freidenberg resorts to another metaphor she developed during the blockade: "I was in a quagmire that no number of buckets could dry up" (XXXII: I, 28). She continues, "Something stinking flowed at my feet, amorphous and irrepressible, and increased with every hour" (XXXII: I, 29). As during the blockade, she imagined herself overcome by a flood of human waste. The metaphor leaves little doubt that she, too, was tainted.

In the fall of 1948, Freidenberg reports, she submitted another resignation letter, claiming poor health. This was a very painful move: her department was "her last link to life." As on other occasions, she felt that she was losing the two main things in life—love and work (XXXII: I, 34).

One day, she was walking along Leningrad's spectacular main street, Nevsky Prospect, thinking, as she often did, about her "life path" in general and the degradation of her department in particular. Suddenly someone called out to her: "In front of me stood Tronsky." She decided to speak to her "enemy" (XXXII: I, 34). On impulse, she told him "the whole truth . . . about myself, about him, about all of us." Freidenberg confessed that she was leaving the department not for health reasons but "because of Vulikh." Tronsky admitted that he had agreed to take on the chairmanship of what she called "my department." But at this moment, "seized by a deep feeling of inner joy," Freidenberg did not pay attention to such "ignoble facts." They shook hands and parted in peace—or so it seemed (XXXII: I, 35). By the time she described this scene (it took place in October or November 1948, and she wrote a few weeks later), Freidenberg, as she made clear, was again convinced that Tronsky was "a scoundrel and usurper," but at that solemn moment on Nevsky Prospect, she had believed in the possibility of a human connection, and she put this on record (XXXII: I, 36). And for us, Freidenberg's notes on this period, attentive to such intimate encounters and inner feelings, capture the rapidly shifting dynamics of the terror process as it unfolded within one university department, implicating its members in the drama of mutual mistrust, betrayal, and occasional magnanimity.

At this tense moment in her narrative, Freidenberg shifts into another mode, interrupting the chronicle of events to reflect on the workings of the Stalinist system. She considers the structure of authority: "Behind Tronsky was Vulikh, and behind Vulikh was the dean, behind him was Dementiev, behind Dementiev was the [Communist] Party's City Committee, behind the City Committee was the Central Committee, and behind the Central Committee was Stalin" (XXXII: I, 39). Thus, she creates a chain that leads from her squabbling colleagues—via representatives of the university and party administration—directly to Stalin. Having built this great chain of power, Freidenberg returns to the departmental intrigues, drawing a direct connection between the petty academic squabbles and the state system of repression: "That was the whole point. There have always been and will always be intrigues. But this is not about intrigues, but about the state system, which everywhere, in all institutions ferociously pitted people against each other...." These "psychic attacks," she adds, undermined any project or action (XXXII: I, 39).

Seen in this perspective, conflicts among colleagues over the adoption of textbooks, dissertation defenses, or department chairmanship are a product of the country's system of governance. With this in mind, Freidenberg turns the narrative of petty academic intrigues into a symbolic testimony to the workings of the Stalinist state, using the names of her enemies in the plural pejorative form: "The Berdnikovs and Dementievs, the Vulikhs and Sharovs were symbolic figures reflecting the Stalinist system. Everywhere and everywhere the working environment was the same" (XXXII: I, 44).[17] She seems to admit that she, too, was inextricably implicated: "How to break out of this system? There is no way" (XXXII: I, 40).

Freidenberg then returns to her chronicle. The department was required to hold a public discussion of Tronsky's textbook, and Freidenberg, still the department chair, was expected to conduct the meeting, which took place on November 11, 1948. Freidenberg believes that the representatives of the party administration (Vulikh and Dementiev) intend to justify the continuing use of Tronsky's textbook, excusing even the criminal reference to Veselovsky. With this in mind, she wants to express her intellectual objections to the book while avoiding the political minefield. Writing after this meeting, she states that she believes that she spoke "very correctly" and yet said everything she wanted to say. She reports saying the following:

> I do not impose my opinions on anyone. The divergence of our views is a natural and healthy thing in scholarship.... I would have kept my personal attitude to Tronsky's flat evolutionary methodology to myself if he had not taken on the role of my scholarly judge and censor last spring. When our personal views clashed at an intense political moment, in the midst of an attack on me, I found it possible to express my disagreement with Prof. Tronsky. Then I did so in a harsh form, calling the method of the textbook perverse and Prof. Tronsky's attacks a dictate to which I was unwilling to submit. He pissed me off then (*laughter*). Today I can say the same thing in a proper and comradely manner. (XXXII: 3, 64–65)

As Freidenberg writes this account, she seems convinced that her complex strategy has been successful in all respects: she has preserved her "honor" and her "sense of truth," and she has managed to avoid a "trap." (As for the trap, she believes that she was expected to sharply attack Tronsky again, thus showing her opposition to the party-sanctioned opinion of the "scholarly community," which endorsed Tronsky's textbook and his views on literary evolution [XXXII: 3, 65].) She is also aware that, in the eyes of her colleagues, she suffered a crushing defeat. As if looking at herself from outside, she speaks in the voice of her enemies: "I have met with complete moral failure. Dementiev has settled accounts with me. Tronsky's textbook turned out to be excellent, Tronsky made no mistakes.... Thus, the representative of the City Party Committee was right in discrediting me and elevating Tronsky. The prestige of Dementiev has been fully restored" (XXXII: 3, 66).

Having related the position of her enemies, Freidenberg responds in her own voice, "Fools! They did not suspect that I had won." Her goal, she explains, was "to reinforce the department with cement" and "to restore her former normal business relations with Tronsky," and this could not be done by any other means. It troubled her that with her methodological criticism, she was participating in a political attack against Tronsky: "How many nights I did not sleep, trying to find a means that would relieve me of the vile role of his castigator." (Freidenberg uses the Soviet term, *prorabotchik*.) "But could the party members, the bandits, the whole subversive scum understand it?" (XXXII: 3, 66).

Here Freidenberg carefully defines her contradictory objectives: to preserve her professional honor by voicing her legitimate objections to Tronsky's textbook; to avoid a deeply disturbing role of making a political denunciation of her colleague; to preserve her professional, businesslike relationship with Tronsky for the sake of peace in the department; and to not fall into the trap set for her by the Communist Party organization in the person of Dementiev and Vulikh (whom she believed had expected her to repeat her attacks on Tronsky).

Was it possible to realize this paradoxical desire? And did her actions reach the intended results? What the notes make clear is that at this tense moment, Freidenberg thought, contrary to the general opinion, that she had succeeded in achieving her contradictory goals. But a question remains: immersed (as she knew) in that pernicious system, could she even tell success from failure?

If there was no clarity in Freidenberg's mind regarding the tangled political situation in the department, the picture seemed clear to her when she thought about the general direction of the repressive campaigns from a theoretical perspective. She again draws a parallel between the internal politics in her department and the big politics of the Stalinist state: "In big international politics the same things are going on as in my department. Stalin has created a special apparatus of subversive agents, of spies, a special system of clandestine subversion that can be neither encompassed nor defined or caught red-handed. I am describing this system not because it undermines my life, but because it is, so to speak, over and above me, and it is a fact of university life, the life of the state, a historical fact. The completely unprincipled nature of Stalinism clearly shows itself in the recent events at the department" (XXXII: II, 52).

Here she concludes that covert subversion aimed at destroying community and creating enmity between people is a product of a deliberate Stalinist policy that can be "neither encompassed nor defined" (XXXII: II, 52). In fact, encompassing and defining the workings of the Stalinist system is precisely what she is trying to do in her notes. By following what is going on in her department, she seems to catch that state red-handed. And, as she observes, she aims for a stance that is suprapersonal. It is important for Freidenberg to affirm that she is *not* describing this system merely as a force that undermines her own life—although the traces of damage done to her life and self are quite evident in her intense and tangled accounts. In her own eyes, Freidenberg is recording historical facts, testifying to life at the university and in the state at large, and this feeling seems to have brought her a measure of moral relief.

Addressing a future historian, Freidenberg switches from political to symbolic description: she needs to convey the special quality of "deadness" all around her: "Will the historian understand the deadness of our existence? A dead country. Dead schemes. People with uprooted souls are dead in work and dead in life" (XXXII: II, 48). She imagines the future historian's next question and provides a bitter answer: "The historian will not understand how the population could endure such a system of repression and violence. So, I answer him: the population cannot endure this system. The whole population is sick" (XXXII: IV, 77). And she writes as a member of the endangered population.

Turning specifically to the sessions of public castigation and self-denunciation held at the university with increasing frequency, Freidenberg fears that "posterity will never understand the murderous nature of such 'meetings'" (XXXII: I, 42). The word "murderous" is used here in its direct meaning. She provided clinical details: "Even Zhirmunsky had a heart attack. Eikhenbaum was laid up with a myocardial infarction" (XXXII: I, 42–43). Later, on March 1, 1949, she reports that Eikhenbaum had another major heart attack (XXXII: IV, 80). On April 3, 1949: "Azadovsky had a heart attack. Lurie was sent to a hospital in serious condition: myocardial infarction" (XXXII: IV, 81). (Other sources confirm Freidenberg's report.) In the first postwar years, Freidenberg was already writing that diseases of the population were "caused by the state"; now she sees clinical evidence for that conclusion.

In the following months, Freidenberg registers the rapid unfolding of repressive campaigns as they expanded well beyond the humanities. In October 1948, she reports that a new "wave" of repression has covered biology, then linguistics. Freidenberg herself fell under attack for "distorting" the ideas of Nikolai Marr, a scholar long elevated to the role of supreme authority in the field of linguistics and, at one time, Stalin's personal favorite (XXXII: I, 41).

Beginning in early 1949, she writes synchronically with the unfolding events, in diary form; some entries are dated. On March 1, she records "a campaign to lynch theater critics" (XXXII: IV, 80). She was quick to notice that the targets of this new wave were mostly people with Jewish names, writing on April 6 that "Jewish pogroms are going on in the country, but in a 'cultured' form: blood of the body is replaced by blood of the heart. Cultural figures with Jewish surnames are dishonored" (XXXII: IV, 84).[18] Later she provides more details about the antisemitic measures restricting the access of Jews to education and careers (XXXIII, 123). In this situation, Freidenberg's thoughts turn to the proverbial "Jewish question"—a topic that had hardly figured in her notes. She brings up the extermination of Jews by Hitler. Turning to the Soviet Union and to the present moment, she notes that "we have pure fascist antisemitism" (XXXII: I, 68). This is a rare moment when she briefly mentions that she was born Jewish.[19]

The campaigns soon took a new turn, indicating that what had started as a purge of cultural institutions, mostly in Leningrad, could be broadening into another wave of the Great Terror. What historians call the "Leningrad affair" (*Leningradskoe delo*) began in mid-February 1949, when a number of highly placed officials in the Leningrad city government and Communist Party organization were accused of "anti-party actions" and removed from their posts. On April 3, Freidenberg records the names of the officials who had been dismissed or arrested over the last month (XXXII: 4, 82). She speculates that this would not be the end of it, and her political intuition did not deceive her: before long, the dismissals were followed by arrests, sentencing, and ultimately the execution of the government and party officials on political charges. But Freidenberg's main focus remained on events at the university.

Also on April 3, she writes about the "terrible tension at the Philological Faculty": "for two days, more ordeals, this time with 'organizational consequences.'" (The phrase in quotation marks was an official euphemism meaning that people would be fired.) Everybody expected a major attack. And Freidenberg expected that yesterday's "privileged" (*blatchiki*), as she saw her colleagues "Azadovsky-Gukovsky-Zhirmunsky," would be now targeted as well. It was rumored that this time, even Tronsky would be attacked for his textbook (XXXII: IV, 81). Freidenberg is keenly aware that, in both the state terror and the terror campaigns at her university, Stalin's purges touched everybody, including those who tried to make accommodations and those who participated in purging others (and even high government officials).

Writing for history, Freidenberg carefully describes an open meeting of the Academic Council of the Philological Faculty on April 4–5, 1949.[20] The meeting involved a well-prepared attack, aimed mainly at the past and present heads of the departments of language and literature (Viktor Zhirmunsky chaired West European Literatures, Boris Eikhenbaum and Grigory Gukovsky were the former and present head of Russian Literature, and Mark Azadovsky chaired Folklore). Freidenberg was the chair of Classics. She had reasons to expect that her turn would come.

On the first day, the room was crowded and stuffy: "Thousands of students . . . stormed the doors in pursuit of the spectacle of moral execution." Freidenberg nearly fainted and was taken home. "What I later learned was horrible," she writes, referring to attacks on professors' personal lives. "Zhirmunsky had his whole family life exposed" (XXXII: IV, 85). Freidenberg disapproved of Zhirmunsky's liaison with a graduate student, but at this moment, her sympathies were on his side.

On the second day, the meeting was moved to a huge assembly hall. Freidenberg "appeared for a few hours" (XXXII: IV, 85). She saw "a horrifying picture": on one side, the well-fed, self-satisfied designated attack squad (*prorabotchiki*); on the other, the noble faces of professors, pale as death. Each of the targeted professors had his "biographer"—a party man, a student, or a young faculty member who "dishonored" the assigned victim from the podium. Appealing to the distant judgment of "history," Freidenberg discloses the attackers' names. Here, again, she uses the plural pejorative form to emphasize their generic character: "Oh, could it be that history will tolerate these Naumovs, Makogonenkos, Lapitskys!" (XXXII: IV, 85). (In at least one case, her accusations may have been wrong.)[21]

Not long after, Freidenberg again faced the agonizing question of leaving her job. One of the few colleagues she respected, the classicist Solomon Lurie, was to be "purged," and her participation was expected: "Not wishing to take part in the harassment of this scholar, I defended him as a teacher and then filed a petition asking to be released from all work at the university" (XXXIII, 90).[22] That done, she writes of feeling tremendous relief. She would not have to participate in the harassment of a colleague. But she comments on the situation of others: "Such things have long ceased to bother people: coercion untied the hands of both the honest and the dishonest" (XXXIII, 91). Whether Freidenberg was aware of this or not, the observation that coercion frees ordinary people from a sense of personal responsibility could apply equally to her. But now, as she put it, she was "standing at a Rubicon" (XXXIII, 90).

In this situation, Freidenberg stepped down as chair of the Department of Classical Philology: "With disgust, with distaste, I thought of my work and my functions. I deeply mourned the department, the work of my life, to which I had given seventeen years of thought, labor, and talent" (XXXIII, 94). (It remains unclear when exactly she resigned, possibly at the end of the academic year 1948–1949.) She expected that her antagonist Tronsky would be named her successor, but instead a little-known scholar, Ia. M. Borovsky, was selected for this role and "instantly agreed to take on the department" (XXXIII, 95). She would remember Borovsky and his action in the last lines of her life chronicle. For now, no longer a chair, she continued teaching, feeling that she was doing "forced labor" (XXXIII, 94). In the meantime, the repression at the university proceeded to the next phase, as Freidenberg records: "There are arrests. People are dismissed from work or thrown in prison for ten years for 'talking,' for a 'wrong' point of view. . . ." (XXXIII, 97).

In this agonizing situation, Freidenberg again thinks of suicide: "Throw the body out the window? Drown? I can't." She feels that her life is something imposed on her: "My mind is circling back to the starting point. I'm tired and exhausted. There is no way out. I have to live because it's impossible to die." She sees herself as if from outside, already dead, standing at the entrance to the space of eternity: "Barely dragging my feet, empty, I stand before eternal Space and stare into it, thinking of nothing" (XXXIII, 98). She believes that she is held in this life by her duty to her father: "I should write about him, put him in the history of technology. I'm the last one. I am the end of the lineage. . . . Somewhere, I remember, there was a bundle of patents. . . ." (XXXIII, 99). (Freidenberg's father had invented several devices used in image projection, telephone communications, and printing.) Soon she found these forgotten papers and sorted them out.

By October 1949, she sees no reason to continue with her record: "I will no longer describe Soviet life, the conditions of grueling and forced labor, the most outrageous daily living conditions [*byt*], and the system in which the insulters triumph over the insulted" (XXXIII, 102). She once again turns to the familiar metaphor of Soviet life as a prison camp, but this time with a twist: "No, it is neither a prison nor a concentration camp. Prisons and concentration camps come with specific terms of confinement and an awareness that they are punitive institutions; they do not pass themselves off as conservatories and universities" (XXXIII, 102).

A few months later, she states definitively that "the university has been ravaged" (*universitet razgromlen*) (XXXIII, 103). She concludes that "the question of life is finished" and puts a closing date to her notes: December 5, 1949 (XXXIII, 107).

Then, once again, she returns: "1950. March. I spent several months in an agonizing internal struggle: to retire or not?" Both moves seem disastrous to her (XXXIII, 107). Cursing her fate, she continues teaching within the department she no longer chairs, "in this Stalinist microcosm" (XXXIII, 111).

As she returns to her record, there is a new turn. Freidenberg and her students are summoned to the special university purging "commission." She records a long "interrogation" in the presence of the rector, in which she is insistently asked to "characterize" her colleagues in the department. She tries to evade what she considers a "dirty job" but finally gives in and supplies a political denunciation of Vulikh, whom she considered an instrument of the purges. She records her denunciation without commentary: "She, a party leader, fiercely demands the worship of bourgeois authorities. She hates Marr. She cancels the scholarly literature that I assign to the student I supervise and recommends fascist, Nazi books" (XXXIII, 119).

She thinks that she has triumphed. "Vulikh is dead," she reported to Sonya Poliakova and Beba Galerkina, who visited her at home to discuss the new situation (XXXIII, 119). She soon realizes that she was mistaken: her denunciation has been made in vain. To make matters worse, she believes that, testifying at the same commission, her students "betrayed" her without realizing it. Sonya admitted that she had said that Freidenberg's relationship with Vulikh was a struggle between two "wrestlers" who had long forgotten what they were fighting about; Beba reported to Freidenberg that she had said something similar (XXXIII, 120). Freidenberg is categorical in her judgment: "Alas. The time of villains and vices has passed. The catastrophe was that people did not see the line between what was permissible and what was not. The catastrophe was that such people were not villains at all. Before me, at my table, eating sandwiches and drinking tea, sat my closest students, sweet young women who loved me and frankly confided their betrayal to me. In their eyes, it was a successful ploy" (XXXIII, 121). The institutional terror, she concludes, has taken a moral toll on everybody: "There is complete and cynical decay in the department" (XXXIII, 123). It remains unclear whether she includes herself.

Over the horrible years of institutional squabbling and political purges, Freidenberg's relationships with her closest students were infused with contradictory and painful emotions. The situation became particularly acute when the purging campaign moved to the stage when faculty and students were practically forced to denounce each other. It can be assumed that in this situation the teacher-student relationships were painful for both sides.[23]

Suddenly, in May and June 1950, a new turn in the purges of the humanities caught everybody by surprise. The linguist and cultural theorist Nikolai Marr, Stalin's favorite, had come under attack. As Freidenberg put it, "Stalin crushed Marr, whom he himself had created and nurtured." Not so long ago, "people were killed for criticizing Marr," and "this was done on the orders of the tyrant" (XXXIV, 134). Now, Nikolai Marr's language theory, previously considered a part of Soviet orthodoxy, was declared a subversive force in Soviet scholarship, and his followers were persecuted. Freidenberg, who had enjoyed Marr's personal patronage in the 1920s and early 1930s, was under threat. Although she had long since moved away from Marr's ideas, she expected the most serious consequences for herself.[24]

In 1950, she started preparing the paperwork for retirement. (She finally retired in 1951.) Problems arose: the evacuation of the university during the siege of Leningrad had interrupted the continuity of her service record, and from the perspective of Soviet bureaucracy, she had worked for only six years. Discussing such bureaucratic procedures, Freidenberg again resorts to the metaphor of a siege: "It is a whole cunningly designed system of blockade, impossible to break through" (XXXIV, 136). Siege continued to dominate her thinking. It was the organizing metaphor of her chronicle.

Chapter 4

"To Fill in the Lacuna"
From the University to the Last War (1918–1941)

As we have seen, Freidenberg had chronicled the war (1941–1944) and the postwar years (1945–1950) and even before that had written an account of her early years (1890–1917). But the years 1918–1941 remained unaccounted for. In the winter of 1948–1949, as she was thinking about putting an end to her recordkeeping, she sat down to "fill in the lacuna." Within a few months, she had filled ten notebooks, numbered III–XII.[1] She gave them the subtitle "The Wreath of Dill" (*Venok iz ukropa*), referring to her disappointment with her status in Soviet academia.[2] Freidenberg saw this part of her life story as her "academic biography" (*nauchnaia biografiia*), a curriculum vitae of sorts (XXXII: I, 27). And while this section of her notes includes stories from her personal life, they are inextricably intertwined with her scholarship. The narrative is richly documented. She pasted or copied official documents, intimate letters, her own juvenile poems, and other scraps into the notebooks. At the same time, in notebooks numbered XXXII–XXXIII, she continued her chronicle of current events.

At first, the work of reconstructing the past was agonizing. Her heart overflowing with memories of the dead—her parents; her brother; her coauthor and lover, Khona—she felt exhausted by this act of "necromancy" (XXXII: I, 27). But soon the situation changed: "The world of images overpowered me and eradicated my presence in it. I was possessed by the sweet sensation of a second life with my mother and my scholarship, possessed by the dream of history" (XXXII: I, 27). But while it seemed to Freidenberg that she was fully possessed by the past, as if vacating her present self to write this history, the time of writing is palpably present in her narrative. Speaking about her earlier years, she constantly relates "then" and "now," and she is acutely aware that she is writing "under Stalin" and "after the blockade."

This chapter presents selected moments from Freidenberg's long, hastily narrated description of what happened between 1918 and 1941. The selections are meant as signposts within Freidenberg's biography, in the way she planned it. They should help make her life story comprehensive, if not coherent. But this chapter also has another goal: to show the workings of historical understanding in the notes. Written retroactively, Freidenberg's history of her earlier life shows how the author's present casts a distinct shadow on her vision of the past and how, from this vantage point, various moments in the past relate to each other.

"I Entered Petersburg University"

Freidenberg begins her academic biography with her entry into the university: "I entered Petersburg University. . . . It was the fall of the 1917–1918 academic year. The university still had its old form. Famous old professors gave open public lectures. . . . The revolution had given birth to liberty. The intelligentsia was free to listen to whomever it wanted. There was no bureaucratism yet. After all, I am writing this under Stalin. . . ." (III: 1, 1).[3]

The Russian Revolution opened university doors to women, and Freidenberg is aware that before that happened, she would not have had the opportunity to study. She also makes it clear that her optimism about new opportunities did not endure.

She matriculated as an auditor, without any thought about a future profession, shattered, as she sees herself, "by the storms of experience" (III: 1, 2). The university was a "monastery of the spirit," a "refuge from life" (III: 1,1). Yet, as she reports, she came to lectures elegantly dressed, "in a close-fitting black silk dress," and always wore "a little black hat with a wreath of dark red velvet flowers" (III: 1, 6). She soon started to study in earnest in the Philological Faculty and discovered that "literature—this was my own self" (III: 1, 2).

Freidenberg describes her teachers, with whom she felt a great spiritual communion based on a "mutual penetration" of souls that was not without a touch of eros (III: 2,15). There was A. K. Borozdin, the expert on literature of medieval Rus' and on the Bible. He responded to her passionate interest with a "reciprocal pedagogical passion," or so it seemed to her (III: 2, 14).

Borozdin died in 1918 during the fateful flu epidemic. Another such figure was the demanding teacher V. V. Bush, a medievalist and folklorist whose trust she was privileged to gain. While these were merely "pedagogical" passions, she fell seriously in love with her first instructor in classical (Greek) philology, I. I. Tolstoy, and initially believed that feeling to be reciprocated. Her love for learning and classics had merged with her love for the teacher: "My love grew, and my studies, like my love, kept growing" (III: 4, 35). In the whole of Freidenberg's notes, just as in Freud, "love" and "work" form the fundamental modes of life, but for Freidenberg, the two modes are closely intertwined and practically inseparable. And it was maternal love that continued to hold her life together: when Freidenberg learned about Tolstoy's marriage, she turned to her mother for comfort, sleeping at her side, and her mother's "sweet, warm body" healed her pierced heart (IV: 12, 103).

In August 1922, she had written about her hopeless love for her teacher in a very long lyrical poem; in her notes, she reproduces that poem in full (V: 18, 25–30). Now, in 1948, she comments that, having lost her love, she immersed herself in scholarship, where she found "the highest possible happiness." She adds that in later years, Tolstoy, having lost his wife and young son in World War II, "found happiness in vanity, the Order of Lenin, a car, and the rank of a member of the Academy of Science" (V: 18, 31). Tolstoy's wife, like Freidenberg's mother, had died during the blockade, and after the war, the two survivors had exchanged warm letters of sympathy. But by the time Freidenberg was describing her youthful love in her notes, they had grown apart under the pressure of departmental squabbles.

In the early 1920s, Freidenberg had made two attempts to leave the university, one after the collapse of her love for her teacher. She comments that "now, when I write this, in 1948, close to old age, I also have to force myself to resist the urge to leave the department" (III: 8, 61). Both then and now, she makes clear, she found refuge and renewal in scholarship.

Freidenberg concludes her story of entering into the world of learning with a biblical image: "So, from the seed that went into the ground, began my new birth" (IV: 13, 105). In its careful plotting and its use of metaphor and myth, Freidenberg's academic biography relies on techniques mastered and refined in her scholarship.

Petrograd Under Siege

In the 1920s, Freidenberg had written poetry "in the genre of a lyrical diary" (III: 5, 27). In her notes, she quotes these poems, commenting that this poetic diary in no way reflects "the quotidian conditions" in which she lived: "It was a time of the greatest everyday hardship" (IV: 9, 68). "Revolution is a terrible thing! It replaces one form of violence with another, and the process of dragging down one class of exploiters and installing another is horrible" (IV: 9, 68). Freidenberg is acutely aware that the horrible picture she paints reflects her present situation: "Stalin showed the true face of the revolution." And she formulates the general principle of historical understanding: "The past shows its true face only in the future, retrospectively" (IV: 9, 69).

Describing the Civil War winter of 1919–1920, when Petrograd was under siege, Freidenberg writes as someone who had experienced the Leningrad blockade of 1941–1944, and the past and the present reflect on each other.[4] Beginning in November 1919, the whole family lived in one room, where a small makeshift stove provided meager warmth. Her father was losing his mind: "His interests were focused on how many grams of grain there were in the soup that day" (IV: 9, 71). Insensitive to the father's misery, her brother Sashka teased him. Her mother desperately struggled to maintain some order in their domestic life. Freidenberg herself was seriously ill. She remembers a constant feeling of hunger and her envy when her father sat down to eat his bowl of soup when her own bowl was already empty. She interrupts these horrible memories: "Oh, life! What horrors you have not put me through! This was not yet that unspeakable hunger of the besieged city, when. . . . But it is impossible to dwell on this" (IV: 9, 72). Unwilling or unable to recall the other, later siege, she describes the first siege of the city in similar terms: "Terrible days! Life was emptying out. Professors were dying. The living were arrested. The university was covered with dust and decay. . . . The family was falling apart" (IV: 9, 72). She describes the horrible physical and mental disintegration of her gravely ill, hunger-stricken father. Freidenberg's father died on August 1, 1920, and during their last meeting, in the hospital, she felt that he was no longer himself. Contrary to the doctors' expectations, Freidenberg recovered. Back then, at her father's deathbed, she felt no real grief: grief was extinguished by the squalor in which they lived, her own exhaustion, and the shock of his degradation. Now, writing these sober words, she feels closer to her father. Another siege, which took the life of her mother, brought her face to face with her own degradation. Thinking that death is now close, she imagines reconciliation with her father under the sign of eternity: "Having made our mortal journey in the finite, we will merge in the infinite" (IV: 11, 96).

If Freidenberg sees a ray of hope in the memories of the past horrors, it comes from the magic link between teacher and student-disciple, presented in language replete with metaphors: "In those terrible revolutionary years, when everything was disintegrating and decaying, when the whole country was living by way of one state process—destruction, in those years the teacher and the pupil, like a spring, had the energy of a great mutual interconnection...." (V: 16, 2).

When she wrote these lines in 1948, the theme of "teacher and pupil in the terrible years" was tragically relevant. Freidenberg feared that her own students might betray or had already betrayed her. It seemed that in Stalinist society, the sacred bond between teacher and student that had sustained her in the first postrevolutionary years had broken. Still more precious, then, were these memories and metaphors.

"Entry into Scholarship"

Freidenberg's entry into the world of scholarship (*nauka*, the Russian word that refers to scholarship in both the sciences and the humanities) occupies an important part in her peculiar curriculum vitae. Looking back, she sees it as "the fulfillment of a biography": a true "birth" and a blossoming of "the most important." The category of "most important" from the story of her childhood steeped in an ocean of family love (which she presented in her first autobiography, written in 1939–1940) is now redefined: "the most important" is the "suprapersonal" that marks the life of a scholar (V: 19, 31).

To outline her path, Freidenberg describes early intellectual influences absorbed through independent reading. She singles out A. N. Veselovsky, whom, back then, she "used to love" (V: 16, 9); James George Frazer and his *Golden Bough*; and Hermann Usener and *The Names of God*. Reading these books, rather than attending university, was a true "entry into scholarship" (V: 16, 8). Later in the 1920s (as she reports in her notes), she read and assimilated J. J. Bachofen, Lucien Lévy-Bruhl, Ernst Cassirer, and Oswald Spengler, to name the most important authors.[5] But access to foreign sources, as she makes clear, was practically cut off for Soviet scholars in the 1930s.

Still more important for Freidenberg is her first work of scholarship, a study of the Greek apocryphal text "The Acts of Paul and Thecla." It takes her several notebooks to describe the genesis of this work, its scholarly significance, and its significance in her life.

The early Christian text features a young noblewoman named Thecla, who, after an encounter with the apostle Paul, abandoned her worldly life to follow Christian teaching and accept martyrdom. Freidenberg saw in the main plot, the relationship between Thecla and Paul, a transformation of a mythological pattern involving the passions of fertility gods. In its turn, she argued, the story of Paul and Thecla was transformed into a love plot, giving rise to the nascent genre of the novel. Her main thesis was that the early

Christian text turned myth into a moralistic tale about spiritual devotion, which was, in turn, transformed into a love story featuring ordinary human lives, which defined the novel as a genre (V: 21, 39). In her notes, Freidenberg wants to make clear that she was the first scholar to trace the genesis of the Greek novel, one of the earliest examples of the novel in Western literature, to the early Christian texts—and, through them, back to myth.[6] She understands her discovery as having a broader meaning: "I saw that difference is a form of identity, and sameness carries in itself heterogeneity, a thought that has since then not left me" (V: 19, 39). But while she wants to make the theoretical significance of her first work clear, she also has another goal. The way Freidenberg tells this story, her first work of scholarship was deeply embedded in the circumstances of her life. It was also a step on her path to self-understanding.

Freidenberg started her work during the terrible winter of 1919–1920. Much of it she spent in bed, gravely ill. Shortly before her illness, as an assignment for a seminar led by one of her revered mentors, the classicist S. A. Zhebelev, she read the Greek text describing a beautiful young woman named Thecla and her passionate devotion to the apostle Paul. The book remained with her during her illness, and, lying in her cold bed, Freidenberg immersed herself in this text. The story of Thecla and Paul, Thecla's "teacher," resonated with her own life: "The Acts began with Thecla listening, mesmerized, to her teacher Paul. The Apocrypha spoke to me. I felt its erotic, pagan flavor, its artistic quality." She thinks of her own mentors: "Borozdin, Zhebelev, Tolstoy, Bush. . . . My teachers. Everything led me to Thecla and put me at her window" (IV: 10, 83–84). "The Acts of Paul and Thecla" also spoke to her about what it means to write literary scholarship. Writing scholarship, she now understood, was a form of self-understanding and, in this sense, a form of life writing. And in scholarship she found a form of self-writing that was superior to autobiographical poetry: "While working on the Greek novel, I was writing my biography. It was not in [my] feminine poems, but in scholarly work that I was finally finding an outlet for my lyrical essence—that true form of describing my inner self that I had longed for since childhood" (V: 19, 33).

In her first autobiography, written in 1939–1940, Freidenberg claimed that scholarship was autobiography (I–II, 117). Ten years later, she returns to this idea, intimating that, by working on her study, the worldly young woman she had been was transformed into an austere scholar. She became Thecla, and her university teachers became Paul. Scholars have made a different suggestion, tracing the relationship between Thecla and Paul to the young Freidenberg's relationship with Pasternak, the man she listened to for hours—as she describes elsewhere in her notes—entranced by his otherworldly image and understanding almost nothing (I–II, 72).[7] Whatever the case, I do not see this as a matter of direct biographical projection (seeing one's own life in the situation of literary heroes) but rather as a way of relating one's own life to common patterns embodied in myth and literature. Looking at herself through the prism of a literary text, Freidenberg is able to reveal a proto-structure of sorts in her own life that draws on a common stock of meaning embodied in myth and literature: "I found in myself not myself, but a great generalization, an embryo that is similar to all ancestors and devoid of individual features . . . and this explained to me the mysteries of forms and being, the unity of the different, and the singularity generated by what is common" (V: 19, 32–33). Studying "The Acts of Paul and Thecla," she finds deeply rooted patterns like the sacred bond between teacher and disciple, which in her life, as well as in the ancient text, transcended erotic passion in an act of devotion fraught with suffering. For her, doing scholarship was, then, a way of reaching beyond oneself into the world of shared meanings preserved by texts.

In keeping with this idea, Freidenberg describes the creative process involved in producing scholarship as "self-abandonment." She looks for the right word: "Ecstasy, rather, *ekstasis*? Stepping outside oneself?" (V: 19, 32). A work of scholarship was both an act of self-revelation and a way of stepping outside of one's self. Understood in this way, scholarship suited her more as a form of self-writing than lyrical poetry—at least, the self-absorbed "feminine" poetry she wrote as a young woman. And presenting scholarship as a form of creativity analogous with, but not identical to, poetic creativity, Freidenberg may be thinking of Pasternak and their shared quest for a means of self-expression, which she had described in her first autobiography, drawing on their 1910 correspondence.

Concluding her long story, Freidenberg reflects on what remains from this first work of scholarship. It remained unpublished and unknown and "has become dated, as I myself have become dated" (V: 20, 48). But the theoretical principles she introduced as she worked on it have remained valid. And what has also remained is the profound experience of the creative process itself: a sense of self-transcendence. In scholarship, she found the "true"—that is, self-transcendent—form of life writing she had always desired.

And yet, nearing the end of her path as a scholar, Freidenberg also describes her doubts that any form other than art can express the essence of individual human life: "There are things that you cannot narrate without being an artist. Love for one's mother, closeness with one's teacher, a sense of poetry—how can one convey this? Saying 'life,' 'I,' 'autobiography' is not enough" (V: 23, 72). What she says throws doubt on the biography she is now writing in her notes, in which she tries to speak, in a direct and unmediated way, about her love for her mother, her closeness with her teachers, her sense of poetry, and much more. For a moment, Freidenberg, recognizing that she is not an artist, seems to doubt that she stands a chance of fulfilling her lifelong aspiration to reveal that "everything that took place in me and outside of me . . . has a meaning" (I-II, 1).

"Entry into Academia"

Freidenberg separates the story of her entry into the world of scholarship from the parallel story of her attempts to enter academia, or the "academic milieu." As she tells this second story, she is attentive to the workings of the social institutions that functioned in early Soviet society.

For several years after graduating from the university in 1923, she could not find any work. A document pasted into the notebook testifies to her official status as an unemployed person paying obligatory visits to the office of Labor Exchange (Birzha truda) (VI: 27, 108). Then, a dramatic change in her situation was brought about via a fortunate personal connection: "A new life began for my mother and me—a life in Marr" (VI: 26, 98). Thus begins the account of Freidenberg's complex relationship with the linguist, ethnographer, and cultural theorist Nikolai Marr (1864–1934), who played a crucial role in her entry into Soviet academia.

Marr's role in Soviet scholarship is debated by scholars. As the author of a utopian "new theory of language," also known as the "Japhetic theory," Marr often figures in the history of science as a charlatan and opportunist despite his legitimate achievements in linguistics, archaeology, and ethnography. Marr's "new theory of language" mixed wild ideas about the evolution of language, like his notorious claim that all world languages originated from a single source consisting of four monosyllabic exclamations, with elaborate Marxist notions, like the claim that languages go through stages of evolution corresponding to the socioeconomic, class-based development of society. Strange as this may seem, in Soviet academia, this idiosyncratic theory was embraced as a new understanding of the genesis of human civilization befitting a revolutionary society. In the late 1920s, the new theory's author was elevated to the dubious role of "leader" of Soviet linguistics. Rumored to be Stalin's personal favorite, Marr exerted enormous influence in academic life. This situation lasted until 1950, when, on Stalin's whim, Marr, who had died in 1934, was dismissed from the Soviet pantheon and his theory was proclaimed "erroneous."[8]

While scholarly opinions regarding Freidenberg's intellectual involvement with Marr's ideas differ,[9] it seems clear that, while Freidenberg never shared Marr's most eccentric propositions, her ideas on cultural genesis and evolution, including studies done in cooperation with Israel Frank-Kamenetsky in the late 1920s and 1930s, shared common ground with some of Marr's work. Specifically, the principles of Marr's "semantic paleontology"—the method of tracing the genesis of cultural forms to the deep past—influenced Freidenberg's own approach to the origin and evolution of patterns of meaning (plots, genres, metaphors), which she called "genetic semantics."[10] And there is no doubt that Marr's patronage played an important, and paradoxical, role in Freidenberg's academic career. The association with the all-powerful Marr helped her gain her first academic appointments, including the chair of classical philology at Leningrad University in 1932. Then, in 1950, when Stalin anathematized Marr and "Marrism," her association with Marr contributed to her loss of status.[11]

In her notes, Freidenberg presents her first encounters with Marr's work as a discovery of kinship and affinity: "When I started reading Marr, I began to enter a world of concepts that was deeply familiar to me, and there was no limit to my understanding, admiration, and happiness" (VI: 26, 98). She continues, "Each of his works offered me something familiar; what I did confirmed him, and what he did confirmed me" (VI: 26, 98). She claims an elective affinity of sorts, rather than influence, a set of mutual echoes between their ideas on the genesis of cultural forms, though admitting that this had more significance for her than for Marr. When it comes to her career, Freidenberg gives full credit to Marr for easing her entry into Soviet academia, however tentative her first steps may have been.

Thus, Marr's patronage enabled Freidenberg to defend her first dissertation, "The Genesis of the Greek Novel" (*Proiskhozhdenie grecheskogo romana*), or "The Greek Novel as Acts and Passions" (*Grecheskii roman kak deianiia i strasti*),[12] based on her work on "The Acts of Paul and Thecla." Strictly speaking, the dissertation defense was no more than a public debate, since academic degrees were officially abolished in the first years after the Russian Revolution of 1917. The debate took place on November 14, 1924, in the Institute for the Comparative Study of Literatures and Languages of the West and East.[13] Marr arranged the event and presided over it. Freidenberg suggests that, having read her study—written, she insists, before she became familiar with his ideas—Marr saw in her a potential ally in the methodological struggles of the day and decided to take the young scholar under his wing. Freidenberg describes the debate as a battle in which she had to defend herself from attacks that came from all sides, from the traditional classicists to the avant-garde formalists. (Freidenberg indeed stood in opposition to the Russian formalist school.)[14] Pasted into the notebook is a faded note, in pencil, that Marr sent her amid this battle: "Please, don't worry: it's clear that your interpretation is too new and fresh. N. M." (VI: 26, 102). In more ways than one, this defense was a trial and a rite of passage: "On that day I was born as a polemicist and fighter" (VI: 26, 102). Indeed, for the rest of her professional life, Freidenberg was known as a fierce polemicist—a quality that did not endear her to her colleagues.

Pasted into the notebook is the "Qualification Certificate" issued on January 1925 in lieu of a degree certificate, stating that she was qualified "to teach and perform research work in institutions of higher education" (VI: 27, 110–111). Yet her life of unemployment, destitution, and isolation continued. Freidenberg describes how, to sustain the family's precarious existence, she sold possessions from their prerevolutionary life at a flea market. She asks, "Who could I appeal to? Marr wasn't interested in a human being. He lived by his theory. . . ." (VI: 28, 118). Marr, she felt, was not capable of participating in the sacred communion between teacher and student that Freidenberg valued above all (VI: 29, 134).

Freidenberg was also bitterly disappointed in her cousin Borya (Boris Pasternak), who had promised to help through his acquaintance with Anatoly Lunacharsky, the People's Commissar of Enlightenment—the head of the Soviet ministry responsible for education and the arts (VI: 28, 120). Relating the story of her confrontation with Pasternak in 1924 over his failure to come to her rescue, as she saw it, Freidenberg cites a letter she wrote to him in which she tried to formulate the essence of their difficult relationship: "All of this is part of the life program: we have to scold each other, to fall in each other's eyes, to carry on an unworthy correspondence. Then time will cover it over, and there will remain only what we began with—a kindred birth, and volumes of books on different subjects and in different forms" (VI: 28, 124).

Freidenberg's statement contains a program for the future as well as a memory of their past, expressing her veneration of kinship based on the commonality of origin and a shared reading list. In the meantime, they continued what she called their "unworthy correspondence," which she did not reproduce in her notes.[15]

The notebook includes an "epoch-making" letter sent by her uncle Leonid Pasternak from Berlin in February 1925, in which he made an important suggestion about her work: "*Its arena is abroad, not in Russia*" (VI: 30, 138; emphasis Freidenberg's). With his help, Freidenberg then made several attempts to establish contacts in German academia, which she carefully documents. Several letters from Leonid Pasternak, beginning in October 1925, describe his efforts to obtain an evaluation of Freidenberg's dissertation and its main argument based on a German-language abstract from the authoritative classicists in Germany (VI: 31, 149–151). One, in November, describes his visit to Eduard Norden, a student of the famous Hermann Usener (VI: 33, 158–161). Norden's brief evaluation is copied, along with Leonid Pasternak's letters, into the notebook (VI: 33, 162–163).

Then, one day in 1925, Freidenberg heard from a colleague that a book confirming some of her ideas on the origin of cultural forms had appeared in France. This was a study on the origin of folktales by Émile Nourry, published under the penname P. Saintyves. Freidenberg had not heard of him but managed to find his books. In 1925, she comments, it was difficult but still possible to obtain books published in the West. By the late 1940s, as she wrote in her account, maintaining ties with colleagues in the West had long been impossible (VI: 31, 144). And when Freidenberg wrote about Saintyves's publication, she already knew that there would be more. In 1927, a book by the Hungarian Swiss scholar Károly Kerényi (who knew nothing about her work) advanced ideas about the origin of the Greek novel that were very close to her own conception. She lamented that, with her study unpublished, it remained unknown outside a narrow circle of (mostly skeptical) scholars in Soviet Russia (VI: 33, 163).

In 1925, Freidenberg decided to address a letter to Lunacharsky, and she copied it into the notebook years later. In this letter, she introduces herself as the first woman to receive academic qualifications ("in the old terminology, a dissertation") in classical philology, who, at present, lives "at a social status below that of a street beggar." To finance her scholarly work, she was selling family possessions at the Obvodny Canal flea market, alongside thieves and prostitutes. But she would not trouble the People's Commissar of Enlightenment if it were not for one fact: "A study like mine had appeared in France and was met with such honors that the Germans wrote about it with praise, and a German review reached us. . . ." She ends on a solemn note: "It would be beneath my scholarly dignity to ask anything of you, the person charged with the administration of enlightenment. I personally do not need anything. . . ." She will continue her scholarly work in obscurity, hoping it would survive in history. But she considers it her duty to inform the People's Commissar about "the Russian scholarly achievements that had surpassed those of the West" (VI: 31, 145–148).

That was 1925. Now, amid Stalin's official campaign prioritizing Russian science over the Western variety, she looks at her past appeal with scorn: "Now, when I write about 1925, it is 1949, and all the expressions from my letter to Lunacharsky seem taken from [the currently] fashionable political vocabulary: Russian science, Western science, Russian achievements, Russian priority. What nonsense!" (VI: 31, 148).

This makes her ponder the problem of temporal perspective, and she compares her position with that of a novelist: "When a novelist writes the first chapters, he does not know how the last one will end. And I, alas, know: my pluses will turn into my minuses. I know, because I wrote my last chapters first, and then started writing the first ones" (VI: 31, 148). Retrospective vision pervades the story of Freidenberg's entry into Soviet academia. Everything in the past acquires its significance from the present moment of acute political and personal crisis.

Looking back, Freidenberg acknowledges that her letter, with its naive appeal to the "priority of Russian science," played a large role in starting her professional career. One day, she was asked to come to the Institute for the Comparative Study of Literatures and Languages. After reading her letter, Lunacharsky had contacted Marr, and Marr had created a position for her. In retrospect, she knows that this was a pivotal event in her career. And she again imagines her life story in terms of the temporal organization of literary forms: "Big events usually pass unrecognized, like the heroes of an epic. We attach great importance to what disappears without a trace and fail to see what eventually turns out to be important for our entire biography" (VI: 32, 151).

Indeed, in 1925, it was difficult to appreciate her newly found employment as a significant development. To demonstrate this point, she cites yet another official document, showing that while her employment was effective on February 25, 1925, her first salary was paid only on December 18, 1925, in the negligible sum of twenty-four rubles and thirty-three kopecks (VI: 32, 157). As she suspects, as a result of an internal institutional intrigue, the position was handed over to another candidate.

Then there was a further development: in 1926, Marr invited her to join the main institution he then headed, the so-called Japhetic Institute (VI: 36, 189).[16] (In the first postrevolutionary years, a number of small academic institutions with dubious missions and uncertain funding sprang into being, often under the personal tutelage of a powerful person.) There, she reports, in the newly created section for the study of myth, she finally found an intellectual environment and met like-minded colleagues. After several awkward attempts, she formed a close association with Israel Frank-Kamenetsky, a man who would become her most important ally and intimate friend (VI: 36, 190).

In the meantime, as Freidenberg reports, Leonid Pasternak had managed to obtain a favorable opinion on her hypothesis about the origins of the Greek novel from Adolf Harnack, the author of seminal works on the history of early Christian literature, and she cites this document (from October 28, 1926) in the notes (VII: 38, 3–6). She is scornful that back then these few words of approbation from a foreign authority had significantly influenced her scholarly reputation: "my stock rose at once" (VII: 38, 6). And she submits evidence, citing a letter from November 8, 1926, from her former teacher, the distinguished classicist Zhebelev: "He has only to say 'imprimatur,' and all the journals will open their doors. For with the Germans, and perhaps everywhere, Harnack is Jupiter Optimus Maximus" (VII: 38, 5). But this did not come to pass. Freidenberg's study of the Greek novel remained unpublished.

Describing the tangled circumstances that accompanied her first steps in academia, Freidenberg makes clear that both then and now, she was full of apprehension and resentment. The social world that surrounded scholarship, meaning both unpredictable personal relations and the constricting conventions of Soviet social institutions, seemed hostile to her. She felt lost in the tangled paths that led to her "entry into academia" (VI: 32, 153).

Looking back, Freidenberg marks the "two milestones" on her path to professional fulfillment: first, Anatoly Lunacharsky's intervention, which initiated academic employment for her, however tenuous, and second, a word of approbation from an international authority in Berlin, Adolf Harnack, which helped establish her reputation among colleagues in Soviet Russia. This meant entering the carefully guarded "citadel of scholarship," this "structure of reinforced concrete" (VII: 38, 6). Now, at the end of her career, Freidenberg describes its beginnings with bitter irony toward various institutional structures as well as specific people who governed Soviet academia. And she mentions that the hope of entering "real scholarship abroad" (*zagranichnuiu nastoiashchuiu nauku*) continued to inspire her for some years, until it faded, "as all living things faded with the accession of Stalin" (VII: 38, 7). As for Soviet academia, Freidenberg writes, "I understood perfectly well that there were outstanding scholars in Russia, but there was no scholarship" (VII: 38, 7).

If not in 1926 (the time she is describing), by 1949, Freidenberg understood that scholarship did not, and could not, exist in the Soviet Union. She was by then convinced that, as a social institution, scholarship, like science, could not exist in isolation from the rest of the world.

"The Housing Question"

Like her professional life, her domestic life as described in this part of the notes is full of drama, both personal and social. Throughout the 1920s, Freidenberg was still living with her mother and her brother Sashka in the large "bourgeois" apartment they had occupied before the revolution. With Sashka's marriage in 1926, the family was joined by his young wife, Musya, seen as a deeply alien element. As Freidenberg makes clear, Musya was from another social class—the daughter of a janitor—and she brought with her an "alien style" and family discord. In this new household, Freidenberg and her mother "suffered immensely." For one thing, the "janitor's daughter disdained all housework" (VII: 38, 1).

When, in the winter of 1949, Freidenberg described how they had lived back in 1926, she knew that Musya, and then Sashka, had been arrested in 1937. In view of this knowledge, she sees these trivial conflicts somewhat differently (while irritation with the capricious Musya still remains with her): "Oh, if I had known what a terrible fate awaited my brother and this idle, healthy woman, who pretended to be an unearthly creature; how, one day, she would become a manual laborer, a convict—I would probably have washed her feet and kissed the floor under her" (VII: 38, 2). While Sashka disappeared without a trace and the family presumed him to be dead, Musya (as described in chapter 3) suddenly reappeared in Freidenberg's life in the late 1940s, after she was released from a long prison sentence. Freidenberg relates this deeply disturbing encounter in the notebook written at the same time as the memories of Sashka's marriage to the frivolous Musya (XXXII: II, 49–51).

Sashka and his wife left the family apartment in 1927, after which Freidenberg started renting spare rooms to fellow scholars to supplement the family's meager income. But this was only a temporary measure. Because of the acute shortage of living space, the Soviet authorities were expropriating the living space of the former bourgeoisie by forcibly moving in other families, usually from the proletariat. The result was the infamous "communal apartment," in which several families lived in squalor and class enmity in a single flat, sharing the kitchen and toilet. When Sashka left, this possibility became real, and "the housing question" (the official term Freidenberg ironically applies to their personal situation) was very much on her mind. The new Soviet order threatened the established routines of a bourgeois family that, like other such families, could no longer count on the inviolability of their home, their privacy, and their intellectual habitus.

Back in 1927, Freidenberg was aware that such trivial concerns might seem unworthy of a creative person involved in the contemplation of intellectual and spiritual matters, and she broached this subject in her correspondence with Boris Pasternak. In the notebook she wrote twenty years later, she cites a letter to Pasternak dated September 9, 1927, in which she considered the family's housing difficulties from a philosophical perspective. In this letter, Freidenberg referred to the "trivial housing question" as a matter that, unimportant as it might have been, called for immediate interpretation, and she approached this task equipped with concepts from phenomenology and cultural semiotics: "One simply cannot, one cannot fail to interpret the unceasing content of days, which is there, as the given [*dannost'*], albeit composed of small and petty things." ("The given" is a phenomenological term referring to the object that is given to human knowledge as objective reality.) And so, engaged as she then was in the ongoing search for the meaning and purpose—"the idea"—of her "biography," she saw "the housing question" as a "sign" signifying a "stage in the work of the spirit," namely, "an encounter with the everyday [*byt*]," approached in its "gradational quality" (a term drawn from methodological debates about successive, or gradational, stages in the development of culture) (VII: 39, 8). The 1927 letter, written at the very onset of the family's housing difficulties, relies on the conceptual vocabulary the cousins employed in their philosophical correspondence in 1910, combined with the terminology of Freidenberg's practice as a cultural theorist. Not only housing was explained this way. A few pages further, remembering the "unheard-of passion" that linked the star-crossed cousins almost twenty years before (their meeting in Merreküll and Petersburg in 1910, which I described in chapter 1), she presents their current situation as "the relationship of two people thrown into the social everyday [*sotsial'nyi byt*]" (VII: 39, 15). Whether she was ironic or dead serious in employing this language in 1927 is hard to tell.

But when the Freidenberg of 1949 turns to describing the family's increasingly threatening housing problems in her notes, she uses very different language. And this time, the description is clearly devoid of irony. The problem was not trivial but all-consuming: "The whole year 1929, all three hundred and sixty-something days of it, passed under the sign of unheard-of proceedings concerning the apartment" (VII: 53, 186). The family's difficulties started when, in order to forestall the conversion of their large bourgeois apartment into a communal living space, Freidenberg and her mother requested permission to divide it into several units, leaving two rooms with a toilet, bathroom, and kitchen for their own use. Such a move was considered legitimate at the time, but when they applied for the necessary permit, they ran into a series of insurmountable obstacles. In the course of one year, they went through twenty-two on-site inspections and eleven legal procedures, accumulating three volumes of documents, and Freidenberg tries to describe them all in the pages of her notes. Paying special attention to moments of crisis, she tells how, at one point, a lower-class family was illegally installed in the apartment. Freidenberg's description is graphic: "The whole family of a violent, alcoholic laborer moved in, with a mistress and two children" (VII: 53, 187). The Freidenbergs eventually managed to evict them by a court order.

Both then and now, she sees her family's difficulties as stemming from the fact that their large, centrally located apartment was coveted by the high officials of the institution in charge of housing, "party people" who would stop at nothing to get the attractive apartment for themselves. These people—the "enemy"—play a large role in her story.

Freidenberg's account is complete with documentary evidence: a large number of depositions, memoranda, letters of complaint, and more found their way onto the pages of the notebook (VII: 53, 186–214). Aware of the literary potential of this material, she mentions that the case was worthy of the pen of Alexander Sukhovo-Kobylin, the nineteenth-century author of "The Case" (*Delo*), a well-known play satirizing the bureaucratic procedures of the Russian empire (VII: 53, 186). She could not know that, later in the Soviet period, a literary text about a contested apartment, based on original documents, would actually be produced.[17]

Among the documents the notes reproduce in full is an appeal Freidenberg addressed to the secret police, at the time called the GPU (Gosudarstvennoe politicheskoe upravlenie, The State Political Directorate). It was her brother Sashka who had decided to appeal for help to this all-powerful organization, using the slim pretext that he worked at an optical plant that bore the name of the GPU as an honorary title, and she added her own "cry of the heart" to his memorandum. This amazing text, written in a voice that is not her own and far from the one Freidenberg uses in her notes, deserves special attention.

She begins this "very urgent" appeal to the organ of state security by defining the speaker's position as that of a "Marxist-research worker" (*nauchnyi rabotnik-marxist*):

> Very urgent
> To the Head of the Economics Department of the GPU
> Dear comrade.
>
> You are addressed by a Marxist-research worker, an Employee of the First Category of the Research Institute of Literature and Languages at Leningrad State University, the Institute of Marxism, and the Japhetic Institute, with a fervent request to release me from blackmail in the struggle with which I have been overtaxing my strength for nine months and am about to sink completely. Let me familiarize you with the whole case in order to reconstruct the whole picture.
>
> Last year Soviet power gave citizens the right to divide apartments so that they would be given to workers. I took advantage of this right. (VII: 53, 199)[18]

The letter goes on for more than eight single-spaced pages, relating the case in minute detail and characterizing her antagonists in the most damaging terms. Freidenberg concludes by making a passionate appeal to an imaginary officer of state security, begging him to protect her from the arbitrary power exercised by the local authorities: "Comrade. My life is nothing but nightmarish torture: I am at the mercy of blackmail and arbitrariness. . . . One needs the strong and courageous power of the investigative organs to grasp the whole picture rather than its individual parts. My only hope is for your courageous help. I give all my strength to the state, and I ask you to protect me from three predators. . . ." (VII: 53, 207).

Here, addressing the sinister organ of Soviet power, Freidenberg speaks in a voice aimed to evoke sympathy by highlighting the supplicant's Soviet affiliation, helplessness, and ardent trust in state security. Later, Freidenberg submitted another such letter to the Communist Party headquarters, Smolny, also appealing to power in the voice of the new Soviet subject: "Comrades! I am a Marxist. . . . I am an ordinary worker. . . ." (VII: 53, 209).

Reading these documents, one is reminded of the narrative techniques of *skaz*, widely employed in the 1920s by Soviet writers, such as Mikhail Zoshchenko, who played with the voice of the semiliterate Soviet citizen eager to adapt to the political language of the new state. In Zoshchenko's case, this was mostly parody bordering on satire. But Freidenberg's appeal is not literature, and she could not afford parody or irony. Hoping for a reprieve, she tries to speak in the language of the ordinary Soviet man who badly needs assistance from "the strong and courageous power of the investigative organs," and she places herself entirely under their protection. The Freidenberg of 1949 understands that she was using a literary device worthy of a satirical drama. She adds, "But this Sukhovo-Kobylin document did not help one iota either" (VII: 53, 209).

In spite of all their efforts, the Freidenberg family lost their case and faced eviction from their old apartment as well as a catastrophic financial burden. But then a miracle occurred: a complaint Sashka addressed to a higher court landed on the desk of a newly appointed prosecutor who promptly annulled the previous ruling, and in January 1930, the case was decided in favor of the Freidenberg family. This was "fate," Freidenberg comments. Their case was even featured in a Leningrad newspaper on February 27, 1930, as an example of an injustice that was rectified by the Soviet authorities. This is how this "epic" came to an end, Freidenberg writes in conclusion to her story (VII: 53, 210). Now, in 1949, she does not see this as a victory; what is more, she knows that another attempt to turn their apartment (though it had been reduced to two rooms) into a communal space would take place later.

In 1949, the "housing question" was no longer a matter for interpretation in philosophical categories. And the difficulties in the family's living circumstances no longer signify "an encounter with the everyday" as a certain "stage in the spiritual work," as she had put it in her letter to Pasternak in 1927. A lot had changed. For one thing, such everyday problems had become all-consuming. What is more, after the war, Freidenberg thought that the seemingly trivial difficulties were repressive measures created by the Soviet state, intent at reaching its citizens in their no-longer-private homes, kitchens, and toilets. Viewed from this perspective, the housing problems of 1927–1929, which had been resolved through the magical intervention of a higher authority, prefigured the terror that would soon entirely envelop their everyday. In 1929, Freidenberg made pathetic attempts to address the state in the voice of the new Soviet subject, an "ordinary" person who gives all her strength to the state and asks the organ of state security to protect her from predators among the local housing authorities. In 1949, all she can do is create a well-documented record of the yearlong trial. Whether or not Freidenberg was fully aware of the change in her vision of her daily life, her narrative makes the progression clear: from initially reflecting philosophically on the "encounter with the everyday," she passes to adopting a Soviet persona with the aim of gaining sympathy from the secret police and, still later, to writing an "epic" about the "housing question" for posterity in her notes.

"I Lived Through Khona"

"My scholarship was inextricably connected with love. I lived through Khona" (IX: 69, 157). This is how Freidenberg starts the story of her love for her colleague and close ally in scholarship, the cocreator of "genetic semantics," Israel Frank-Kamenetsky (born Israel-Chona, he was known to family and friends as Khona). Their involvement was "an exchange of scholarly souls," with an "intimacy . . . such that the individuality of one was lost in the other. Nature made us, two strangers and distant people, into twins" (VI: 37, 204). Pasted into the notebooks covering the years 1928–1937 is the voluminous correspondence between the lovers. Writing in 1949, Freidenberg feels that the correspondence did not reflect the essence of their relationship, so she supplements the documents with her story.

Having met as colleagues in 1924, the two became close in the spring of 1928: "We were wedded by the commonality of lives and loves. Our destinies merged" (VII: 44, 70). Khona's wife, Dora, soon learned of their love, and Freidenberg's mother, from whom she hid nothing, disapproved of her association with a married man; a heavy atmosphere of restrained hatred prevailed in both homes (VII: 46, 95). The lovers spent whole days wandering the city together: through streets and back alleys, along crowded Nevsky Prospect and empty embankments, often holding hands (VII: 44, 70–71). Freidenberg presents the city as the site of their love and misery: "O, where have we not whispered, hugged, and cried?" She answers, "In entryways, the dark corners of vestibules, under the vaults of churches...." (IX: 69, 166).

Although they lived in the same city, they exchanged long letters, addressed to a post office poste restante. Sometimes they wrote on the same day they managed to see each other or talk on the phone. They discussed the nuances of their relationship. For a long time, they addressed each other formally by first name and patronymic and used the formal, second-person plural pronoun (*Vy*). Frank-Kamenetsky wrote: "I told you [*Vy*] this 'morning' (by telephone) that after yesterday's conversation I had a great deal of confusion in my soul, but when you answered that there was much to be clarified, I had a glimmer of doubt about the very possibility of such clarification" (VII: 45, 80).

Nevertheless, he attempted a clarification. The next day, May 12, 1928, Freidenberg replied with a long "philosophical" letter of her own—eleven double-spaced pages when typed: "Today, when you [*Vy*] told me on the telephone that you had a letter for me . . . suddenly such a great, such an airy, light joy seized me that I understood the nature of my soul, for which the dearest thing in the world is language speaking from heart to heart, with a complete withdrawal from life, from the world of sounds, from everything sensual (in the philosophical sense!)" (VII: 45, 83).

In this way, in their letters, the lovers discussed the meaning of love and the workings of language. Freidenberg wrote about the "fusion" of souls that was "qualitatively different" from accepted forms of communion inasmuch as it led to "unity" as an object of desire and a value in itself. And she made clear that she understood such things as "fusion" and "unity" "in a philosophical sense" (VII: 45, 73–74). They often talked about love, fate, and death. In addition to philosophical concepts, both used the conceptual tools of their profession as philologists and cultural historians. Thus, when Frank-Kamenetsky brought up the topic of "interdiction," referring to their avoidance of sex, Freidenberg suggested that such "interdictions," or "conventions," belonged to "prehistoric semantics" (VII: 45, 74). This objection did not, apparently, result in any change in their behavior. "He meant the ordinary denouement of love," explained Freidenberg, referring, it seems, to sexual consummation, "and I thought that he was talking about fate, about the predestination of our encounter in this life" (VII: 45, 79). She then suggested the "possibility of transforming the physical into the spiritual" (VII: 45, 87). In their discussions of the painful problems of their love, including the indefinite deferral of sexual consummation, the lovers were heavily dependent on the conceptual apparatus of cultural studies—and it seems that, at least in some cases, they used this language without irony.

In the summer of 1928, when Frank-Kamenetsky's wife was away, Freidenberg rented a room near Leningrad, in Tsarskoe Selo. While the pair was meeting in that room, they continued to write each other lengthy letters affirming their resolve to keep the relationship "pure." But in July, they switched to the informal address (*ty*).

Dora returned. Soon Freidenberg learned that Khona had resumed carnal relations with his wife (VII: 47, 133). A new stage of love began, "bitter" and "burdensome" for both of them (VII: 47, 139). Freidenberg soon decided that they "had a right to act as their love demanded," but this time Khona held back (VII: 51, 169). Thinking this over in 1949, when she wrote her notes, Freidenberg claims that she never felt sensual love for any person she loved, who was thus "spiritualized by my love." She continues, "Strong passions shook me precisely when I did not love" (VII: 51, 169). Back then, on sleepless nights, she was tormented by one question: "Could it be that the passion that was given to me by nature in such a strong measure is sublimated into scholarly creativity?" (VII: 51, 170). More than one year passed in this way.

While Freidenberg lived through Khona, her mother, as she puts it, "lived through me." In simple terms, her mother felt that her daughter's life belonged to her. She hated Khona. At home alone, she waited impatiently for her daughter's return (X: 80, 116). And yet, Freidenberg insists, jealousy and possessiveness did not disrupt the deep bond between mother and daughter. She recalls, "I thought about her always, worried about her every hour. . . ." What is more, Freidenberg realizes that she had been consumed with the fear that her mother would eventually leave her: thirty years older than her daughter, she would die first. At night, listening to her mother's breathing, she sobbed at the thought of the inevitable separation. This feeling, she thought, was mutual: "We both, hiding from each other, thought our terrible thought about the same thing" (X: 80, 116). As a result, "our life of those years, filled with the greatest happiness of closeness and the greatest mutual understanding, was at the same time a silent devastating drama" (X: 80, 117).

When Freidenberg wrote these lines, she was still mourning her mother, who had died in terrible conditions during the siege, and hence her remorse for the discord they experienced during her troubled love affair with Khona and her obsession with the separation inevitably brought by death.

Tristan and Isolde

In 1929–1932, Freidenberg, Frank-Kamenetsky, and their colleagues worked on a collective edition devoted to the myth of Tristan and Isolde. The project had been launched under Freidenberg's direction but appeared in print, featuring Freidenberg's introduction, as an edition of the Japhetic Institute "under the editorship of N. Ia. Marr."[19] Khona, as Freidenberg mentions in 1949, considered the book his own project—and she obliged by ascribing, in her book *Poetics of Plot and Genre*, the leadership to him (VIII: 58, 31). Now, writing her notes, she implies that she had played a large part. This edition, which traced the medieval legend of Tristan and Isolde (or Tristan and Iseult) to its roots in early mythology, in accordance with the principles of Marr's semantic paleontology, received highly positive reviews and found a way into Stalin's personal library.[20]

After publication, in the summer of 1932, Frank-Kamenetsky, who was touring the Caucasus with an "antireligious brigade," gave several public presentations about the myth of Tristan. In his letters to Freidenberg, he imagined himself as a latter-day Tristan repeating the mythic plot as he proceeded on his journey. "Without moving across the water," he noted in one letter, "the whole structure of the plot would have been violated" (VIII: 58, 43). He added that "the motif of love" was an "intimate tale" that he could not trust to paper (VIII: 58, 43). Adding "forgive me these awkward jokes," he signed, "Your Tristan" (VIII: 58, 43–44).

Upon his return, Frank-Kamenetsky wrote to Freidenberg about his love with unadorned despair, counting on her instant understanding: "Olya, I think about you every day, of course, not about you alone, but about the two of us. The situation is becoming purely tragic. I am not saying everything, but you will understand. Of course, I am not afraid of the worst: I believe in you, in your resolve no less than in my feeling. But still, it is impossible to go on like this, and I don't know what to do. I think that life itself will bring resolution—there is nowhere else to expect it from" (VIII: 58, 45). When Freidenberg cited these words in her notes in 1949, she knew that the resolution of their love would come with Khona's death.

The theme of death seems to have pervaded the lovers' conversations: "He spoke about death—he always spoke about death. . . ." (VII: 44, 72). Khona's tragic death (in a traffic accident in 1937) was of course on Freidenberg's mind, but the emphasis on death was more than retrospective. Writing in 1949, Freidenberg cites a letter she wrote to Khona, undated but from a time when they were still addressing each other formally: "You [Vy] upset me a lot on Saturday, making my heart contract. It was when you spoke about death" (VII: 44, 72). She also thinks about dying together, asking Khona to wait until she too would have "the right to die" so they could die as a pair, "without breaking either a link between mother and me, or a link between you and me" (VII: 45, 92). Responding in a philosophical mode, Khona turned to the nature of time and eternity: if "two beings have come together in limitless space," then "past, present, and future are fused, and the moment is equal to eternity." He continued, "There is no duration of time, and certainly there are no stages. What both felt once is, was, and will be" (VII: 46, 102). Here he evokes the theory of stadial evolution advanced by Marr, though only to reject it. In this poignant moment, contemplating the end of his life and the fateful meeting with his beloved, this scholar-lover linked love and death and, switching to professional discourse, made a reference to "so-called 'meaning'": "If someday, at the end of my life, death does not take me by surprise, and there is a moment when I will look back at my whole life in a single moment—all my experiences, all life with its so-called 'meaning' and that unknown thing called 'nonbeing,' would not all of this be colored differently for me because fate has finally sent me that meeting in which there is happiness—and joy, and 'pain and reconciliation'. . . ?" (VII: 46, 102).

As Freidenberg's notes suggest, the myth of Tristan and Isolde, which the pair had explored in their joint research project—and which they also knew from Wagner's opera with its celebration of death as the only consummation of forbidden love—was realized in their lives.

"My Department"

Beginning in 1929, writes Freidenberg, "my entry onto the broad public-academic arena" began; "the preparatory period of my life was over" (VII: 48, 142). From 1930 on, Freidenberg held responsible positions and was involved in collective projects, mostly at the State Institute for Speech Culture (GIRK). Then, she says solemnly, "And so I reach the year 1932, the beginning of my university activity" (VIII: 57, 20). Yet Freidenberg pointedly describes her appointment as head of the newly opened Department of Classical Philology at Leningrad University in 1932 as something that happened against all odds and took place almost against her will: "There was an order to open a department of classical philology, and they asked me to organize it. . . . I refused again and again. . . ."[21] She explains that "any entry into the gates of the kingdom," by which she means a social institution with its forbidding rules and conventions, was a burden for her. She was not an administrator. What is more, she had never taught—how would she become a professor? And in recent years, she had withdrawn from classical philology, becoming involved in the study of mythology (VIII: 60, 57). But finally, she agreed, "almost coerced" into the role of the head of the department. Freidenberg does not mention what her biographers and historians claim: her association with the all-powerful Marr may have played a role in this appointment.[22]

114   CHAPTER 4

She marks the day, December 24, 1932, when she entered a classroom with students—of whom there were only a few—for the first time. Soon she was "captivated" by her work (VIII: 60, 58). She starts saying "my department" and "we," and she describes the atmosphere of trust and cooperation in her department in its early days (VIII: 62, 76). When Freidenberg writes these phrases at the end of the 1940s, they are full of bitterness: she is about to be ousted from her department. These circumstances may have influenced her vision of the events of the early 1930s.

"Looking Back, You See"

Freidenberg looks back at the political developments of the years 1929–1936, striving to "understand." She starts with signposts: "These were the years of the first five-year plan, the emergence of socialist competition, the 'six conditions of Comrade Stalin.'. . . ." From her present vantage point, she sees these events as leading to the emergence of a murderous regime that was soon too entrenched to be resisted. "For a long time, we did not understand its nature," she writes, meaning "the intelligentsia." Freidenberg now sees the limitations of this kind of collective understanding (VII: 56, 247).

She writes as a person who did not have "a taste for factional politics" but held an interest in "broad international politics and had aspirations and expectations." There are confessional moments: "In 1931, I was already a Soviet person who wanted to explore, understand, respect, and build new things." This statement is immediately qualified: "But with the reign of Stalin, a system established itself, the essence of which no one understood, but against which they bumped their heads." Next, she switches into a self-consciously retrospective mode: "Looking back, you see how simple it was: the strangulation of the country by means of famine and carefully cultivated ruination; the complete suppression of individuality, thought, ideas, and the human self. This system maintained itself by denunciations of an unheard-of scale, political and 'ideological' persecution, and also public humiliations. I remember the general confusion at the first appearance of printed insults with name-calling and mudslinging. I remember the first campaigns to undermine all authority, institutional, political, and moral. Destruction as a political end in itself was just beginning" (VII: 56, 247).

The retrospective vision of "looking back, you see" pervades Freidenberg's comments on the political history of the Soviet Union and the problem of understanding it. Her past life is largely a history of the misunderstanding she shared with others, a misunderstanding whose contours are now obvious from the vantage point of 1949. Looking back, she recalls everybody's "confusion" at the first purges and the first insulting public attacks at public figures that took place in the 1930s. In a parallel notebook, she describes the public insults and persecutions unfolding in front of her eyes in 1948–1949. From her current position, she sees the destruction and suppression of the individual that began in the 1930s as the foundation of Stalin's regime.

She now sees 1933 as the last "good year." It was a year that "passed under the sign of creative work, a sense of being necessary, progressive upward movement." Now she understands it could not last: "It is clear that Stalin had to sharply cut it off." It is "clear now," but back then, people dismissed the ominous events. Now she understands the limitations of her past vision, but the joy of belonging she experienced then, in the first years of her public activity, seems to remain with her. The year 1933 was "good" (VIII: 62, 76).

The tone soon changes to that of foreboding: "And so, came the year 1934" (VIII: 62, 79). Now, in 1949, she links the beginning of large-scale repressions to the assassination of Kirov in 1934, a view generally accepted by scholars today. Maintaining a double perspective, "then" and "now," Freidenberg again and again affirms the limitations of her then-understanding: "Of course, I was very naive then. . . ." (VIII: 64, 107).

Soon after bringing up the murder of Kirov, Freidenberg starts describing the death of "millions" in the camps and in the war (VIII: 62, 91). She briefly stops herself, commenting that in her agitation, she had been carried far away from the year 1934, but then decides that, after all, this leap in time is faithful to the logic of history (VIII: 63, 92). Back then, her knowledge was just beginning. She returns now to the 1930s equipped with that knowledge: "Now begins what ended in my just written words" (VIII: 63, 92).

Freidenberg also wants to reconstruct the general mood of the first part of the 1930s, which, for most people, bore no inkling of the terror that was to follow. She invokes Stalin's slogan from 1935: "Life has become easier, comrades; life has become more fun. . . ." (VIII: 63, 92). As she now understands, Stalin was the malevolent force behind the carnivalesque atmosphere of joy and happiness: "Dancing, wine, flowers, banquets were created by the directive of the secret police. . . . Anniversaries, soirees, toasts, balls went on in all institutions" (VIII: 63, 93). In a time of famine (as we now know, it peaked in 1932–1933), "the country rattled with fanfares and champagne corks" (VIII: 63, 95). During the blockade, Freidenberg wrote about the "fictitious world" created by official propaganda, which presented life in the besieged city with no correlation to "real-life experience" (XVII: 133, 33). Now, looking back, she sees fictions within the Soviet life of the 1930s. One of the tasks of her notes is to reveal such fictions.

Turning to the university, she notes that then, as now, "the university was a barometer of politics." This was the time of continuous institutional change: "Departments were being expanded or shrunk; faculties and institutes were being renamed." What she saw at the time was expansion and broad prospects (VIII: 63, 95). The academic year 1933–1934 was "happy," and she worked with great enthusiasm.

In this way—with many contradictions, some of which may have escaped her attention—Freidenberg describes the first part of the 1930s. It was a time of fictitious joy and intense work. Real enthusiasm was punctuated by occasional recognition of ongoing repressions, but not by a sense of what the future had in store. The same mode of retrospective vision prevails as she moves forward to 1936: "The year 1936 was approaching. We all thought that the repressions that made up the political system in which we then lived were the response to Kirov's assassination. We did not know what awaited us" (IX: 70, 170).

"Your Book Has Been Confiscated"

In 1935, Freidenberg was faced with the requirement of defending a doctoral dissertation. By this time, degrees and titles had been restored in Soviet academia, and the qualifying work she had defended in 1924 was counted as equivalent to a "candidate" degree. (The Soviet system followed the German one in distinguishing between the first doctorate, or "candidate" degree, and the second doctorate, which was required for the title of full professor.) Faced with this new requirement, Freidenberg revised an unpublished study which she had worked on since the late 1920s and submitted it as her second dissertation, *Poetics of Plot and Genre: The Period of the Classical Literature* (*Poetika siuzheta i zhanra: Period antichnoi literatury*) (IX: 66, 119). The public defense that took place on June 9, 1935, was a significant academic event, and Freidenberg cites with pride the newspaper article that presented her as "the first woman to defend a doctorate degree in literary scholarship" (IX: 67, 141).

This is one of the rare occasions when Freidenberg makes a reference to her situation as a female scholar in Soviet academia, where appointments of women were encouraged. On the whole, paying attention to sex or gender remained as alien to her as claiming her Jewish ethnic origin as a factor of personal or social significance. Like many of her contemporaries, she simply did not want to think in those terms.

She then relates the dramatic circumstances surrounding the publication of *The Poetics of Plot and Genre*, the only book she managed to publish during her lifetime.[23] Her story starts off well: "In May 1936, my *Poetics* was published. It was a big day in my life. . . ." (IX: 71, 184). It was not long, or so it seems to her, before her fortune reversed. A telephone call: "Your book has been confiscated" (IX: 71, 186).[24]

What precipitated the removal of the book from circulation was a blisteringly critical response to Freidenberg's study written by an obscure Moscow author named Ts. Leitenzen and published in the main government newspaper *Izvestiia* on September 28, 1936, under the threatening title "Harmful Gibberish" (*Vrednaia galimat'ia*). Freidenberg explains, "A huge article in the official press was in itself a harbinger of political persecution. But even more murderous was the note in bold type from the editorial board, which was a signal for harassment. The situation was not a joke" (X: 73, 24).

At the university, she became a pariah for everyone from rector to students. Colleagues avoided her "like a leper" (X: 73, 26). Only Khona and Sonya remained loyal (X: 73, 27). It was then that Natalia Moreva, "my favorite student," a person for whom she had high hopes and dreams, "dropped away" (X: 73, 28). (By the late 1940s, when Freidenberg wrote this account, Moreva—now known under her married name, Vulikh—had become her "political overseer, spy, and provocateur" [X: 73, 28].) The confiscation of her book seemed to Freidenberg no less than the disappearance of a loved one in the terror: "I felt a terrible longing for my arrested book. Now as I write, I have no words to convey this longing, this yearning, this craving, the passion to see the book alive" (X: 73, 28).

What was she to do? Freidenberg now admits that, in secret from everybody, except her mother, her brother, and Khona, she had addressed a passionate appeal to Stalin: "I wrote to Stalin. . . ." She felt that the one weapon she had in her life was her pen (X: 73, 26). At the time, she now explains, she honestly believed that Stalin was just and that he read everybody's letters. (In fact, such an appeal was not at all unusual among people who lost loved ones in the terror or met with administrative injustice, even among those who did believe that Stalin was actually responsible for their woes.)

In telling the story of her book, Freidenberg shapes the action as a classical drama, or tragedy, and she follows the Aristotelian principle of peripeteia. Her fortune continues to shift rapidly from good to bad and bad to good. The good was that the letter to Stalin worked: she received a summons to see the People's Commissar of Enlightenment, B. M. Volin. Freidenberg hurried to Moscow. At the meeting on November 10, 1936, she received Volin's personal resolution, a statement featuring the magic words "in its content, the book contains nothing damaging" (X: 76, 57). A triumphant return to Leningrad followed, and Freidenberg was welcomed as a hero by the same colleagues and students who had recently shunned her as a leper. On November 13 came the day of her "complete rehabilitation" (X: 76, 57).

But the next day, November 14, another smear article appeared in *Izvestiia*, this time by a Leningrad correspondent. It was necessary to "throttle this article as well" (X: 77, 58). As Freidenberg remembered it, Khona was dispatched to Moscow to fulfill the mission.[25] The plan was to ask Boris Pasternak to appeal to Nikolai Bukharin, the editor of *Izvestiia*, with whom he was acquainted (X: 77, 59). By pure luck, Pasternak's letter to Bukharin did not reach its addressee. As they soon learned, Bukharin was under house arrest (X: 77, 61–62). (He was put on trial in February 1937 and executed in 1938.)

This was not the only episode in which the bizarre logic of Stalinist terror produced reversals of fortune befitting an ancient Greek drama. Soon after its labeling as "harmful gibberish," Freidenberg's book was put on "trial," as she wrote—that is, it was subjected to scrutiny and condemnation at a public session, organized by the Rector of Leningrad University, M. S. Lazurkin. Freidenberg describes this humiliating procedure in painful detail (X: 74, 29–34). Then, in 1937, Lazurkin was arrested, as were many in his cohort of Old Bolsheviks. Freidenberg describes how one day she ran into her persecutor—"yesterday's judge"—in the university lobby, surrounded by guards. Burning with pity and shame, she averted her eyes. Lazurkin soon died in prison from a heart attack (X: 77, 62–63). As she now understands, the terror encompassed all, including those who in one way or another enacted it.

In the end, Freidenberg's epic struggle for the liberation of her captured book ended in a victory. The book was released from under arrest, but, as she insists, that fact brought her neither relief nor joy.

Plotting the story of her book as an ancient tragedy, Freidenberg sets the action against the backdrop of the terror. Writing for history, she attaches documents. The fateful article from *Izvestiia*, letters, minutes of meetings at which her book was condemned, and more are carefully copied or pasted into the notebook. She asserts that what helped her survive these ordeals was her "unshakeable faith" in history, which could not be deceived. She felt sure of "history's" true existence, as if she had seen it with her own eyes. She states, "All powerful people could do anything: kill, distort, pervert. . . . But they had no means to influence history, no matter how omnipotent they were" (X: 73, 29).

With a future historian in mind, Freidenberg presents a clear picture of the workings of Soviet academic institutions. First, a philological study was negatively evaluated in the state's primary newspaper. That evaluation served as a signal for the author's immediate colleagues and students to denounce her. Next, a judgment on the merits of this highly specialized work was rendered by a high-ranking official of the Soviet ministry of culture. The new evaluation was couched in terms of whether the book was damaging to the socialist society (it was decreed that "in its content, the book contains nothing damaging"). And books, like their authors, could be put under arrest. Finally, Stalin's personal intervention in the publication of a specialized philological work could resolve the crisis. By the late 1940s, these procedures were familiar to many of Freidenberg's contemporaries from personal experience, but she realized that they might be incomprehensible to the historian of the future.

"I Don't Know How Historians Will Describe 1937"

When she reaches the year 1937, Freidenberg turns to the scattered records she made at that time. She hopes that these immediate records will supplement her plotted narrative, allowing "history" to look into her life as though through a magnifying glass: "When you write retrospectively, you are forced to see only the main lines of your life. Letters, documents, diaries are magnifying glasses, spectacles to let history see" (X: 78, 69).

Looking through her old notes, she chooses one that provides glimpses into the intimate spaces of private life:

> Conversation with Khona:
> —What's going on with you? What are you experiencing? . . .
> —I'm experiencing fear.
> —Fear? But who, what are you afraid of?
> —I don't know. It's beyond me.
> And he would add, pulling me close to him, quietly:
> —Fear. (X: 79, 110)

On June 1, 1937, Freidenberg learned from a casual remark made by a colleague who did not know about their intimacy that the day before, on his way home from the institute where he worked, Frank-Kamenetsky had been hit by a truck and taken to a hospital, his chest crushed. Three days later, on June 4, 1937, Khona died in great pain. Freidenberg did not have an opportunity to visit him in the hospital, and she decided not to go to the funeral, dreading a meeting with his wife. A note she made at that time tells "how it all happened": "On the 31st, near the Institute of Language and Thought, a motor vehicle [*mashina*] ran over Khona, who was apparently walking, as he had been doing lately, self-absorbed, depressed" (X: 83, 139).

Writing about her loss in 1949, she passes from the description of Khona's horrible death to a characterization of the terror campaign that was unfolding at the time: "Still in Khona's lifetime, Stalin launched the extermination machine known as Yezhovshchina. . . . Terrible political trials, arrests. and exiles began...." (X: 84, 142). The "extermination machine" metaphor draws Khona's death under a motor vehicle—in Russian, "under a machine" (*pod mashinoi*)—into the system of terror. It seems that in 1937 (and in 1949, as well), it was difficult to accept the idea of an accidental death.

Having lost her beloved, Freidenberg spent days walking through the streets, "feeling complete emptiness." Looking at the urban landscape, she thought, "So this is what it looks like after I die! This is what it will look like" (X: 84, 144). She pictures herself as a living dead who walks through the city of Leningrad.

Other tragic events occurred in 1937. Musya, the wife of Freidenberg's brother Sashka (Alexander), was arrested.[26] The secretary to the director of a military plant, she had had a love affair with her boss, an Old Bolshevik, and when he was arrested, as were many Old Bolsheviks, she too attracted the attention of state security. On August 3, 1937, Sashka was arrested as well. The ordeal that many families then faced—standing in prison lines, trying to obtain information on the victim's case—started for the Freidenberg family. On January 30, 1938, they were finally notified that Sashka had been exiled to Siberia for five years "without right of correspondence." She writes, "What devil but Stalin could have devised such torture for a man?" (XI: 85, 157).

From the time of his arrest, his mother and sister lovingly gathered supplies to prepare him for exile—warm clothing, dry goods, canned food—but they did not have a chance to send a single parcel. Those unsent supplies, untouched for several years, would help them survive the blockade of Leningrad.

When Freidenberg described these developments in 1949, the family still had not had any news about Sashka. The uncertainty weighed heavily on her mind: "For 12 years now, I've seen him every night in my dreams. He comes home and I am crying, throwing myself at him, screaming: 'It's a dream, I am dreaming!'—and I realize that this is real. Then, shaken, I wake up" (XI: 85, 158). This double dream ends in a cruel awakening to a reality that seems stranger than any dream.

From the notes, it remains unclear whether the family ever learned that the sentence "without right of correspondence" was a frequently used euphemism for the death penalty. On the day when the five-year sentence would have ended, August 3, 1942, Freidenberg wrote in her notebook that she and her mother "felt" that Sashka was no longer among the living (XIII: 84, 32). As we now know from archival sources, Freidenberg's brother Alexander had been executed in Leningrad on January 9, 1938.

Back in the winter of 1938, Freidenberg wandered the streets of Leningrad, imagining her brother destitute, freezing, and alone. When she saw a tramp in rags, she thought: if he can survive the winter, maybe Sashka, wherever he is, will survive as well (XI: 85, 158). As happened after Khona's death, she projected her feelings onto the cityscape.

Freidenberg's narrative then switches from her family to the condition of Russia. She thinks of future historians: "The year 1937 will go down in Russian history as the chapter of the Apocalypse that marks the social and moral end of the country.... I don't know how historians will describe 1937." She adds that this was a year of "a political plague" (XI: 86, 158–159). In attempting to capture the enigmatic essence of the terror, she appeals to mythological imagery: Stalin "chopped off heads," leaving only the "severed torso" of the monstrous body politic (XI: 86, 159). She also attempts to describe the bizarre process of terror, the inexplicable, indiscriminate arrests: "They arrested everybody, all around...." (XI: 86, 159). Then, turning to denunciations, she again resorts to mythmaking: "Betrayal burst from the womb of black Russia as an elemental force...." (XI: 86, 160).

As for her own experience, Freidenberg writes about the ever-present expectation of arrest: "Every person waited at night for a search and arrest. The vast majority of people did not go to bed or went to bed clothed" (XI: 86, 161). She recalls, "I, like others, kept a fur coat and a small prison suitcase at my bedside at night...." (XI: 86, 161). Since connections with foreign countries became dangerous, from that time on, the family was no longer in touch with her "dear and wise uncle" (XI: 86, 168).[27] Fear reigned in her department: day after day, exhausted after a sleepless night, colleagues came to the university and, in a whisper, exchanged the news about the recent arrests (XI: 86, 162). From among her immediate colleagues, the scholar of ancient Greek literature A. I. Dovatur was arrested. Released ten years later, in 1947, he paid Freidenberg a visit and told her the story of his camp experience. At about the same time, she describes his visit in another notebook that she used to record current events.

Freidenberg concludes her history of the fateful year 1937 by pronouncing a moral judgment on her contemporaries from the point of view of the future. Now she knows that "the terror did not pass without a trace for those who survived it." Its main heritage was a "terrifying fear," or the "horror of fear" (she uses two tautological phrases, *strashnoe ustrashenie* and *uzhas strakha*, to define a sense of fear that in itself creates terror). This terror of fear became "the driving force of everything in society," bringing "a complete moral emptiness" to the whole country. "From that time," she concludes, "the Russian nation lost its honor and its will to live" (XI: 86, 168). Now, more than ten years later, she writes from that space of moral emptiness and deadness.

What she experienced in the year of the Great Terror (as historians call the 1937–1938 campaign) affected Freidenberg in many ways, and she spares no detail. In its immediate aftermath, she found herself in a moral conundrum. One day, probably in 1940, Freidenberg was summoned to the headquarters of state security (the notorious Bolshoy Dom, or Big House) in an attempt to recruit her as an informant. She tries to fathom who could have "recommended" her for this role. Freidenberg "does not dare" to think, as she puts it, that this could have been B., the man she loved (XII: 95, 235). And yet she does think of this possibility, and she records her thoughts in her notebook. She believes that she confronted the recruiters with cunning and boldness, but as she emerged from the horrifying building, she felt relief that she was still free. But this was not the end of the ordeal. Freidenberg was asked to write down "everything" about the department she chaired, and once back home, she sat down to this terrible task. Relating this episode in her notes, she calls the document written "for them" "Testimony" (*Pokazanie*). She cried as she wrote this thorny document and tried hard not to disclose anything that might damage anyone. In this degrading situation, Freidenberg sought consolation in the thought that she wrote not only to inform the state security about her department but also to leave a document in its archive for "posterity": "My mind wandered in the distant future, and I wanted to tell posterity, which would find this paper in the archives, that I was not writing denunciations, but only giving testimony as a witness. I drenched them with tears of despair and shame. . . ." (XII: 95, 235).

In her despair and shame, Freidenberg envisioned the files of the state security as a repository of testimony to be read at a future Nuremberg-type trial of the Stalinist regime. Her hope was not a complete delusion. For a brief period in the late 1980s through the early 1990s, the Bolshoy Dom and other organs of Soviet state security indeed released to the public some documents pertaining to the terror, including coerced denunciations and self-denunciations. Some were visibly drenched in blood and tears.[28]

Freidenberg was soon visited in her home by an agent who came to collect her report, and it seemed to her that he was unhappy with it (XII: 95, 237). Fortunately, this episode, which was not at all unusual for the time, did not have obvious consequences. And while the archives of the state security did not release her "testimony" to posterity, her own home archive documented her fear, despair, shame, hopes, and delusions.

"I Wrote My Autobiography for Him"

"Life is a strange creature," Freidenberg writes when her narrative reaches the late fall of 1938 (XI: 88, 178). She started to suspect that it was more than a shared involvement in academic squabbles that made her constantly think about B., the new dean of the Philological Faculty, with whom she often discussed university business. Soon there were no doubts: she was, once again, in the grasp of passion—a hopeless and shameful passion (XI: 89, 182). Feeling that she was betraying Khona, she analyzes the situation in terms of her theory of form: the new feeling, she muses, was a result of her loss—it is "the same love in a different form" (XI: 91, 197). And so, in 1939, at the age of forty-nine—after the terror, Khona's death, and her brother's disappearance—she feels herself to be "in a state of 'vita nuova,' a complete spiritual and bodily renaissance" (XI: 91, 201).

In the bitter cold winter of 1939–1940, at the time of the troubling Winter War between the Soviet Union and Finland, Freidenberg wrote her first autobiography. She wrote it for her new beloved. And in 1949 (when she described how she wrote the autobiography), she formulated her hermeneutic theory of love as "a special Weltanschauung," as seen in chapter 1.

As she prepares to tell this story, Freidenberg cites a note made at the time: "I read myself: 'The second semester, 1940. It's cold, cold. . . . B. returned from Moscow . . . I kept my life going by writing my autobiography for him (the beginning, before the university)'" (XI: 92, 208). The note describes how she sent the notebook to B. and waited. About ten days later, he called on her. She recalls, "He said he read it at once, read it all night till morning. . . ." It seemed to her that he did not want to part with the notebook, but he remained cold to its author. Freidenberg felt crushed by the rejection of her love offering: "The denouement. There's nothing to connect us anymore. Dead despair. Nothing to live by" (XI: 92, 208–209). Back then, in 1940, with her love unrequited and her "autobiography" ineffective, she felt that she had "nothing to live by."

And yet she continued to work on her scholarship. Freidenberg concludes her "academic biography" with the story of her unpublished studies. Between 1933 and 1940, among other projects, she worked on Hesiod's poem *Works and Days*, her "third book" (VIII: 61, 76). Submitted for publication in March 1941, this study met with a negative evaluation. The reviewer felt that Freidenberg's generalizations and conclusions far exceeded the confines of the text at hand and that it would not be appropriate, or advisable, to publish the work. He mocked what he found particularly objectionable, if not ridiculous, and Freidenberg reproduces the reviewer's mockery in her notes. Ironically, it is from this hostile evaluation that the readers of her notes learn about this work: Going beyond Hesiod's poem, Freidenberg also went beyond the confines of our ideas about human behavior "in society, in the family, at work." The reviewer found it far-fetched that she wrote about the parallelism of the political, mythological, and ethical planes, tracing the transformation of the historical into the eschatological. He ridiculed her thesis that the eschatological doctrine takes political form, or her view of man as a microcosm in which, as in Plato's *Republic*, the idea of the state and the universe is reflected (XII: 95, 243–244).

Citing this passage, Freidenberg takes pride in those aspects of her study that the reviewer, speaking for the Soviet academic establishment, found far-fetched and even ridiculous. What is more, the description of her work makes clear the parallelism between Hesiod's poem, as Freidenberg interpreted it in her study, and her notes—her own works and days. In her notes, Freidenberg, like her Hesiod, goes far beyond the routine life of a human being, "in the family, at work, in society." Her own ideas about the state and the world are reflected in the microcosm of an individual life—her own life. And describing her own days and works, she fuses the ethical, the mythological, and the political interpretation, envisioning a history of Stalin's terror that takes the form of a chapter in the Apocalypse.

Disappointed in love and in work, Freidenberg was deeply concerned with political events. She was interested "in the life of the Globe, in all things great and small on earth, and suffered from the fact that our society lacked community, views, public opinion. . . ." (XII: 93, 220). She is morally disgusted with the Russo-Finnish War: "It's shameful to count oneself as a Russian." "Friendship" with the Germans causes "moral nausea" (here, Freidenberg cites a note she made in 1939) (XI: 91, 203). In 1949, describing her feelings at the start of World War II in 1939, she writes that she mourned the fall of Poland, "ruined with our help," and the collapse of Czechoslovakia. Her political vision is now clear: "Stalin untied Hitler's hands and thus let the war begin" (XII: 93, 220).

By the spring of 1941, Freidenberg was utterly desperate about her life, about the society in which she lived, and about the world at large. "Death and decay" were entering her. She dreamed of an "irreparable catastrophe" (XII: 95, 246). This is how Freidenberg ends the story of her life between 1917 and 1941, which she wrote in the winter of 1948–1949, with retroactive knowledge of the catastrophes that followed.

CHAPTER 5

The Mythopolitical Theory of Olga Freidenberg in the Context of the Political Thought of Her Time

The New Form of Government

This chapter returns to my suggestion that Freidenberg's "notes" contain what amounts to a mythopolitical theory of Stalinism, couched in terms and images used by thinkers from Plato and Aristotle to Machiavelli and Hobbes and then to Arendt and Agamben. Rooted in Freidenberg's reflections on her everyday experience, it is a theory embedded in a diary-like chronicle: a theory-diary. This is what makes her personal document special.

In the preceding chapters, we saw how, from notebook to notebook, Freidenberg introduced, reiterated, and adjusted a set of theoretical formulations and propositions that encapsulated her understanding of Stalinism as she grappled with new evidence or confronted repeating experiences. The tasks of this chapter are to extract the main postulates of Freidenberg's theory, summarize them, and generalize from them.

The chapter is organized around a set of concepts, some of which we have encountered earlier in other contexts. There is also new material, including Freidenberg's conclusions about Stalinism, which she summarized in her last two notebooks, numbered XXXIII and XXXIV. This chapter also relates Freidenberg's ideas to those of other political thinkers whose work she did not know. Among them are her contemporaries in the West, first and foremost Hannah Arendt. But there is also her compatriot, the literary scholar Lidiia

Ginzburg, who lived on the same street. By contextualizing Freidenberg's ideas within the political thought of her time, with some excursions into our own, I hope to turn her lonely, "homemade" theorizing into a fact of intellectual history. And by relating Freidenberg's interpretations to those of a fellow citizen who also wrote in secret, I hope to show that a shared understanding can link people living in isolation and confined in their writings to diaries and notes.

In one of her postwar notebooks, Freidenberg looks back at her observations on everyday Stalinism from a theoretical perspective and makes a decisive statement: "Hitler and Stalin, two tyrants, created a new form of government which Aristotle could not have known" (XXVIII: 7, 47). Hannah Arendt, writing at the same time, came to the same conclusion: the regime established in Hitler's Germany and Stalin's Russia was "a new form of government" that "differed essentially from other forms of political oppression known to us." This insight became the starting point for *The Origins of Totalitarianism*, written in the 1940s.[1] History knows very few forms of government, writes Arendt, and these "were discovered early, classified by the Greeks and have proved extraordinarily long-lived." Totalitarian government was unprecedented (460–461).[2] Arendt, in New York, carefully developed her ideas about the new form of government in a well-documented treatise of political theory, first published in 1951. Freidenberg, in Leningrad, formulated her thoughts in personal notes, hidden in an iron chest. And yet Freidenberg and Arendt converge in some of their fundamental propositions. Both suggest that for a "totalitarian regime"—Arendt's preferred term—the repression and destruction of human personality is a goal in itself. Both use the camp as a model of sorts to show the basic principles by which this kind of regime molds its subjects. Both note that the image these regimes present to the world at large is pure fiction. And both are intent on theorizing this new form of government and exposing its fictions. In some ways, however, their views diverge.

What did Freidenberg understand as new about this kind of regime, especially as it operated in Leningrad in 1941–1944, where, as she saw it, the two tyrannies, Stalin's and Hitler's, worked in tandem to put "man" (the human being) under siege? And how did Freidenberg understand the workings of this form of government in the postwar years? Unlike Arendt, she was looking at it from within, extrapolating theoretical formulations from her daily life.

Everyday Terror

It was Freidenberg's belief, repeated in many formulations (cited in chapter 3), that the peculiar order of everyday existence—*byt*—bore the unmistakable stamp of Stalinism as a system of government. (The unique Russian word *byt*, as she uses it again and again, embraces various aspects of everyday life: material conditions like food and housing, daily routines, domestic space, established forms of family and community life, and more.) On the basis of her meticulously recorded observations, Freidenberg drew a number of theoretical conclusions.

First, she insisted that the shortages and difficulties were an intentional, calculated "system" aimed at oppressing people. Because a deliberate system of difficulties in daily life had been created, people could think of nothing but how to overcome routine problems. And she saw these conditions as "a state system of dishonor" (XXV: 63, 11).

Montesquieu, as Hannah Arendt noted, famously defined the three forms of government by the main ethical principles they followed: a republic is governed by the idea of virtue, a monarchy by the idea of honor, and a despotic government by the idea of fear. Freidenberg, who may have had Montesquieu in mind (though she did not mention his name), repeatedly suggests that the main principle of Stalinism was dishonor.[3] For Freidenberg, the ordering of the everyday had become a key instrument of oppression and humiliation, forming the essence of political domination.

Second, she saw the everyday threats as the means by which the Stalinist state gained access into each person's home. Recall that in her own apartment, she felt the state reaching her from the leaking sewage pipes or the space under the floor inhabited by flea-infested rats: this is how "the regime reached each person, up into his bed and his toilet" (XXIX: 3, 12.) With all this in mind, Freidenberg formulated an important thesis: the Stalinist everyday is not only a crucial, all-important part of state terror but constitutes one of the major innovations of the new system of government ("Until now, political and religious terror had been known. Stalin introduced everyday terror" [XXVIII: 19, 84]).

Arendt also considered the "identity of public and private interests" in Stalinist society and "the abolishing of the private sphere of life" in the Nazi state, as well as persistent "humiliation," to be the immediate consequences of totalitarian rule (431–432). And she knew that "the iron band of total terror leaves no space for . . . private life" (474). Yet for Arendt, the main evil of totalitarianism was not the destruction of the whole sphere of private life—by which she mainly meant the undercutting of family intimacy and genuine friendship under the conditions of surveillance and terror—but the exclusion of individual people from the sphere of political action. Arendt firmly believed that, from the time of the Greek polis, the political sphere was the main space in which people established and expressed themselves as human beings. And looking at totalitarian society from the outside, she did not know much about the Stalinist everyday or the Soviet domestic order.

Things were different for Freidenberg, who wrote as an insider. For her, the invasion of the private sphere—the penetration of the state into the daily lives, intimate relations, thought patterns, and the body—was the most palpable manifestation of Stalinism as a system of total domination. What is more, like many of her contemporaries in the Soviet Union, Freidenberg placed little, if any, value on the workings of the political sphere, and—her professional knowledge of the Athenian polis and democracy notwithstanding—she did not believe in the human capacity for political action. From her point of view, the invasion of the private sphere and "everyday terror" were the great innovations of Stalin's system of government. And this was unknown to either Aristotle or Arendt.

The Biopolitics of the Everyday

In her wartime and postwar notes, Freidenberg consistently described the condition of the human body, intimate relationships, and the individual's position in community and society from a perspective that present-day scholars call "biopolitical."

For us, the notion of biopolitics is closely associated with Giorgio Agamben, who applied this concept, first introduced in a different context by Michel Foucault, to the operation of the twentieth-century totalitarian regimes. Focusing on Nazi Germany, Agamben sees the concentration camp, as defined by Hannah Arendt, as an apogee of the regime's ambition to control every aspect of bodily, or biological, life. And he suggests that "if Nazism still appears to us as an enigma, and if its affinity with Stalinism (on which Hannah Arendt so much insisted) is still unexplained, this is because we have failed to situate the totalitarian phenomenon in its entirety in the horizon of biopolitics."[4] Freidenberg's observations and theoretical formulations, still unknown, may help in this task. Her notes consistently trace the penetration of political power into every aspect of bodily life, beginning with the most basic physiological functions. Focusing on the everyday, she situated Stalinist life in its entirety within biopolitics.

In her notebooks from the siege years, Freidenberg focuses on the system of food distribution enacted by the Leningrad administration in the besieged city. The state, which took upon itself "the task of feeding people," forbade any forms of trade or exchange and introduced a hierarchical system of food rations that created "people of different categories," some of whom would live and some of whom would die (XII-bis: 29, 80; XIII: 37, 15). She describes the composition of bread distributed to the population as well as the composition of the products of defecation and the frequency of defecation in the people who ate this bread. Her conclusion was forceful: "[Man] was forced to eat and defecate under coercion" (XIII: 37, 15). Observing the changes in her own starving body and in the bodies of other women—the disappearance of hips and breasts, the cessation of menstruation—she presented evidence of the physical transformation of human (physical) nature. And in another remarkable formulation (cited in chapter 2), she blamed both Hitler and Popkov, the head of the Leningrad city administration, for the disappearance of sexual and gender distinctions ("One winter with Hitler-Popkov, and the woman in me is finished!" [XIII: 52, 68]).

Similar conceptual moves are found in Lidiia Ginzburg's blockade notes (also written in private). Reflecting, as did Freidenberg, on the workings of food distribution in a situation of extreme shortages, Ginzburg introduced the concept of "well organized hunger." Analyzing the consequences of starvation, she drew parallels between the dystrophic body of a starving person and the damaged social body of the besieged city.[5]

Freidenberg went further: she did not limit her insistence on the repressive politicization of the body to the exceptional situation of the siege. In the postwar years, Freidenberg viewed the continuing food shortages and extended rationing as forces creating people of different categories (XXV: 63, 9–11). And she described defecation and copulation in the presence of others that took place in the coerced cohabitation of overpopulated communal apartments as a direct result of housing shortages caused by the policies of the Stalinist state. From this perspective, the shortages and the policies governing the distribution of basic resources like food and housing directly affected the condition of people's bodies and the configuration of communities. Stalinist power was thus a controlling and coercive force that reshaped both the individual and the collective body.

Surveillance and Ideology

In her last notebook, concluding her years-long analysis of Stalinism, Freidenberg turned her attention to the workings of all-embracing surveillance, which she linked to enforcement of Stalinist ideology. Here, too, her starting point is the everyday. First, she comments on surveillance as a result of coerced cohabitation. Both at home and at work, a person is under the watchful eyes of other people: "At work, he is thrown into a 'collective' where he is watched, and he is denounced in his own apartment, in his own room, and even in his own family" (XXXIV, 144). From this generalized individual, Freidenberg moves on to "the intelligentsia," describing the system of political surveillance that surrounds the university faculty, at work and at home. She begins by mentioning the obvious, the phenomena that are not even worth elaboration. And yet she elaborates, listing different kinds of surveillance she encounters in her own everyday life as a professor and author:

> I am not even talking about the surveillance, the regular denunciations, the snooping by the special department, the [Communist] Party committee, the Party representative, the students and graduate students, the janitors, the house superintendent, the neighbors, all kinds of eavesdroppers, informers, and covert and overt agents from the ranks of one's acquaintances. I am not talking about the "secret agents" who swarm around each individual, about the typists who notify the Soviet Gestapo regarding private manuscripts, about telephone espionage, about opening private correspondence. All this is a familiar, inalienable condition of Soviet everyday life. I have something else in mind. (XXXIV, 144)

What she has in mind is that at the university, not only everyday life, but thinking itself, becomes the object of surveillance and coercion. Freidenberg links surveillance to the enforcement of Marxist ideology in its Stalinist version.

The faculty is made to study Stalin, and also Marx, Engels, and Lenin, "by force." In many institutions "they lock the doors, trapping employees who run away from forced lectures and meetings after a hungry day of slave labor" (XXXIV, 144). In Leningrad University, as she knows from her own experience, people are coerced into absorbing ideology through a strict system of accounting. Every hour of their regular work life—every conversation with students, every seminar and lecture—is already recorded on special time sheets. "But this is not all," she continues. A special system of accounting keeps each faculty member's political education under control. Every topic and every "work" assigned for "study" (the quotation marks are Freidenberg's) are recorded on a special form, complete with the deadline for completion. She states, "Another column on the same form indicates who your 'consultant' (i.e., guard) is, when you last saw him, what grade he gave you, when you will report to him next. . . ." (XXXIV, 144–145). This system of coerced ideological implementation, Freidenberg surmised, also operated in factories, offices, and elsewhere as a part of the overall system of surveillance and control that extended to people's thinking or minds (XXXIV, 146).

Arendt, in her *Origins of Totalitarianism*, also considered the implementation of ideology—a system of pseudo-scientific ideas based on the fiction of irrefutable logic—to be a crucial part of a totalitarian regime, be it Hitler's or Stalin's. According to Arendt, the combination of "ideology and terror" formed the core of this "novel form of government."[6] She was aware that totalitarian regimes relied on compulsion, which finds its ultimate force in terror. But she assumed that ideology was inculcated through "inner compulsion," by way of the mental "tyranny of logicality," which explains everything in the past, present, and future. In other words, totalitarian rulers rely on "compulsion with which we can compel ourselves," on ideology as a "self-coercive force." And this, Arendt believed, accounted for the popularity of Marxism in the Soviet Union (473–474).

Not paying any attention to the postulates of Marxism or its self-compelling power, Freidenberg focused on something else: a detailed description of the procedures by which the study of Marxist ideology, as defined by Lenin and Stalin, was implemented in institutional routines, from universities to offices and factories. For Freidenberg, Soviet ideology was a part of the system of surveillance, control, and coercion that permeated everyday life. Addressing naive foreigners who believe that "Marxism is being developed and elaborated in our country" (XXXIV, 146), she concludes, "Marxism in Stalin's country is neither a worldview nor a method, but a lash. It is a police-punitive category" (XXXIV, 146).

The Great Terror

Freidenberg developed her conception of the new form of government in the period when she kept regular notes—during the siege of Leningrad and the first postwar years. In the late 1930s, during the so-called Great Terror, she did not keep a diary, though occasionally she recorded her impressions on pieces of paper that she later used in writing her retroactive notes (then destroyed). When, in the winter of 1948–1949, Freidenberg wrote the story of her life between the revolution and the war, she made several attempts to describe the year 1937 as an aid to future historians. Trying to complete this far-from-easy task, she reached for mythological and historical imagery: "The year 1937 will go down in Russian history as the chapter of the Apocalypse that marks the social and moral end of the country. For Russia here must begin the Peloponnesian war, followed by the fall—and ruin. I do not believe that everything is permissible for a people [*narod*]. A moral Nuremberg still awaits it. I don't know how historians will describe 1937...." (XI: 86, 158–159).

Trying to imagine a future history of Russia that could accommodate the year 1937, Freidenberg envisions it as a chapter from the apocalypse. And here, as elsewhere in her notes, *Nuremberg* stands for the Last Judgment.

As her mention of the Peloponnesian War indicates, some of Freidenberg's moves could have been prompted by Thucydides, whose *History of the Peloponnesian War*, as she knew, was a combination of historiography and mythology. Originally planned as textbook of politics in the form of a journal, Thucydides's treatise grew into a history of the war in which he shaped historical events into mythological patterns and literary plots. This strategy influenced Hobbes, who translated Thucydides's *History* into English. This strategy could have also influenced Freidenberg, who perused the study of the English classicist Francis Macdonald Cornford, *Thucydides Mythistoricus* (1907), which described the method of "mytho-history."[7]

Freidenberg used an array of mythic images and metaphors. The Great Terror is a personified epidemic: "Political plague roamed the whole of Russia." Anybody could be swept by this evil force, regardless of their place in the social hierarchy, "members of the Academy of Sciences, janitors, street sweepers, beggars. . . ." A party membership or a high position in the Soviet hierarchy did not protect an individual from falling victim to the elemental forces of terror (XI: 86, 160).

For Freidenberg, it is especially important that, by way of denunciations, the whole nation participated in terror: "People crushed each other, smothered each other. Denunciations knew no limit" (XI: 86, 160). Freidenberg envisioned denunciation as a physical force, akin to the elements, whose origin is the body of the Russian nation: "Betrayal burst from the womb of black Russia as an elemental force. . . . People betrayed each other, one betrayed another. Neighbors in the [communal] apartment, family members, fellow workers, tenants in the same building, passers-by, janitors" (XI: 86, 160).

Judging by this elaborate imagery, Freidenberg associated the idea of all-embracing betrayal, when every person was being pitted against every other person, with the Hobbesian idea of the war of all against all in the body politic, or, in this case, the terror of all against all.

Freidenberg's contemporary Lidiia Ginzburg also singled out "the all-pervasive betrayal that spared nobody" as the main principle of the Great Terror. For Ginzburg, too, the Stalinist terror, which mobilized the human capacity for betrayal for its own purposes, was tied to the Hobbesian notion of the war of all against all.[8]

The War of All Against All

Freidenberg returns to the idea of all-inclusive enmity in Stalinist society throughout her notes, and Hobbes's famous notion of the war of all against all underlies her imagery (though she never mentions his name). She describes mutual denunciations as the main force behind the success of the terror campaign of 1937. What preoccupied her even more was the enmity and hostility that manifested itself in the routine situations of everyday life. During the blockade, writing about hungry and exhausted people, she notes the outbursts of resentment and hostility that tore apart families and homes (XIV: 80, 25). Freidenberg then makes a poignant comment, presenting the human tendency toward animosity as a universal phenomenon that can be mobilized by the state: while "there is envy, slander, and intrigue among all nations of the world," under Stalin such "spiritual waste" acquired the character of an "organized social system" (XVII: 129, 19). After the war, she describes virulent conflicts that ruled everyday life in communal apartments and academic departments; her term for them, "squabbles" (*skloki*), elevates an otherwise trivial word into a concept that designates an instrument of terror. Describing how the well-organized ideological campaigns at Leningrad University involved faculty and students in mutual accusations and denunciations, Freidenberg concluded that creating enmity was Stalin's "methodology." On the last pages of her last notebook, she addresses universal strife (fighting and quarreling), which she calls "squabbling" again. Generalizing this phenomenon, she presents the "squabble"—a principle that operated in all social institutions of society, from families and communal apartments to universities to the state as a whole—as one of the fundamental innovations of the Stalinist form of government:

> Stalin created an entirely new concept and a new term that cannot be translated into any cultured language: the squabble [*skloka*]. Everywhere, in all institutions, in all apartments, there is squabbling. It is difficult to explain what it is. It is a low, petty enmity, a malicious grouping of some against others; it is ultra-unconscionable spitefulness that breeds petty intrigues. It is denunciation, slander, surveillance, backstabbing, clandestine accusation, inciting the base passions of some against others. Nerves strained to the extreme and moral degradation lead a group of people into rancor against another group of people or one person against another. Squabbling is the natural state of people pitted against each other, helplessly furious people who have been kept by Stalin in captivity. Squabbling is the rudder of Stalin, the "helmsman of communism." The squabble is the alpha and omega of his policy. The squabble is his methodology. His international policy, his diplomacy is built on squabbling. (XXXIV, 150–151)

In this remarkable formulation, Freidenberg calls squabbling, or enmity of all against all, the "natural state" of people living in Stalinist society. Using

Hobbes's phrase, she has radically reinterpreted its meaning. While, for Hobbes, the "natural state of men" is to be at war with each other, the state is a solution to this natural condition. An authoritarian state ruled by a strong sovereign prevents society from falling into the perpetual war of every man against every man. Not so for Freidenberg. Using Hobbes, she inverts his famous principle: the war of all against all stems from a deliberate policy of Stalin the sovereign who is intent on "pitting people against each other." This is Hobbes turned inside out.

The New Leviathan

In the 1930s and 1940s, political thinkers who witnessed Hitler's rise to power—Carl Schmitt, Leo Strauss, Hannah Arendt, and quite a few others—turned to Hobbes and his conception of the state as a monstrous and powerful Leviathan. These thinkers saw political myths as a way to conceptualize the new political regime and explain its influence on the minds of contemporaries. Hobbes and his Leviathan inspired both those who accepted Nazism, like Schmitt, and those who did not, and both sides believed in the power of myth.[9] Freidenberg, isolated in the Soviet Union, did not know the work of these new theorists of unfreedom, and yet she could be considered part of the revival of political myth and reformulation of Hobbes, which emerged as a notable intellectual trend in the age of Hitler and Stalin. Needless to say, Freidenberg knew Hobbes and his sources in the political thought of classical antiquity. And in the 1920s, she closely followed scholarship that dealt with mythological thinking and the power of mythological metaphors—specifically, the work of Ernst Cassirer.

For Hobbes, who wrote his treatise during one of England's long civil wars, the Leviathan stood for the political unity of society under the rule of a strong sovereign who protects the population from the "natural state" of war of all against all. Suffice it to recall the iconic image that appeared on the frontispiece of the treatise: a huge man made from a multitude of tiny human bodies, subsumed under a towering head. This was Hobbes's optimistic view of sovereignty, but some of those who used the image of Leviathan in the age of Hitler and Stalin viewed it differently.

Hobbes's most influential proponent in the 1930s was Carl Schmitt, a political theorist who offered his services to the Third Reich. Schmitt expressed regret that, since Hobbes and his Leviathan, the idea of the state as a single body under the absolute authority of the sovereign, benign in Plato, had turned into a symbol of something monstrous and threatening. Schmitt decided to rehabilitate the monster as a reassuring image of political unity.[10]

In his book *The Leviathan in the State Theory of Thomas Hobbes*—written in 1938, after his career as Hitler's court jurist had failed—Schmitt carefully analyzed the symbolism of the Leviathan. Schmitt noted that Hobbes used several distinct and contradictory images to represent the "mythic totality" of the state: the Platonic "huge man"; a "giant animal" ("sea monster"); "an artificial being, an *automaton* or a *machine*"—in sum, a "huge man, huge animal, huge machine." And following scholars of mythology who traced the origin of the biblical Leviathan to Babylonian mythology, Schmitt explicitly brought up the goddess Tiamat as a predecessor of Leviathan.[11] In his book, Schmitt took the myth very seriously, arguing that the figure of Leviathan in itself had considerable power over political thinking and imagination.

The political theorist Leo Strauss, who emigrated from Nazi Germany to the US, also dedicated a book to Hobbes, *The Political Philosophy of Hobbes: Its Basis and Its Genesis* (1936). And while Strauss definitely did not consider Hobbes's vision of the state a model for imitation, he also thought that the mythic image had considerable power and claimed that the idea of all-powerful Leviathan was rooted in human experience.[12]

The thinker closest in spirit and language to Freidenberg, Hannah Arendt, was also thinking of Hobbes's mythic image when, after the war, she worked on the study of the genesis of Hitler's and Stalin's rule. While this seems to have passed unnoticed by her readers, in *The Origins of Totalitarianism*, without using the word "Leviathan," Arendt likened the totalitarian state to a huge man. She lamented that the plurality of individuals had disappeared "into One Man of gigantic dimensions" and that total terror, "by pressing men against each other," had destroyed their "capacity of motion which cannot exist without space" (466).

In the Soviet Union, Lidiia Ginzburg used the image of the Leviathan when, during World War II, she reflected on the relationship of the intellectual to the Stalinist state in this new situation.[13] For her, this was "another phase in the age-old relationships with the Leviathan . . . as Hobbes called the all-powerful state" (427). Ginzburg writes about the attempt of Soviet intellectuals to establish relationships with the "New Leviathan" based on voluntary participation and initiative (297). These feeble hopes, in her view, stemmed from the idea that during the war, with the country facing an external threat, cooperation from the intelligentsia might diminish the hostility the state had previously shown toward it as a potential internal enemy. But in the end, all hopes for social participation under wartime conditions were crushed. Moreover, Ginzburg came to see the war as the "ultimate unfreedom" that penetrated into every aspect of human existence, "up to the smallest ones" (297). In one of her wartime notebooks, modifying the famous mythic image, she writes that "everything presses and crushes the individual, but the individual himself does not participate in anything until the Lev[iathan] extends its tentacles toward him, so as to grab and use him for its own good" (297).

As we have seen, the image of Hobbes's Leviathan figures prominently in Freidenberg's notes, appearing in different forms—though, like Arendt, she does not use the word "Leviathan." During the blockade, Freidenberg used the image of the Babylonian goddess Tiamat, which (as Schmitt knew) is a variant of the Leviathan, to personify the penetrating power of the Stalinist state, the "Soviet Tiamat." Both during the blockade and after the war, Stalin and the Stalinist state appear in the image of a serpent who held her and her family in its evil power.[a] In the postwar years, echoes of Hobbesian imagery showed up on the pages of Freidenberg's notes when she brings up the ever-present pressure from the state and its institutions. An example is a memorable passage about the exploitation of man by the state, in which the state appears as a "colossal beast-like machine that is much more threatening and inescapable than an individual person" (XXIII: 34, 20).

Using Hobbes's apparatus, Freidenberg created a myth of the state that differed from Hobbes's version. And needless to say, while Freidenberg used imagery similar to that of Schmitt in Nazi Germany, she evaluated quite differently the idea of society united in a single body. For Schmitt, the "huge man, huge animal, huge machine" was protection; for Freidenberg, the "colossal beast-like machine" was, by contrast, a threat.

Freidenberg's postwar notebooks, as we have seen, use images of Soviet society as a beheaded social body: "Having beheaded Russia, killed the whole intelligentsia, Stalin made the body alone into a country" (XXIII: 34, 21). "The human body devoid of the head became promiscuous" (XXV: 63, 11). Remembering the year 1937, Freidenberg explicitly speaks about a new myth, based, like the myth of Leviathan, on the conceptual metaphor of the body politic: "[Stalin] was carrying out a process of ruthless massacre of the population also by chopping off the people's heads; henceforth there was only the torso left. Such a version of the myth has never been invented by mankind. . . . There were myths about the hydra, about the head of [Alexander Pushkin's] Ruslan, but no one thought of the horrifying picture of severed and functioning torsos—not even John the Theologian himself" (XI: 86, 159).

---

[a] In one of her blockade notebooks, Freidenberg writes, "What could have released us from the underworld where the human being has been driven by a blood-thirsty serpent?" (XIX: 163, 71). In another notebook, citing her note from 1939, she writes, "Will this serpent, covered with blood and tears, ever expire? He is only sixty years old!" (XI: 91, 23). Here, the serpent is clearly Stalin.

Judging by this image, Freidenberg separates society from the state. In her myth, the state is not a force that unites society into one body over which the head of the sovereign looms large, as Hobbes had it, and Schmitt after him. The body politic is a victim of the tyrant who has beheaded (and not "headed") it. And this body is frightening in its immorality.

One thing is especially important about such mythmaking: for Freidenberg, as well as Schmitt and a number of other scholars, the Leviathan is not a rhetorical figure. At the start of his treatise, Schmitt insists that, for Hobbes, the Leviathan is not a mere illustration, emblem, or allegory. It is an image in the mythical sense, and its power transcends the "philosophical-intellectual sphere." The Leviathan is a creature conjured into existence by means of "irrational" or "mythic" (that is, magical) thinking.[14] This understanding of the power of a political myth applies to Schmitt's own work, as his political theory relies heavily on anthropology. Schmitt focuses on emotions, seeing political myth as a reaction to fear, and when he speaks about the mythic power of images like Leviathan, he treats this phenomenon as a part of a belief system, or "political theology." And Schmitt seems to accept political myth, especially the myth of the Leviathan, as an affective instrument of state power.

Some critics of the Nazi regime also took the power of myth seriously, but for them a return to mythical thinking was a sign of regression, a retreat from Enlightenment ideals and a return to "a new barbarism."[15] For Cassirer in *The Myth of the State*, on which he worked as a German refugee in the United States during the war, myth was a defensive instrument to which people resorted in desperate situations, when reason failed. He believed that this principle worked both in "primitive society" and at "highly advanced stages of man's political life." Cassirer made it clear that he had the political thinking that brought Hitler to power in mind and that, for him, the rise of "political myths" after 1933 was as dangerous as Germany's rearmament. On the concluding pages of his cautionary essay, he illustrated the power of myth by drawing on the Babylonian legend of creation involving the struggle of the chief god Marduk with the evil serpent Tiamat. Cassirer had invoked Tiamat earlier, in a nonpolitical context, in his *Philosophy of Symbolic Forms* (published in the 1920s). Now, during the war, he used the Tiamat figure as an allegory about the emergence of National Socialism. Conquered by the god Marduk, the monster was not entirely destroyed but, as a force of chaos, remained a submerged threat to world order. The same, Cassirer intimated, is true of the power of myth itself. Lurking in the cultural and social depths, the chaos of mythical thought was rising again in Germany in dark times.[16]

Freidenberg's position on the question of the power of myth appears to be at once similar to and different from Schmitt's or Cassirer's (whose late book *The Myth of the State* she could not know). For Freidenberg as a scholar, mythical thinking was the main object of analysis, and her view of language and myth were obviously influenced by Cassirer's philosophical anthropology. Following Cassirer's early work (which she knew well), she believed in myth and metaphor as primary instruments and repositories of cultural meaning.[17] Her political theories found expression in her ethnographic diary, the notebooks in which she recorded her field observations on the "double barbarism, Hitler's and Stalin's" (XVIII: 138, 10). Subjecting to anthropological analysis a society that had regressed to a primitive state, a new barbarism, she reveals the workings of mythical thinking in such a society. She also applies the analysis to herself. Recall that during the blockade, as she observed her own reactions from the position of self-ethnographer, Freidenberg described situations in which she felt incapable of thinking in terms of cause and effect or using "reason" to understand the calamities that befell her. Facing the backup of sewage in her bathtub, she was like an "ancient man" confronting an intrusion of the mythical goddess Tiamat—the "Soviet Tiamat" (XV: 115, 27).

Leadership: The Führer Principle and Political Religion

Under totalitarianism, wrote Arendt, "authority is not filtered down from the top . . . to the bottom of the body politic, as in the case of authoritarian regimes." Not only does the Führer have an "absolute monopoly on power and authority"—she wrote with Nazi Germany in mind—but there is no other authority. "The Führer principle" entails that any functionary represents the unitary power of the Führer so that any administrative action emanates from the one and only source (404–405).

Freidenberg, in her turn, believed that the leader played a very special role in Stalinist society, which she saw as a direct parallel to Hitler's. Once she heard on the radio a summary of the speeches at the Nuremberg trial: "'The organized foundation of Hitler's party'—said the Nuremberg prosecutor—'was "the Führer principle," which governed the leadership of the German state from top to bottom. . . . A person endowed with power was obliged to look after everything that took place in his domain'" (XXV: 72, 47). Freidenberg added, "Replace the word Hitler with the word Stalin," and you will get the picture of "our system" (XXV: 72, 48).

Analyzing the structure of power in Stalinist society, Freidenberg concluded that the elevation of Stalin led not only to the complete denial of power or authority to anyone else but also to the downgrading and humiliation of any other authority: "I don't know whether there was anything comparable in history! This official state acknowledgment that everyone is stupid, blind, a 'deviationist' [*uklonist*].... In primitive societies, people know that only shamans possess the truth. In our society neither the academies nor universities possess the truth. Only the pontifex maximus, Stalin" (XXV: 63, 13).

Developing this idea, which Arendt entertained as well, Freidenberg notes the presence of Stalin behind every public figure: "If a soccer or chess player ... or musician won [a competition], it was not that person's doing, but the force of Stalin and 'the people' standing behind Stalin, for whom the winner was only an instrument. All victories, successes, and achievements in war or labor went into Stalin's pocket. This was reflected in language" (XXV: 63, 13).

Once, thinking about how repressive campaigns at the university were conducted, Freidenberg identified a chain of power that went from the head of her department's tiny Communist Party cell via the dean of the Philological Faculty to the City Party Committee to the Central Committee of the Communist Party and finally to Stalin. She concludes that behind a minor party functionary in her department—her former student Natalia Vulikh—"stood Stalin himself" (XXXII: I, 39).

As a philologist, Freidenberg was attentive to changes in language, noting new developments indicative of the leader cult in phraseology, semantics, and phonetics. In similar fashion, the philologist Victor Klemperer in Nazi Germany made observations in his diaries on "the language of the Third Reich" that were published after the war as a separate book, subtitled "A Philologist's Notebook" (*Lingua Tertii Imperii: Notizbuch eines Philologen*).[18] Freidenberg's notes from Stalin's empire include the following:

> A stable epithet appeared: "stalinist" [*stalinskii*]. It was applied to everything positive, to people, events, seasons, things, locations. The word "good" [*khorosho*] disappeared because the concept as such ceased to exist. People said: "not bad" [*neplokho*].... Such words as "dear" [*rodnoi*], "beloved" [*liubimyi*], "friend" [*drug*], "father" [*otets*], "teacher" [*uchitel'*], which were constantly applied to Stalin, lost meaning and became almost comical (the same with the word "wise" [*mudryi*]). The same is true of the words "zeal" [*pod"em*], "inspiration" [*voodushevlenie*], "enthusiasm" [*entuziazm*], and Stalinist phrases with high market value ("the assembly adopted with great enthusiasm an appeal to Comrade Stalin," and other cliches). The language was filled with commonplaces, a politicized epic language. (XXV: 64, 13–14)

Freidenberg also duly noted changes in the pronunciation and stressing of certain words in imitation of Stalin's personal speech habits, often mediated by radio announcers. She provided lists of words, complete with their phonetic transcriptions (XXV: 64, 14).

Closely observing the elaborate celebrations of Stalin's seventieth birthday in December 1949, Freidenberg arrived at another important conclusion: that the cult of Stalin constituted a "political religion": "Stalin's seventieth anniversary has clearly shown that our Soviet 'socialism' is an age-old religion, just like militant Catholicism, but in twentieth-century form. Not a religion of God, but a religion of man, a political religion" (XXXIII, 111).

Here, the phrase "political religion" (amply used by historians)[19] is a concept conceived on the basis of Freidenberg's ethnographic observations. She describes how the cult works: "From morning to night, they celebrate masses for this god-man. Stalinist political liturgy has its own established ritual order. There are hymns to Stalin and glorifications of Stalin" (XXXIII, 111). Then, she turns to the situation of individual people within the political cult: "All of individual life, up to the minutest detail, has been put under the microscope, and made into a 'vessel unto honor' imbued with the godhead-Stalin. . . . The ideal party man is a god-imbued, Stalin-imbued man, a man without will or reason who believes in the ultimate kingdom of God despite everything that logic tells him and his own eyes show him" (XXXIII, 112).

The reference to the "vessel of honor" comes from Timothy 2:21: "Man shall be a vessel unto honor, sanctified, and meet for the master's use." Modifying this biblical phrase, Freidenberg creates an image that fits Stalinism as a political religion. Man is a Stalin-imbued vessel, ready for the master's use. Soviet socialism is therefore a new gospel, and Bolshevism is a "theocracy" with the ambition to become a new world religion: "They are creating another new Rome from Moscow (the third one? the fourth?). The Bolshevik theocracy rules the country, spreading out into the whole world, recruiting the dispossessed by sword and purse. . . . The party functionaries are the clergy. Party membership is divine grace" (XXXIII, 112).

Describing the rituals of the Stalin cult, Freidenberg finds equivalents to them in historical forms of political religion, which featured similar rituals: "All of Stalinist messianism, its flower-strewn idols resembling the Catholic Virgin Mary, the special intonation in pronouncing his name . . . the ritual of rising to one's feet, [Stalin's] invisible chairmanship ('honorary chairman') at all meetings, collective prayers addressed to him by the assembly of the faithful—all of this is very old. . . . Again Augustus, 'Pater Patriae,' the eschatological cult of Frederick Barbarossa. . . . Again we have a punitive or benevolent *Weltlicher Herrscher*, or, as he was recently called, 'the commander of the twentieth century'" (XXXIII, 113).[20]

In this way, extending the idea of the "Führer principle" from the speeches at the Nuremberg trial, and employing the concept of "political religion" from historical scholarship, Freidenberg conceptualized the cult of Stalin as she observed its manifestations in the everyday.

Concentration Camp or *L'état de Siège*

In her *Origins of Totalitarianism*, with the Nazi case in mind, Arendt famously posited concentration camps as the "laboratory" of the totalitarian regime. Once in power, the totalitarian state "erects concentration camps as special laboratories to carry through its experiment in total domination" (392). Inflicting physical suffering and extreme deprivation, the camps develop ways to "manipulate the human body—with its infinite possibilities of suffering—in such a way as to make it destroy the human person. . . ." (453). The camps, in which "everything is permitted" (441), function as "the laboratories where changes in human nature are tested" (458). When she created such a vision, Arendt had at her disposal the first published reports about the Nazi camps, including some memoirs of survivors, but Arendt knew very little of the Soviet camps.[21]

For Freidenberg, besieged Leningrad was the symbolic equivalent of a camp: "The besieged city languished within a domestic concentration camp. . . ." She explained her metaphor: "Here, human beings were subjected to violence, death, all the horrors of starvation and the struggle with physical nature. . . ." (XV: 108, 5). And judging by the phrase "a domestic concentration camp," she was also thinking of the Nazi camps, which were not entirely unknown to the people in the Soviet Union. She found it pertinent to add that "international public opinion" did not know or suspect that this was the case (XV: 108, 5). Freidenberg's blockade notes of 1941–1944 describe life in the besieged city in terms that are quite similar to those later used by Arendt in her reflections on the camps. According to Freidenberg, it is a life of extreme physical deprivation and complete domination, and, like Arendt, Freidenberg wrote about "changes in the physical nature of the human being" (XIII: 52, 69).

For Arendt, one of the results of the regime of total domination is the creation of living dead: in the camp, human beings become totally passive and indifferent to their fate, resembling living corpses. (Primo Levi, and Agamben after him, describe a person in this state as a "Musselmann.") Freidenberg is like Arendt in characterizing the people confined in the besieged city as living corpses, indifferent to their fate. And she insists that it is precisely the "Russian, and what is more, the Soviet person" who found himself in this situation. "European man could have perished in such conditions," but the Soviet man, who had lived through the terror in the 1930s, could "die and then return to life" (XII bis: 23, 62). In the Great Terror, the Soviet people died and returned to life as living corpses. Now, during the blockade, they died and returned in the image of the living dead yet again.

The parallel between siege and camp was also noted by Lidiia Ginzburg in her blockade notebooks (453), where she writes about the "absolute power" and "absolute unfreedom" that ruled in both situations (427).[22] Like Freidenberg, Ginzburg notes the readiness of "contemporary man" to endure hardship. She sees this new individual as possessing a "relative indifference to life," stemming from a conviction that "adversity constitutes a normal form of being." And while Freidenberg ascribes this passivity specifically to Soviet man, Ginzburg is more inclusive. She notes that passivity and lack of initiative as a result of repression and violence are also found in the West, where "Fascist man" responds to coercion with the same apathetic patience as "Soviet man" (296).

For Freidenberg, the image of the blockade retained its uncanny power long after the war ended, and she continued to describe the situation in postwar Leningrad as life under siege or in a concentration camp (a "city-camp"). In her last notebook, summarizing her analysis of life under Stalinism, she coins a new formula: "The human being is blocked" (*chelovek blokirovan*) (XXXIV, 143). She explains that in the Soviet Union, people are restricted in their ability to move to another city and even to change apartments, and once again, she returns to the familiar image of a communal apartment as a place of confinement and surveillance (XXXIV, 143).

Throughout her notes, Freidenberg paints a picture of the circles of hell: first, a room where members of the family eat, defecate, and copulate in each other's view; then an apartment in which an educated person shares a kitchen and toilet with "thieves and bandits"; then the "city-camp," in which residents live under the surveillance of the secret police; and finally, a country in which citizens are locked in total isolation from the outside world. All this falls under the concept of blockade, or siege. This is a metaphor, of course, but, as we know from her scholarship as well as her notes, Freidenberg believed in the experiential reality and cognitive power of metaphors.

The metaphor of the siege-camp as a special regime gains additional force from its association with the political concept of *l'état de siège*. The concept became relevant in Germany in the 1920s–1930s, when it attracted the attention of Carl Schmitt, and it has later gained considerable currency as elaborated by Giorgio Agamben.[23] Agamben begins with the notion of "the state of exception," equivalent to *l'état de siège* as Schmitt advanced it in the 1920s.

To simplify this complex argument, Schmitt argued for the necessity of a "state of exception" to be enacted by the sovereign as a temporary suspension of the rule of law at the time of an external threat ("siege") or internal danger. Theoretically, the state of exception helps normalize the situation. As we now know, in practice, the state of exception put into effect by the Weimar Republic helped Hitler come to power in 1933. In the early years of our own twenty-first century, Agamben reexamined the idea of the state of exception, offering a radically different understanding of the concept of normalization. His main goal was to show that the state of exception had the potential to transform a democracy into a totalitarian state. Following Hannah Arendt, Agamben used the Nazi concentration camp as the "matrix" of the totalitarian regime. Following Walter Benjamin, he focused on the situation in which the state of exception gains permanence, becoming the rule or norm. The camp is an institution that comes into being when *l'état de siège* is normalized. In the camp, a state of exception—initially a temporary suspension of the rule of law—becomes the normal order, permanently abolishing the legal order. In this space, according to Agamben, human life becomes an object of radical biopolitics and is threatened with elimination.

To return to Freidenberg and her metaphor of the siege in light of these ideas, from its origins in the blockade notes and into the postwar years, Freidenberg used the siege, along with the concentration camp, as a model of life in the city and in the whole country. In Russia, she once wrote, "a person is always under siege" (XIII: 59, 88). The phrase "the siege of the human being" turns into a metaphor for the Stalinist system, and the image of the human being under siege stands for the human condition in Stalinist society. It is this special human condition that Freidenberg purports to describe in her notes, and to this end, she employs various analytical instruments. As we saw in earlier chapters, she subjects everyday conditions to scrutiny akin to ethnographic analysis, describing forced labor, organized hunger, coerced cohabitation, all-embracing surveillance, and much more. As shown here, she also draws on the conceptual metaphors and categories of political philosophy.

Among her most important theoretical concepts is the normalization of the exceptional condition under the state of siege. Remember how, during the blockade, she describes a whole family cramped into a single room—the only heated room in the apartment—and then concludes, "The tyranny normalized this into an everyday routine" (XVI: 119, 6). Also during the blockade, she notes how "starvation was accepted as a normative condition" (XVI: 89, 47). And she describes the normalization of death in the daily shelling of the city streets by the German artillery (XVIII: 138, 10–11). On the basis of these observations, Freidenberg formulates an important theoretical conclusion: "History has known sieges and catastrophes. But never before have human disasters been conceived as a normative everyday phenomenon" (XVIII: 138, 10).

Freidenberg's concept of the normalization of the exceptional seems remarkably similar to Agamben's, but there is a difference. Agamben, following Schmitt, is interested in the legitimacy of the *l'état de siège* as a condition that places power outside the "normal" legal order. Freidenberg was not in the least interested in the legal status of the regime; rather, she focused on everyday life. For her, *l'état de siège* was a situation when exceptional, inhuman living conditions were turned into the normative, habitual order of daily life.

Unlike her contemporaries who worked with the concept of *l'état de siege*, for Freidenberg, the siege was a metaphor rooted in everyday experience, in what she saw with her own eyes and lived in her own body. It is no surprise, then, that while Freidenberg shares with Arendt the image of the concentration camp, it is the state of siege that stands out for her as the all-embracing symbol of the new form of tyrannical government.

The Philosophy of History

Significant differences between Freidenberg and Arendt come to the fore when we compare their views on history. Freidenberg (as we have seen) imagined history as a "supraindividual," "objective process," as she put it, borrowing from Hegel, in which "nothing is ever despised or forgotten." History was a force that linked her to the "brotherhood" of the whole world, "an absolute being" that would preserve her besieged life, recorded in her personal archive, for future generations (XXVI: 75, 56–57).

The idea of the redemptive power of history stands behind the image of a "Moscow Nuremberg" that appears in the notes time and again, perhaps echoing Hegel's famous formula *Weltgeschichte ist Weltgericht*. Even though Freidenberg had no faith in her personal role in this salvation scheme ("I will not live to see the retribution. I will not see the Moscow Nuremberg" [XXVII: 83, 9]), she maintained her faith in the world tribunal of history to the end of her notes.

Many diaries and memoirs of the Russian intelligentsia—the personal archives of the Soviet experience—pictured the fractured lives of people caught in revolution, terror, and two world wars as a part of an absolute process that promised redemption—and constituted evidence for the international tribunal of history. Lidiia Ginzburg, who did not share this veneration of history, wrote about Hegelian historical consciousness in her scholarship. She also referred to it as a belief held by her contemporaries when she spoke about the experience of the Stalin terror and World War II in her notebooks.[24]

Such a vision of history was not alien to European intellectuals, even in the twentieth century, among them Dilthey, whose views of history followed Hegel's.[25] But as the twentieth century unfolded, it proved increasingly difficult to maintain belief in the eschatological potential of history.

Karl Löwith's book *The Meaning of History* exemplifies their predicament. Published in 1949 in the US, some years after the author's escape from Hitler's Germany, the book analyzes the teleological understanding of history that overtook European thought in the nineteenth century as a secularized version of the Judeo-Christian notion of divine providence. These ideas, Löwith showed, culminated in Hegel's vision of history and were then recast as social theory in the work of Marx. It is in this vein that Löwith interpreted Hegel's formula *Weltgeschichte ist Weltgericht*, or (in my paraphrase) world history is an international tribunal. Löwith considered this view to be an inextricable part of European intellectual history. But after Hitler, he regarded such optimistic visions of history as hopelessly outdated.[26]

The idea of history as an absolute process leading to salvation was well known—and deeply alien—to Hannah Arendt, especially in the postwar years. Arendt's radical rejection of the philosophy of history derived from Hegel and Marx was a part of her antitotalitarian impulse. In her *Origins of Totalitarianism*, she subjected the Hegelian-Marxist idea of History as a "world-historical force" moving in accordance with its own laws toward the predetermined end to a sharp critique. Arendt famously argued that the Stalinist terror was legitimized by the idea that the death sentence on the dying classes had already been pronounced by the "higher tribunal" of History, while Hitler's terror condemned certain races to extinction by appealing to the laws of Nature (464–465). Later she explicitly rejected the Hegelian idea of *Weltgeschichte als Weltgericht* in favor of the Kantian principle of the autonomy of the human mind.[27] On one occasion, speaking about the tendency of Marxist intellectuals in Western Europe to put their trust in the historical process, Arendt wrote that "the Hitler-Stalin pact was the turning point for the European Left; now one had to give up all belief in history as the ultimate judge of human affairs."[28]

Freidenberg found herself in an entirely different situation. Living and suffering in total isolation in Stalinist society, under the double assault of Hitler and Stalin, war and terror, Freidenberg—like many of her compatriots—could not afford to doubt the redeeming power of an objective historical process. She had lost too much; she had been deprived of too much. And the desperate hope, against all odds, for a "Moscow Nuremberg"—the image that appears on the last page of her notes—was necessary for her. In the same vein, Freidenberg found it necessary to hold onto the presumption of total meaning (the feeling that "everything had a meaning"), which figures on the first page of her notes.[29]

Stalinism Introduced Many New Things

At the very end of her last notebook, Freidenberg drew a line across the page and began to summarize her theory of Stalinism: "Stalinism, without a doubt, introduced many new things. It threw the outdated and naive Machiavelli into the attic...." (XXXIV, 148). She focused on what she calls Stalin's "methodology": Stalin introduced "a different state methodology: mystification" (XXXIV, 148). While Machiavelli used the concept of "mystification" to describe strategies of deception employed by the prince to manipulate the population, Freidenberg clearly means something else: the propaganda of freedom that deceived some "fools" in the international arena (XXXIV, 148). Here, as elsewhere in her notes, Freidenberg sought to explain the nature of Stalinism to both an uncomprehending future historian and the naive inhabitants of the West. (Arendt also came to the conclusion that totalitarianism used different methods of mystification and political manipulation than those described by Machiavelli.[30])

Among other innovations, Freidenberg mentions the all-embracing reach of Stalinist power. Stalinism set itself a goal "to conquer the whole universe, from the single individual to the universe" (XXXIV, 148). Looking at Stalinist society itself, she sees the secret police as an all-pervasive force: "With us, the secret police is not an organ of the government, but a regime covering the whole scope of the public and the private, the whole scope of personal life" (XXXIV, 149). (In her *Origins of Totalitarianism*, Arendt also posited "the secret police" as "the sole organ of power," which permeates "the entire texture of totalitarian society" [419, 430].) And looking from inside the regime, Freidenberg found it particularly important that terror was enacted not only through the secret police but also by mobilizing the internal strife between people into an all-embracing system of mutual surveillance and self-perpetuating denunciation. And it is here, summarizing her analysis of Stalinism, that Freidenberg coined her definition of the "squabbles" as Stalin's main "policy" and "methodology" (XXXIV, 150–151).

The last pages of Freidenberg's last notebook offer one final image of the body politic: "Stuffed like herrings in a tightly corked barrel, sick, half-dead human beings swarm and crush one another" (XXXIV, 150). This picture may serve as an alternative to the solemn icon of society from the frontispiece of Hobbes's treatise.

Concluding her political analysis of Stalinism as a new, unprecedented form of government, Freidenberg again returned to the idea of the war of all against all and modified Hobbes's idea (without naming Hobbes). The Stalinist state, she writes, "also introduced a new system, unheard of until then—the state of war with each individual person who is part of the population of Russia" (XXXIV, 148). In other words, rather than providing protection from the war of all against all, the sovereign enters into a state of war with each one of them.

In conclusion, Freidenberg makes one last list of the main principles, or "methods," of Stalinism. Her notes offer a number of these lists, with variations. This one says, "Mystification of nations, death in prison cells, suffocation of each individual human being, and universal squabbling—these are Stalin's methods" (XXXIV, 151).

In summary, Freidenberg's theory-diary introduces many new ideas that modify the political principles of Aristotle, Machiavelli, and Hobbes. She takes the same components—*corpus politicum*, tyranny, Leviathan, war of all against all, mystification, and more—and recombines them, trying out a variety of patterns and images. What she does not do is bring her ideas to definitive conclusions or link her array of concepts and images into a coherent system. This was not a theory formulated in a treatise but a theory embedded in a diary. And a diary remains open-ended.

The Testimony of Lazarus

Reflecting on how difficult it was to describe the experience of concentration camp prisoners, Arendt turns to the language of mythological metaphors: "Seen from outside, they and the things that happen in them can be described only in images drawn from a life after death...." (445). Arendt surmises that from the internal position of camp survivors, it would be nearly impossible to describe the experience in a way that would make those who had not been there understand the full horror of totalitarian domination. She sees the return of camp inmates to the "psychologically or otherwise intelligible world" as resembling "the resurrection of Lazarus" (441). Try as they might, they cannot impart their experience to those who have not shared it. She further speculates that they cannot relate easily to their own memories. Memories of the concentration camp "must seem just as incredible to those who relate them as to their audience" (441). The experience of these survivors would be indispensable for the understanding of totalitarianism, but "recollection," as she sees it, is insufficient. An "eyewitness report" from the camps remains "uncommunicable" (441).

Freidenberg could have recognized herself in this image of Lazarus. After the war, she repeatedly wrote about herself as a corpse who was forced to live, a corpse who walked the streets of the city, visited the theater and the cinema, and taught in the Department of Classical Philology at Leningrad University. Yet Freidenberg proved capable of relating her experiences to others. While her reports were not, in the strict sense, those of someone from a concentration camp, she assembled a meticulously detailed eyewitness account of all-embracing everyday terror for which the concentration camp was a major metaphor. Working from within, she created a personal chronicle of life in a totalitarian society, as well as a theoretical analysis of that experience: a diary-theory.

CHAPTER 6

"Conclusion" (1950)

More than once, Freidenberg felt that her life and her notes had come an end. On two occasions (August 5, 1947, and January 14, 1948), she put a "final" date to her notes. As time went on, she filled in gaps in her life story. She prepared her father's archive, which documented his inventions, and handed it over to the Museum of Communications (Muzei sviazi). She made a notarized will, leaving her archive to Sofia Poliakova. (Later, she changed her will, making Rusudan Orbeli her heir and executor.) Under pressure, she stepped down as chair of the Department of Classical Philology and began preparing to retire from the university. She made a plan to summarize all her "intellectual experience" in a scholarly study with the title *Image and Concept* (XXXIII, 96).[1] Now, on December 5, 1949, she wrote that "the question of life" was finished for her (XXXIII, 107). And her thoughts turned to her notes:

> Notes, these notes! I was afraid of a search, not for my own sake, because of myself, but for theirs: I was afraid—that the notes would be destroyed. How many times was my soul touched by hesitation: my notes or my freedom? Destroy them and be free, fear nothing, not a search and nor death! But I could not even value freedom more than these notes. I did not want to die voiceless. That would mean I was accepting the worst that the world had ever known—the mystification

of good, the ideological cynicism, the dehumanization. I remembered the ideals that covered up the killing of a human being, remembered how conscience, my own conscience, lay on the anatomy table when the tyrant forced us to face our biological physiology, and we lived half-dead, jealous of a piece of bread eaten by our loved ones, longing, in secret from our own selves, to take their food. Oh, these torments of conscience, torments that never pass and deprive life of the right to exist! What did Stalin not do to a man, what did he not kill, what did he not put him through? What in history has he not mocked? (XXXIII, 110–111)

She prepared to conclude her notes but soon (in March 1950) resumed writing. She started a new notebook, numbered XXXIV; it is subtitled in parenthesis, "(Conclusion)" [(*Okonchanie*)]. After describing the summer and fall of 1950, she drew a line and turned to formulating conclusions to her analysis of Stalinism. With that finished, she drew another line and composed a page and a half of final conclusions to her own life, lived, as she put it, in opposition to the "state machine" (XXXIV, 153): "That is really all about my life. What can be the epilogue and what is its meaning? Whether I live a long or short life is asemantic. Nature gave me an abundance of moral strength and abilities, but I have been losing them in the incessant struggle to resist the state machine, a machine of violence and the murder of living people" (XXXIV, 153).

She ends with a list of her losses: "My husband, given to me by life, as grace is given by god, was crushed by a drunken machine" (XXXIV, 153).[2] She imagines the death of her brother, who disappeared without a trace after his arrest in 1937: "My brother died amid the most horrible tortures of the Stalinist dungeon." She puts side by side the death of her father (in the Petrograd blockade of 1920) and her mother (in the Leningrad siege in 1944): "My father and my mother died of starvation and shock." She speaks about her work, "My scholarship was strangled by Stalin's fingers," and about her "love": "My love was debased, as was my honor." Honor remains one of her most important losses throughout the notes. Finally, she comes to her work at the university: "My students moved away from me, scared by the Stalinist state. I had to give up the last thing I held dear—my department" (XXXIV, 153).

Of all the catastrophes she experienced, one was the worst: "The most terrible thing was the siege, which I saw with my own eyes, that scalping of the living human being no soul can endure" (XXXIV, 153).

She describes her notes as a weapon in an apocalyptic struggle and asserts her readiness to continue her armed resistance: "Inwardly, of course, I will continue not to give up. These notes, written amidst searches, arrests, and executions, are my human protest against the artillery of the Antichrist. I will go on digging in the earth in search of a healing root and speaking out against the headquarters of Maria Lazarevna and the cretinism of Borovsky, I will rebel, make efforts to write my final book; I will believe in science and in history" (XXXIV, 154).

To the end, Freidenberg did not surrender her belief in history, her rebellion against all forms of tyranny, and her readiness to oppose evil. And even in this solemn moment, she alludes to the squabbles on the faculty (the wife of her colleague-rival Tronsky, Maria Lazarevna, and the new department chair, Borovsky). University squabbles remain a part of the state arsenal of tyranny.

In the last lines of her notes, Freidenberg tries for something inaccessible to a diarist and autobiographer: to write the chronicle of her life to its end—that is, to the point of death. Imagining that moment, she is left with two images: one personal—her mother, who died in the siege—and one mythic—the Last Judgment of history:

> I don't know when and of what I'll die. But I know one thing: if I am conscious when I die, standing before my eyes will be two images: one of my mother—and the other of the Moscow Nuremberg.
>
> 10 December 1950 O. Freidenberg
>
> (XXXIV, 154)

At the end of the academic year 1950–1951, Freidenberg retired from the university. She died on July 5, 1955, from cancer. Her notes remain unpublished to this day.

Appendix: The Russian Original of Major Quotations

Listed here are the original Russian texts of major quotations found in the book in the English translation, keyed to the first words of quotations.

Introduction

"From the first days of childhood..."
С самых ранних дней детства, как только во мне проснулось сознание [...] у меня было чувство [...] что все то, что находится во мне и вне меня, не исчерпывается собой, а имеет значение (I–II, 1).

"In Russia... whether there is a blockade or not... a person is always under siege..."
В России [...] есть ли блокада или нет [...] человек всегда в осаде... (XIII: 59, 88).

"I have never been able to make barriers..."
я никогда не могла ставить перегородок между научной теорией и непосредственным восприятием жизни; одно выражало другое (XVI: 122, 17).

"What happened at the university..."
то, что происходило в Университете [...] ничем не отличалось от любого советского учреждения.

"Hitler and Stalin, two tyrants, created a new system of government, unknown to Aristotle."
Гитлер и Сталин, два тирана, создали новую форму правления, о которой Аристотель не мог знать (XXVIII: 7, 47).

"And though I do not know whether [these notes] will see the light of day..."
И хоть я не знаю, увидят ли они свет (кто их спрячет? Куда?), я не хочу отказаться от того, что я считаю своим долгом перед

историей. [. . .] Лучше рисковать жизнью, но тайно писать (XXXII: I, 45).

"(my notes are free from coercion, incoherent, inconsistent . . .)"
(мои записки свободны от принуждения, сбивчивы, непоследовательны и написаны бедным языком, отражая утомленный и обедненный мозг) (XXVII, 83, 12–13).

"Do they know [about us] abroad?"
Знает ли заграница?

Chapter 1. "Overture" (1890–1917)

"I spoke to you about the childhood of one's inner world . . ."
Я говорил тебе о детстве внутреннего мира, которое связывало нас. И даже не говорил, а м. б. слушал твои воспоминания об этом. Но постепенно эта романтика духовного мира, который отличает детство и кульминирует в 15–16 лет, захватывает внешний мир, который до этого момента мы просто наблюдали, схватывали характерное, имитировали, умели или не умели выразить (I–II, 76).

"Twenty-one pages!"
21 страница! Это было письмо, полное молодого, сильного чувства, которое не смеет назвать себя (I–II, 78).

"I did not yet know that Borya would be a poet . . ."
Я еще не знала, что Боря будет поэт, и что ему дано лирически говорить за всех. В этом письме он выразил и всего себя, но и всю меня (I–II, 78).

"He talked, usually for hours, and I walked in silence . . ."
Он говорил, обычно, целыми часами, а я шла молча. Признаться, я почти ничего из того, что он говорил, не понимала. Я и развитием была неизмеримо ниже Бори, и его словарь был мне непонятен. Но меня волновал и увлекал простор, которые открывали его глубокие, вдумчивые, какие-то новые слова. Воздвигался новый мир, непонятный, но увлекательный, я вовсе не стремилась знать точные вес и значение каждой фразы; я могла любить непонятное; новое, широкое, ритмически и духовно близкое вело меня прочь от обычного на край света (I–II, 72).

APPENDIX: THE RUSSIAN ORIGINAL OF MAJOR QUOTATIONS

"from an early age, there smoldered in me . . ."
Так, начиная с раннего возраста, во мне тлел интерес к формам, которые принимала жизнь, к ее метаморфозам и перелицовкам. . . (I–II, 117).

"And after all, scholarship, like all creative work, is autobiography . . ."
И ведь научная работа, как всякое творчество, есть автобиография. И когда я впоследствии стала заниматься теорией литературных форм, семантикой смыслов, рождавших форму; когда я порывалась охватить многообразие и пестроту форм единством перевоплощенной в них семантики—я только и делала, что рассказывала о жизни своей души и своего тела (I–II, 117).

"I did not know that this was the beginning of my life at its major turning point . . ."
Я не знала, что это есть начало моей жизни на ее главном переломе. Что все пережитое было только вступлением и увертюрой. [. . .] И что только теперь начнутся мои увлечения и страсть, и настоящая любовь . . . (I–II, 179).

"He is your brother not only by blood!"
Он брат вам не только по крови! (XI: 90, 192).

"Love is a special Weltanschauung . . ."
Любовь—это особое мироощущение. Время останавливается. В нем нет протяженности. Все, что было, остается жить во всех деталях [. . .] если связано с «ним». [. . .] Каждый пустяк получает особую значимость. [. . .] Все требует толкования, все полно глубочайшей символики (XI: 91, 201).

Chapter 2. Blockade (1941–1945)

"How Freidenberg Wrote"

"The Germans killed Leningraders with inhuman cruelty."
С бесчеловечной жестокостью немцы убивали ленинградцев (XII-bis: 17, 40).

"Day after day, week after week, a human being was given nothing to eat."
День за днем, неделю за неделей человеку не давали ничего есть. Государство, взяв на себя питание людей и запретив им торговать,

добывать и обменивать, ровно ничего не давало (XII-bis: 29, 80).

"No one had any choice in anything . . ."
Не было ни у кого ни в чем ни выбора, ни возможности свободы, ни избежанья (XII-bis: 23, 62).

"May 27, 1942. There was an air raid at night."
27 мая 1942. Ночью был налет. Мама плохо спала. . . (XIII: 59, 90).

"Today I donned my childhood coat . . ."
Сегодня одела детское свое пальто. [. . .] Меня уже, в сущности, нет. Мое тело заживо истаяло. У меня структура восьмилетнего ребенка (XIII: 59, 90).

"It's time to face this catastrophe."
Этой катастрофе пора взглянуть в глаза. Чего ждать, на что надеяться? (XIII: 59, 90).

"This is how an inmate of a concentration camp must feel . . ."
Так должен себя чувствовать мученик концлагеря . . . (XIII: 59, 89–91).

"A person is placed, as in a concentration camp, in a hopeless situation."
Человек поставлен, как в концлагере, в безвыходное положение (XVII: 127, 12).

"Where could a person hide from the enemy-aggressors who besieged him . . ."
Куда было укрыться человеку от осаждавших его агрессоров-врагов, от государства, от тирании чужих и родных, от этой громадной и мощной системы насилия, в которой не учитывалась свобода? (XV: 112, 15).

"Yes, this day, like many others, was experienced and lived through."
Да, был пережит, был прожит и этот день, как многие другие. Но жизнь, даже жизнь в СССР, в России, не может оставаться одноцветна, даже в осажденном городе среди осажденных людей (XV: 112, 15–16).

APPENDIX: THE RUSSIAN ORIGINAL OF MAJOR QUOTATIONS

"Life protected me and carefully led me on a difficult path over an abyss."
Жизнь оберегала меня и осторожно вела за руку по тяжелой тропе над пропастью. [. . .] обобщая и символизируя, как всегда, явления жизни [. . .] я увидела в этом неожиданном факте [. . .] глубокую сущность матери-жизни (XIV: 96, 72–73).

"How have we lived? . . . [We lived] like everybody else . . ."
Как мы жили? Как мы прожили эти годы? [. . .] Наравне со всеми: в будущее не заглядывали,—о завтрашнем дне не думали. Погибающие люди научились, не сговорившись, жить вершками. Время скорчилось и застыло судорогой (XVIII: 154, 79–80).

"Life is horrible. It is replete with torments . . ."
Жизнь ужасна. Она полна мук, она состоит во всей своей общественной сути из одних фикций (XVII: 133, 33).

"Life in its humiliating downfall went on as normal."
Жизнь шла нормально в своем унизительном паденьи (XVIII: 157, 87).

"International public opinion did not know, did not suspect . . ."
Международное общественное мнение не знало, не подозревало, что осажденный город изнывал в отечественном концлагере; здесь человек подвергался насилию, смерти, всем ужасам голодного истощения и борьбы с физической природой, всем лишениям заброшенного государством, но им эксплуатируемого, существа (XV: 108, 5).

"The Germans targeted peaceful citizens, women, crowds of civilians."
Немцы метили в мирных обывателей, в женщин, в гущу гражданского населения (XVIII: 142, 25).

"This was a double barbarism . . ."
Это было двойное варварство... (XVIII: 142, 25).

"The Germans pounded the streetcar stops . . ."
Немцы били снарядами по трамвайным остановкам и по всем местам скопления публики, мирной безоружной публики, которую наш тиран заставлял жить и работать на передовых

позициях. Трамваи обращались в кровавое месиво (XVIII: 155, 80).

"The problem of form and content . . ."
Проблема формы и содержания есть проблема жизни и судьбы, небытия и божества, космоса в физическом и духовном началах. Живя и страдая, научно работая над текстами и книгами, я вынашивала только один этот страстный вопрос, обращенный к безмолвному универсуму (XVI: 122, 17).

"I could never set up barriers between a scientific theory and . . ."
я никогда не могла ставить перегородок между научной теорией и непосредственным восприятием жизни; одно выражало другое (XVI: 122, 17).

"Famine and the Total Abolition of Civilization"
Голод и полная отмена цивилизации

"The bread was so horrible that it came out . . ."
Хлеб был так ужасен, что выходил в испражнениях непереваренными крупинками [. . .] и целыми кучками той самой структуры, которая у него была до пищеваренья [. . .]—словно это был хлеб, но не экскременты (XII-bis: 29, 81).

"We were no longer protected by everything that civilization had developed."
Мы не были защищены всем тем, что выработала многовековая цивилизация. У нас не было ни домов, ни жилищ, ни топлива и теплых вещей, ни воды и уборной, ни отлива для нечистот, ни еды, ни света, ни защиты законов (XV: 111, 13).

"The whole day was spent in overcoming unfortunate everyday obstacles . . ."
Целый день уходил на преодоленье несчастных бытовых препятствий, о которых человеческая цивилизация давно забыла; они усугублялись тем, что разыгрывались не среди природы, а посредством сложной машины государственного насилия и сложнейших выкрутасов самой передовой техники, направленной на уничтожение и мучительство людей. Ни Робинзон, ни палеазиат [sic!] не знали налогов, карточек, аэропланов и снарядов. . . (XV: 113, 17).

APPENDIX: THE RUSSIAN ORIGINAL OF MAJOR QUOTATIONS

"There were different categories of people, rations of different categories . . ."
Были различной категории люди, различной категории пайки. [. . .] Рассказывать о них не позволялось (XIII: 37, 15).

"Some people died with blue lips . . ."
одни умирали с синими губами, исходя поносами, а другие носили на спине рюкзаки и бодрым шагом несли домой жиры, белки и углеводы (XIII: 37, 15).

"[Every person] was forced to swallow and defecate under coercion."
Глотать и испражняться он вынужден был по принуждению (XIII: 37, 15).

"My God, how emaciated and ugly I was."
Боже мой, какая я была исхудалая, страшная. [. . .] Я, полногрудая с малых лет, оказалась кастрированной, словно это не структура моего тела (XIII: 52, 67–68).

"One winter with Hitler-Popkov, and the woman in me is finished!"
Одна зима с Гитлером-Попковым,—и уже конец женщине! (XIII: 52, 68).

"And we have all became like this. Women without hips . . ."
И такими были мы все. Женщины без бедер, без грудей, без живота, женщины с мужской структурой (XIII: 52, 68).

"There was no person and family, no apartment without acute diarrhea . . ."
Не было человека и семьи, не было квартиры без острого поноса, иногда доходившего до 19–20 раз в сутки (XIII: 34, 3).

"The yard, the floor, the street, the snow, the square . . ."
Двор, пол, улица, снег, площадь все было залито желтой вонючей жижей (XII-bis: 31, 86).

"The communal apartment above us flooded us with waste from above."
Коммунальная квартира заливала нас сверху испражнениями. Я выносила по 7 ведер в день нечистот, да еще поджидала, чтоб экскременты были горячими, свежими, иначе они замерзали бы через 10–15 минут и создали бы безвыходное положение (XII-bis: 31, 86).

"The hot liquid rushes out and floods my legs, my dress."
Горячая жидкость потоком вырывается и заливает мои ноги, мое платье (XIV: 78, 18).

"The Soviet Tiamat"
Советская Тиамат

"Once upon a time, suffering consisted in . . ."
Когда-то страданье заключалось в том, чтоб выпить до дна чашу: так древний человек метафоризировал несчастье. В советском быту метафорой беды была пролитая чаша. . . (XV: 115, 25–26).

"I heard the momentary gurgle of pipes in the corridor . . ."
Я услышала в коридоре мгновенное бульканье труб, и это наполнило меня непередаваемым ужасом. Заглянула в уборную— сосуд снова наполнен до краев дрянью, но инстинкт подсказал, что дело уже не только в этом. Открываю, с замиранием сердца, ванную и вижу: ванна до самых бортов полна черной вонючей жидкости, затянутой сверху ледяным салом. Это страшное зрелище ни с чем несравнимо. Оно ужасней, чем воздушные бомбардировки и обстрелы из тяжелой артиллерии. Что-то жуткое, почти мистическое, в напоре снизу, а не сверху, при закрытом чопе (пробка). Страшно, гибельно, угрозой смотрит огромное вместилище с черной, грязной водой. Она бесконечна и необузданна, эта снизу прущая стихия напора и жидкости, эта советская Тиамат, первозданный хаос и грязь. Я с трудом выносила и поднимала свои ежедневные несколько грязных ведер. Но могла ли я вычерпать и вынести 30–50 ведер нашей громадной ванны. Ее черное, страшное содержимое смотрело на меня своими бездонными глазами; это наполнение до самых бортов вселяло ужас и ощущенье еще никогда не испытанного бедствия. Еще миг—и нас, наш дом, наши комнаты зальет эта вонючая черная жидкость, и она будет снизу подниматься и выпирать, и будет разливаться, и это будет потоп снизу, из неведомой и необузданной, не подвластной взору пучины. А я одна, и слаба, и уже вечер, а на дворе зима. Бежать? Куда? К кому? Как оставить тут беспомощную старуху? (XV: 115, 26).

APPENDIX: THE RUSSIAN ORIGINAL OF MAJOR QUOTATIONS

"I am writing this in April, and the bathtub is still full . . ."
Вот я пишу в апреле, а ванна так-же [sic!] полна, черна и страшна (XV: 116, 27).

"This state of siege, created by tyranny, has kept the city, me . . ."
Осадное положение, созданное тиранией, держало город, меня, мое тело и психику, в особом ультра-тюремном укладе. Я уже привыкла считаться только с краями наполненной ванны и смотреть исключительно на ее борта. Не поднялся ли уровень? Перельется сегодня или нет?—Больше ничего меня не интересовало [. . .] Причина явлений и устранение бедствий—это отошло, как химера. Только борт! Только семантика того тонкого верхнего края, который служит границей жизни и смерти, символом, отображающим мой сегодняшний день (XV: 115, 27).

"Dependency, Hunger—and the Unbearable Lifelong Obligation!"
Зависимость, голод,—и непосильное обязательство по гроб!

"She had a chance to tie us hand and feet with her favors."
Ей представлялся случай связать нас по рукам и ногам собственными услугами. Пошли трудные морально и физически дни. Антонина убивала нас, через день принося нам хлеб. . . (XIII: 43, 33).

"Dependency, hunger—and the unbearable lifelong obligation!"
Зависимость, голод,—и непосильное обязательство по гроб! (XIII: 43, 33, 34).

"She did the hard work of charity naively and purely . . ."
Тяжелый подвиг благотворенья она совершала наивно и с ясным чистым сердцем, не понимая, как он труден и как трудны мы с мамой. . . Мы страдали ожогами гордости (XV: 107, 2).

"What I took for lofty, heartfelt feeling . . ."
То, что я принимала за высоту сердечного чувства, теперь рисовалось мне, как преходящее поверхностное увлеченье. [. . .] Она меня сломала, завоевала. Теперь интерес был погашен. . . (XVIII: 155, 82).

"My soul at last recoiled from her . . ."
моя душа, наконец, отшатнулась от нее, уже не могла никогда ни забыть, ни простить ей (XIX: 164, 75).

"I had forgotten all the petty things."
Все мелкое было мною забыто (XIX: 171, 89).

"A human being is complex . . ."
Человек сложен, многообразен, думала я. . . (XIX: 171, 89).

"Romances and dramas don't happen in love alone."
Романы и драмы бывают не в одной любви. Они и в дружбе, и в мысли (XXVIII, 89–90).

"Characterizations of a person . . ."
Характеристики человека, обычно, лживы. Только одно искусство может человека охарактеризовать. [. . .] Говорю ли я о маме, о Тамаре, о Раисе, о Лившиц–я везде вру, поношу или восхваляю. . . (XVI: 119, 8).

"Only art can characterize a person."
Только одно искусство может человека охарактеризовать (XVI: 119, 8).

> *"Stalin's Blood-Soaked Regime and My Mother's Blindness Have Destroyed My Life the Way a Prison Does"*
> Сталинский кровавый режим и слепота матери замучили, как в застенке, мою жизнь

"My thought was constantly focused on my relationships with my mother."
Моя мысль постоянно работала над взаимоотношениями с матерью. Я думала об этом днем и ночью, на улице и в очередях, за всякой работой и роздыхом (XV: 118, 35).

"My bitterness was in direct proportion to the analysis . . ."
Моя ожесточенность шла в прямой пропорции к анализу, который я день и ночь производила над матерью и нашими отношениями (XIV: 80, 25).

APPENDIX: THE RUSSIAN ORIGINAL OF MAJOR QUOTATIONS

"I called upon the god of patience."
Я призывала бога терпенья. Но где он, как его имя? Такого бога не было (XIII: 44, 38).

"Mother was losing her mental equilibrium."
Мама теряла душевное равновесие. Ее раздражительность становилась патологической. Она мучила меня… (XIII: 44, 37–38).

"I was no longer my former self."
Но и я уже была не собою прежней. Мой тихий нрав, мое терпение были утеряны. Чахлая, злая, с отвислыми щеками, без груди и бедер, я проходила через ожесточенье и раздражительность (XIV: 80, 25).

"Then we would open our souls to each other…"
Тогда мы открывали друг другу души, и одна находила одинаковые переживания в другой, и мы вместе ужасались и скорбели (XIV: 80, 25).

"It seemed to me that this could not end well…"
Мне казалось, добром этого не кончить: "Или я ее убью—или она меня" (XIV: 93, 61).

"I found it impossible for two close people…"
Я считала невозможным сожительство двух близких людей в обстановке ссор, молчанья, забастовок, деланья "на зло" [sic]. Это было мне невыносимо, эта духовная неопрятность и осада внутри семьи. Но она крепко сидела и здесь, пробираясь еще глубже, в самое сердце человека, удушая и преследуя его везде, даже наедине, даже ночью, даже в своем глубоком "я" (XIV: 106, 109).

"She intruded into my love…"
Она вторгалась в любовь… […] Она вторгалась в мои дружбы и воинственно становилась между мною и моими друзьями. Она подтачивала мою науку, сделав меня прислугой (XV: 118, 35).

"I could not forgive her for her tyranny…"
Я не прощала ей тирании (XV: 18, 35).

"The state of siege created by tyranny."
   Осадное положение, созданное тиранией *(*XV: 115, 27).

"This retrospective view of a life . . ."
   Этот ретроспективный взгляд на жизнь, даром загубленную, впитанную без пользы чужой душой, жег меня днем и ночью. Нигде я не могла от него укрыться. Он настигал меня на улице, в постели, за столом и за книгой, он рос во мне, подобно злокачественной опухоли и наполнял меня ожесточеньем (XV: 118, 36).

"My mother, meanwhile, was in a constant state of intense and bitter irritation."
   Мать, между тем, находилась в состоянии постоянного и язвительного, возбужденного раздраженья. В такой атмосфере мне приходилось жить. Она во всем корила меня. Если мое состояние было мирное, я вечно вчем-то оправдывалась—[. . .] в отсутствии канализации, в плохих макаронах, в войне (XV: 118, 36).

"Then, I would relent and be overcome with pity."
   Потом я смягчалась и жалела. Моя мольба просила теперь одного: чтоб я могла забыть, простить; победить светом дракона в своей душе. И я стала перевоплощаться в материнскую природу и покидать себя. Я почувствовала себя хилой, ветхой, дряблой. Иждивенка—вот кто я была, лишенная самостоятельности, одинокая в душе, все утратившая, всех пережившая, в тягость и мученье мне, единственному живому дитяти.
   Я трепетала от состраданья. . . (XVI: 118, 1–2).

"When I got food, I would divide it equally . . ."
   Получая продукты, я поровну делила между нами, чтоб она ела и пила, сколько и когда хотела (XVI: 118, 1–2).

"Observing her from the outside (especially later on, in the winter) . . ."
   Глядя на нее со стороны, я утешалась тем (особенно позже, зимой), что ее преодоление двух ужасных зим уже само по себе, совершенно объективно, говорит в мою пользу. Я делилась с нею половиной своей жизни и своего дыханья. С пайком, с рабочей карточкой я могла бы прекрасно жить, не испытывая голода. . . (XIV: 90, 50–51).

APPENDIX: THE RUSSIAN ORIGINAL OF MAJOR QUOTATIONS

"Once she told me:..."
Однажды она сказала:
—Не думай, что я обязана тебе тем, что в такое время жива, что это ты меня так хорошо содержишь и кормишь. Мне дана здоровая натура, а не ты это. Я обязана только своим родителям (XIV: 90, 50–51).

"Humiliation at the hands of a typist..."
униженья перед машинисткой, униженья перед секретаршей с распущенными волосами. [...] О эта страшная сталинская машина! О, эти колеса папок, резолюций, сухих сердец, распущенных волос и юбок до колен, злобных взоров, нечеловеческой черствости (XVIII: 144, 38).

"O yes, the soul was already stained..."
Да, душа уже была запятнана, ее чистота утрачена. Жизнь ожесточала и срывала покровы с заветного и стыдливого. Функционировал замаранный тощий зад (XIV: 93, 60).

> *"Our Drama Was That We Were Locked Up and Crammed into a Common Crypt"*
> Наша драма была в том, что нас заперли и забили в общий склеп

"Our drama was that we were locked up and crammed..."
Наша драма была в том, что нас заперли и забили в общий склеп. Цивилизация поняла индивидуальные особенности каждого человека и соорудила дома, квартиры, комнаты. [...] Она поняла, что человек—не скот; что самых близких людей нужно отделять и уединять. Совместное, в кучу, проживание было изобретено цивилизацией, как форма государственной кары за преступление. Только в тюрьме люди скучены; если они в одной и той же комнате совместно проводят день и спят, и испражняются тут же, где едят—то это и есть тюрьма. Тирания создала из этого нормативный быт (XVI: 119, 6).

"It was as if it had been decreed that..."
Было как бы декретировано, что все обстоит «в основном, благополучно» и только имеет отдельные «неполадки»,

«трудности» и «лишения». Тем самым методы временных пыток получали постоянство и узаконение, как один из компонентов жизни. Человеческая природа отменялась. Есть не нужно было. Голодание было признано нормативным явлением (XVI: 89, 47).

"History had known sieges and catastrophes."
История знала осады и катастрофы. Но еще никогда человеческие бедствия не бывали задуманы в виде нормативного бытового явления (XVIII: 138, 10).

"[A Russian] submitted to the shelling and silently died . . ."
Он подчинялся обстрелам и молча умирал в расцвете дня и здоровья, как умирал в застенках чеки, в изнуреньях концентрационных лагерей (XVIII: 138, 10–11).

"But when the Russian comes face to face not with power . . ."
Но там, где русский человек оставался с глазу на глаз не с властью, а с человеком, он становился зверем (XVIII: 138, 11).

"There are bad people everywhere, in all countries."
Плохие люди есть везде, во всех странах. Зависть, клевета, интриги у всех наций на свете, как испражнения—у всех милордов и миледи. Это верно, но нигде никогда эти духовные нечистоты не носят, как при Сталине, характера организованной общественной системы. Здесь человека травят, гнетут, удушают и преследуют в официальном, узаконенном порядке, всем государственным аппаратом во всей его страшной мощи (XVII: 129, 19).

"the Stalinist system was such that it was a breeding ground for . . ."
эта сталинская система была такова, что в ней находили питательную среду самые страшные людские бактерии—продажность, предательство, ложь, корыстолюбие, подлость (XVII: 129, 20).

"It was Stalin to and Stalin fro, Stalin here and Stalin there."
Это был Сталин туда и Сталин сюда, Сталин тут и Сталин там. Вся жизнь людей, весь быт людей, весь отдых людей фаршировались, как колбаса, этим Сталиным. Нельзя было ни пойти на кухню, ни сесть на горшок, ни пообедать или выйти

APPENDIX: THE RUSSIAN ORIGINAL OF MAJOR QUOTATIONS

на улицу, чтоб Сталин не лез следом. Он забирался в кишки и в душу, ломился в мозг, забивал собой все дыры и отверстия, бежал по пятам за человеком, звонил к нему в комнату, лез в кровать под одеяло, преследовал память и сон (XVIII: 156, 85).

"One does not have to describe battles and bloodshed . . ."
Не нужно описывать сражений и кровопролития, великих мук и дел. Достаточно, для освещения эпохи показать обыкновенную повседневность в ее среднем, самом обычном уровне (XVIII: 152, 72).

"Only a Catastrophe Could Get Us Out of This Underworld"
Только катастрофа могла вывести нас из этой преисподней

"Only a catastrophe could get us out of this underworld . . ."
Только катастрофа могла вывести нас из этой преисподней, из которой мы не могли выбраться, как ни страдали, собственными силами. Все теперь было ясно исторически и биографически ясно. Я не в состоянии была пережить муки воспоминаний и угрызений поруганной совести. Мама вставала в ее настоящем духовном облике, в ее ужасных страданиях, в ее глубочайшей ко мне любви, преданности, жалости. Я вспоминала ее голод, ее жажду хлеба, как я не покупала его и не верила ей, как задавала себе вопрос—какова же ее функция в моей жизни, зачем впилась она в мою жизнь. Я сгорала от боли. Все вещи вдруг получили свой истинный смысл. Человеческое паденье, мое паденье, мою слепоту я почти ощущала руками, я осязала их (XIX: 159, 66).

"Moments of clear logical consciousness emerged . . ."
Потом рядом с бредом стало появляться ясное логическое сознание. Мама воскресала. Но она воскресла не той, что была в блокаду, а прежней собой, той нежной, мягкой, бесконечно светлой и дорогой матерью (XIX: 163, 71).

"What could have released it from the underworld . . ."
Что могло вывести нас из этой преисподней, куда загнал человека кровавый спрут?—Только катастрофа. Только полное перерождение. И мы его проходили (XIX: 163, 71).

"We have experienced the total bliss of meeting again."
   Мы пережили все счастье новой встречи (XIX: 163, 71).

"Our hearts melted with love."
   Наши сердца исходили от любви. Голова к голове, прильнув друг к другу, мы ловили дыхание одна другой, мы упивались чувством бесконечной близости и полного духовного и биологического единства. [. . .] Нет, теперь уже нам не оторваться! Эта была основа моя, ткань моей жизни. Все, что звалось мною, было в ней (XIX: 163, 71).

"I combed her hair, washed her . . ."
   Я ее причесывала, мыла, содержала в чистоте и сухости. Я косы ей заплетала вокруг головы (XIX: 163, 71).

"In the night of March 28, the very might when . . ."
   В ночь на 28 марта, в ту самую ночь, в которую 54 года тому назад мама в муках меня рожала, в эту ночь я присутствовала опять при страшных родильных муках 84-х летней женщины. Как-то она подозвала меня и сказала:
   —Выпусти мне дитя из живота!
   Я проходила теперь через единственное из страданий, недоступных человеку. В эту ночь я видела свое рождение (XX: 176, 99).

Chapter 3. After the War (1945–1950)

"A Second Birth into the World as a Corpse"
Второе рожденье мертвецом в мир

"I looked biology in the eye. I lived under Stalin."
   Я видела биологию в глаза. Я жила при Сталине. Таких двух ужасов человек пережить не может (XXI: 1, 2).

"My eyes are shrinking and dimming."
   Глаза уменьшаются и тускнеют. Руки давно умерли. Кости оплотнели. . . (XXI: 1, 1).

"What are students and scholarship to a heart that has no life in it?"
   Что ученики и наука для сердца, в котором нет жизни? (XXI: 4, 6).

APPENDIX: THE RUSSIAN ORIGINAL OF MAJOR QUOTATIONS

"dead heart could not be taken to the Volkovo Cemetery . . . a second birth into the world as a corpse.

мертвое сердце нельзя было увезти на Волково кладбище [. . .] второе рожденье мертвецом в мир (XXI: 4, 8).

"It was hard for me to return to these notes."

Мне было тяжело возвращаться к этим запискам. Они связывались у меня с записью о маме, в блокаду, в преисподней, где бились наши совести против законов физиологии. Но я к ним вернулась, готовая преодолеть самые кровоточащие травмы, чтоб только донести до чернил и бумаги рассказ о сталинских днях. Это— мой посильный протест против удушенья человека! (XXI: 6, 11).

"Two years separate the last lines of these notes from today."

Два года разделяют последние строки этих записок от сегодняшнего дня (XXI: 9, 18).

"There is not much left to do: pass through time."

Это смерть. Осталось совсем немногое: пройти через время (XXI: 5, 13).

"I want to delimit it by caring for things, fill it in . . ."

Я хочу его отграничить заботой, забить движением в пространстве, но ничто не укорачивает его. Сколько у меня ни было бы дел, время не сокращается (XXI: 4, 7).

"Time flows, streams. And I walk through its tunnel . . ."

Течет, льется Время. И я прохожу по его тоннелю, ожидая окончания пути (XXI: 9, 18).

"I stop writing. The so-called things-to-do have no significance for me."

Я перестаю писать. Так называемые дела не имеют для меня никакой значимости. Вот я сажусь в стороне от стола. Вот я хожу. Вот я у окна (XXII: 16, 14).

"Time. A bottomless wasteland."

Время. Бездонная пустошь. Страшно от этой бескрайней временной пустоты. Оголенное время. Боже мой, а если я умру нескоро? (XXII: 16, 15).

"Is this how we imagined this meeting after death?"
Так ли мы представляли себе эту встречу после смерти? (XXII: 15, 13).

"A person who held a certain position with the Bolsheviks yesterday . . ."
Человек, занимавший известную должность у большевиков—вчера, а сегодня лишившийся этой должности, с несомненностью ощущает изменение в своем теле. [. . .] Ты вдруг лишаешься свойств физического тела. Твоего вида не видят, твоего голоса не слышат. Ты делаешься невесом, как райские пэри (XXI: 10, 22).

"Maria Lazarevna ran the headquarters, in which everything was instantly known."
у Марьи Лазаревны был штаб, где все моментально делалось известно (XXI: 3, 4).

"Soiled, humiliated, having lost everything, I stood face to face with that day."
Заплеванная, униженная, все потерявшая, стояла я лицом к лицу с этим днем (XXII: 24, 41).

"Who Can Describe the Soviet Everyday?"
Кто может описать советский быт?

"Who can describe the Soviet everyday, the everyday life of Stalin era?"
Кто может описать советский быт, быт сталинской эпохи? Он со временем будет непостижим, как фантазм.

Была создана нарочитая система «трудностей»—Сизифов камень, который неизбежно скатывался вниз. Непередаваемы эти мученья—то нет электричества, то нет воды, то испорчен телефон, то молчит радио (XXIII: 34, 19).

"Everyday life was indescribable."
Быт был непередаваем. Часто можно было слышать: «Этого никто никогда не поймет» или «никогда никто об этом не узнает». Мысли заключенных! (XXV: 63, 12).

"From the outset of Stalin's reign, the state developed a whole system . . ."
Государство, с воцареньем Сталина, выработало целую систему, в которой барахтался человек. Продуманная система голода

APPENDIX: THE RUSSIAN ORIGINAL OF MAJOR QUOTATIONS

и унижения не позволяла людям ни о чем думать, кроме преодоленья тяжелых условий. Непосильный труд при грошовом заработке был эксплоатацией [sic!] человека не человеком, а государством—колоссальной звероподобной машиной, куда страшней и непреодолимей, чем отдельный человек. Эта государственная эксплоатация [sic!] охватывала людей со всех сторон и нигде не отпускала их ни дома, ни наедине (**XXIII**: 34, 19–20).

"Forced slave labor at an assigned place without the right to leave or protest . . ."
Рабский принудительный труд, с «прикреплением», без права ухода и протеста. Голод, и, наконец, дом, где в каждой комнате живет целая семья, где одному человеку вселяют в его жилище чужих людей, где у всех общая кухня и общая уборная с вечно испорченными плитами, водопроводами, стульчаками, полами, фановыми трубами. Драки и пьянки в квартирах, громкоговорители и радиолы, площадная брань и склоки женщин, вонючие пеленки, клопы; без разбора, культурный человек попадает в соседство с негодяями и бандитами. . . (**XXIII**: 34, 20).

"Coming home from the job she had been forced into . . ."
Приезжая домой с насильственной службы за Товарной Финляндской ж. д., она, измученная ездой в трамвае, после тяжелого и голодного дня, едва поспевает поесть, как наступает ночь. И в своей квартире, у себя дома она подвергается оскорбительному соседству (**XXIII**: 34, 20).

"Having beheaded Russia by killing the whole of the intelligentsia . . ."
Обезглавив Россию, убив всю интеллигенцию, Сталин создал из страны одно туловище (**XXIII**: 34, 21).

"no one could breathe any more, not only scientists or artists, but any person."
никто не мог дышать—не одни люди науки и искусства, но любой человек (**XXV**: 63, 10).

"People are locked up, but they are not fed."
Люди заперты, а есть не дают. Без карточек на хлеб живет огромное количество людей. Создано много категорий людей, не

получающих карточек. Продажи хлеба нет, она запрещена. [...] Спекулируют все. Но иначе нельзя. Этого требует само естество. [...] Неравенство страшное. Академикам и партийцам создают жизнь такую, что они обнаглели. В одном и тот же магазине люди получают различную пищу, в зависимости от чина. [...] Такой иерархии не знало ни одно государство (XXV: 63, 10–11).

"Thought is stifled. The human body, deprived of its head, has become promiscuous."
Мысль задушена. Человеческое тело, лишенное головы, стало распутным (XXV: 63, 10–11).

"People get together and split apart—the whole of Russia . . ."
Сходятся и расходятся,—вся Россия сходится и расходится, просто, без драм (XXV: 63, 11).

"They live like cattle, in the same room."
Живут по-скотски, в одной комнате. Тут родители, тут новобрачные. Тут дети, тут отцы лежат с матерями. Это система, государственная система бесчестья (XXV: 63, 11).

"The illnesses in the population are caused by the state."
Болезни населения вызываются государством (XXV: 71, 43).

"Russia was made to look like a victorious power."
России придавали вид победившей державы. Сейчас, в 1947 году, уже видно, что она не выиграла войны. Но и в 1945 году было ясно, что народ-победитель был смертельно болен. Его спасала численность и невежество. Сколько бы людей ни умерло, ни было больных и нищих, все равно это терялось. Россия вышла из войны в депрессии, психически больная, еле волочащая ноги. Трудно было встретить человека без сердечных припадков или гипертонии. Кровоизлияния и удары сделались обычным явлением, уже не связанным с возрастом (XXII: 28, 51).

"This Is an Ordinary Soviet Day"
Это простой обыденный советский день

"Torturers! Gas. Light. The queues are deliberate."
Мучители! Газ. Свет. Очереди нарочно (XXVIII: 7, 46).

APPENDIX: THE RUSSIAN ORIGINAL OF MAJOR QUOTATIONS

"I look above history."
Смотрю поверх истории (XXVIII: 7, 46).

"Everyday life is maintained in a distinctly Stalinist way."
Быт строго выдержан по-сталински (XXVIII: 8, 49).

"Over one day, first the telephone malfunctions . . ."
За одни сутки то телефон не работает, то радио замолчало, то воды не было, то электричество не горело (XXVIII: 8, 49).

"But everyday life is not only a matter of these 'temporary difficulties' . . ."
Но быт не только в этих "временных трудностях". Он—в нарочитой разрухе (XXVIII: 8, 49).

"I told myself that one should always prepare for a siege . . ."
Я говорила себе, что нужно вечно готовиться к осаде, ждать ее всегда, что наша власть всюду подстерегает нас, подобно врагу (XXVIII: 10, 56).

"And so, Stalin makes life into the rock of Sisyphus."
Итак, Сталин делает из жизни Сизифов камень. Но он еще хочет, чтоб никто ничего не имел, ни надежды, ни спасенья, ни покоя (XXVIII: 12, 58).

"Take today. I get up, there is no electricity . . ."
Вот сегодня. Встаю, нет света. [. . .] Холодно. [. . .] Писать? Читать? Темно. . . (XXVIII: 14, 68–69).

"State torture joins forces with domestic torture."
К государственному мучительству прибавляется домовое (XXVIII: 14, 69).

"I am not a historian, and therefore I would like to speak about my era with indignation."
Я не историк, и потому мне хотелось бы говорить о своей эпохе с негодованием (XXVIII: 15, 70).

"Here is my ordinary day—and I am a 'professor.'"
Вот мой очередной день,—а я «профессор». Встала—морозный день. Снежит. Метелица. Ставлю чайник—электричества нет. В

темноте налаживаю вонючую старую керосинку. [. . .] Свечки, спички, керосин, вонь.

Когда все утренние церемонии были проделаны, загорелся свет. Ах, эта радость советской жизни, как она ослепительна! На миг забыты все горести. Прощаешь всему миру. Тащишь кастрюли и чайник, ловишь горациевский «миг», включаешь все плитки, все приборы.

Я препарирую суп из кипятка, масла и капусты. Всё приготовив, спешно одеваюсь, проветриваю квартиру от керосиновой вони и иду, успокоенная и отдохновенная, подышать морозным воздухом (XXVIII: 17, 76–77).

"I am returning home. These damned Soviet winters . . ."
Я возвращаюсь домой. Эти проклятые советские зимы, эти непроходимые дворы, обледенелые скользкие улицы с переломами костей и сотрясением мозга!

Возмущенная, расстроенная раздеваюсь, чтоб приняться за дела. Включаю на варку обед. Электричества опять нет! (XXVIII: 17, 77).

"The day is lost. I stand, arrested, by a cold window."
День пропал. Стою арестованная у холодного окна (XXVIII: 17, 78).

"I stand and think about the blockade, think new thoughts."
Стою и думаю о блокаде, думаю новыми думами. Мне становится ясно, что вся блокада была паспортом советского строя. Вы внезапно открываете дверь и видите человека в неубранном естестве. — Все, что пережито в блокаду, было типичным выражением сталинской нарочитой разрухи и угнетения, затравливания человека. Но это было краткое либретто. До и после блокады—та же тюремная метода, разыгранная медленно и протяжно. [. . .] Я эти строки пишу почти в темноте. Мне светит история. Я замерзаю. Это даже не блокада и не осада. Это простой обыденный советский день (XXVIII: 17, 78).

"Until now, there was political terror and religious terror."
До сих пор был известен политический и религиозный террор. Сталин ввел и террор бытовой (XXVIII: 19, 84).

APPENDIX: THE RUSSIAN ORIGINAL OF MAJOR QUOTATIONS

"*Both in the everyday and in the state, there is the same system of pressure.*"
И в быту и в государстве одна и та же система тисков (XXVIII: 19, 84).

"*Here is one more example . . .*"
Вот один образчик. . . Сегодня. . . (XXVIII: 19, 84–85).

"Departmental Squabbles"
Склоки на кафедре

"*It was time for the special session. In accordance with the ritual . . .*"
Но вот подходила сессия. По заведенному в СССР ритуалу, я должно была сделать отчетный торжественный доклад на совете факультета. Должен был быть зачитан приказ ректора "с благодарностью", которой отмечались все личные юбилеи, окончание учебного года и всякие даты. Должны были быть приветствия декана и факультетских кафедр. И, наконец, после традиционной выставки и научной сессии [. . .] в последний вечер—банкет вскладчину (XXVI: 77, 64).

"*Spring 1945 went by for me under the sign of Sonya's defense.*"
Весна 1945 года прошла для меня под знаком Сониной защиты (XXII: 26, 43).

"*I stood up . . . I spoke loudly and sharply . . .*"
Встала я [. . .] громко и резко я сказала, и воздух затихал, отсекался и падал снарядами:—Здесь происходит балаган [. . .] предают осмеянию и шельмуют молодых научных работников (XXIII: 43, 63).

"*In my presence, he appealed to everyone . . .*"
"И потом он всех агитировал при мне. "Тут нужна жертва. Галеркина все равно безнадежна. Нужно спасать Мореву" (XXIII: 43, 64).

"*It was horrifying: the prospect of getting under Fortuna's feet.*"
Было страшно, чтоб не попасть под ноги Фортуне (XXIV: 51, 31).

"*While Galerkina is on her way, I inscribe these lines into the notebook of history.*"
Пока Галеркина едет, я записываю эти строки в тетрадь истории (XXXII: IV, 70).

"Don't lose heart. Remember the historical nature of this moment . . ."
"Не теряйтесь. Помните историчность минуты. Все равно победители мы, а не они" (XXXII: IV, 70).

"I have various papers, documents, long, scribbled notes . . ."
У меня лежат бумажки, бумаги, длинные исписанные записи, короткие памятки, иногда газетные вырезки. О, эти следы волнений и жара крови, эти старые бумаги, почти всегда имеющие надпись «заявление»! Это кладбища моих горячих пульсаций сердца, взвихренных и кипящих мозгов, кривая моей жизни.

Неотосланные письма, неподанные заявления—вот что это. Когда я умру, у меня останутся мои работы, мебель, деньги и эти неподанные заявления и неотосланные письма.

О них никто не слагал лирики, романисты о них не знали. Но сколько за ними скрыто! Сколько они говорят о советской эпохе, о страстях человека, который постоянно вел оборонные войны, замышлял, стрелял, истекал кровью, носил глубокие психические раны. Они напоминают мне волосы, которые остригались немцами у жертв «фабрик смерти». Груды волос (XXIV: 47, 10).

"Public Humiliation Was Revived"
Возродились публичные поруганья

"The first victim was Eikhenbaum."
Первой жертвой стал Эйхенбаум. [. . .] Он держался превосходно, с достоинством, и за это его били еще больней (XXIV: 59, 60).

"After Zhdanov's speech, the final sprouts of emerging life were strangled."
После речи Жданова все последние ростки жизни были задушены. Европейская культура и низкопоклонство были объявлены синонимами. Создавалась искусственная культур-изоляция. Воскрешался тайной полицией русский XVII век, с ненавистью ко всему чужеземному. [. . .]

Иоанн Грозный—наш политический идеал. Петр Великий попал в крамольники, поскольку прорубил окно в Европу. Оживлен полицейский панславизм. Да что! Это держат в секрете, но этой зимой появилось тайное распоряжение не выдавать работникам науки никакой заграничной научной литературы, даже старой. Были составлены тайные списки, кому выдавать можно (например, западниками, классикам), но фамилии попавших тщательно «проверялись». Затем, нас секретно «инструктировали», что иностранной литературой нужно пользоваться только отрицательно: разоблачать, полемизировать и т. д. Сталин бросил лозунг «превзойти иностранную науку» (XXV: 64, 16–17).

"The agent, aka head of the Writers' Union, Fadeev . . ."
Агент, официально именуемый руководителем Союза писателей, Фадеев, недавно выступил с большой речью [26 ноября 1947], где он «проработал» в площадных выражениях А. Н. Веселовского («раба романо-германской школы», псевдоученого, «основоположника низкопоклонства перед заграницей»). Идет опять волна публичного опозориванья видных ученых. Когда знаешь, что это старики с трясущейся головой, с урологическими старческими болезнями, полуживые люди, от которых жены скрывают такую «критику»,—впечатление получается еще более тяжелое. Сейчас публично опозорили, не пощадив площадных выражений, старого почтенного Шишмарева, больного Азадовского, немолодого и честного Проппа. Ждем дальнейшего. Сталин из года в год держит в напряженье. Из года в год идет новая волна чисток, проработок, арестов, ссылок, травли. Человека давят всевозможными способами, физическими и психическими (XXV: 64, 18).

"I lost the last vestiges of life force in my soul."
Я потеряла последние остатки живых соков в душе. Тяжелое, свинцовое лицо стало у меня. Люди, видевшие это лицо, отшатывались. [. . .] И я сама, глядя на себя со стороны, поражалась этой мертвой давящей убитости, стараясь найти для нее термин. Его не было. Нет, никакая «подавленность», никакая «депрессия», даже «убитость» не передавала этого холодного, каменного состояния. [. . .] Все было кончено. Я жила насильственно, как насильственно умирают. Нужно жить? Ха! (XXV: 66, 23).

"my brother was exterminated. The mind can't fathom this! . . ."
брата заморили. Не может мысль дотронуться до этого! [. . .] Потом осада. Нет, подняться может живая душа, мертвые не воскресают (XXV: 67, 24).

"I thought a lot about death. Suddenly an idea struck me: starvation!"
   Я много думала о смерти. Вдруг меня осветила мысль: голод! Ведь я видела, как от голода можно, лежа у себя дома, обессилеть и умереть. Дома, у себя, длительно, с подготовкой—это отвечало всем моим желаньям. Но нужен был срок. Нужно эти записки закончить во что бы то ни стало. Я не умру молча. Нет, свое дело я доделаю. Я ненавижу молчащих перед тиранией жизни (XXV: 67, 25).

"But what will be the fate of what I've written? To whom do I hand this over?"
   Только какова будет судьба написанного? Кому передать? [...] Соню я уже давно не считала своей наследницей (XXV: 67, 26).

"I cannot be hurt by any person or phenomenon that I don't respect..."
   Меня не может задеть ни человек, ни явление, которого я не уважаю: травля, нападки, публичное советское обвинение; или то или иное поведение лиц вроде Мещанинова или Жирмунского—людей завистливых, продажных и патологически тщеславных. Не они поражают меня, эти стоки советских академических нечистот. Но жизнь всегда меня поражает. Мой ум обобщает ничтожные явления, видя в них голос целой эпохи (XXV: 71, 43).

"It's not about the Zhirmunskys."
   Дело не в Жирмунских. [...] Бывает так: живешь-живешь. И вдруг стукнет тебя по голове то самое, что ты давно видел и знаешь.
   В эту зиму [1947–1948] я стала захлебываться и задыхаться от подступившего к горлу итога жизни. Я уже не верила в спасение. Мысль, что я все-таки не опубликую своих работ, вдруг стала огнестрельной раной. Любовь и наука! Для одного человека две катастрофы—это слишком много (XXV: 72, 46).

"Our eternal, common question: 'Do they know abroad [about us]?'"
   Наше вечное, всеобщее "знает ли заграница?!" [...] Да, знает! И эта мысль дает спокойно умереть (XXV: 72, 49).

"I Tear the Fabric of Time to Finish the Tale of My Last Love"
я разрываю ткань времени, чтоб окончить рассказ о своей последней любви

APPENDIX: THE RUSSIAN ORIGINAL OF MAJOR QUOTATIONS

"What if he is an informer, an agent of the secret service?"
А вдруг—осведомитель, агент тайной службы? Кто мог поручиться в этой кошмарной жизни за своего брата, друга, мужа, возлюбленного? (XXIII: 41, 54).

"Who decided that hell is under the earth?"
Кто выдумал, что преисподняя под землей? Она в человеческом тоскующем сердце (XXIV: 52, 33).

"This was amid [department] squabbles, anxieties, strong pulsations of the heart."
Это было среди склок, волнений, сильных пульсаций (XXIV: 52, 33).

"Maybe these notebooks will perish?"
Может быть, эти тетради погибнут? (XXIV: 52, 33).

"And so, it was summer."
Так вот, было лето. Была вторая половина июня. Было лето. Был понедельник (XXIV: 52, 33).

"Today is my name day, this is why I am crying so much."
(Сегодня день Ольги, оттого я так плачу) (XXIV: 52, 33).

"I tear the fabric of time to finish the tale of my last love".
Я разрываю ткань времени, чтоб окончить рассказ о своей последней любви (XXIV: 54, 46).

"Time does not consist of segments."
Время не состоит из отрезков. Ее [sic!] поток соединяет и переливает прошедшее с будущим, которых на самом деле нет (XXIV: 58, 57).

"[Love is] a strong feeling that is beyond will or desire."
сильное, вне воли и желанья, чувство, непреоборимое, раз навсегда данное, нечто не становящееся, а "ставшее", почти лишенное субъективности (XXIX: 2, 8).

"Soon he came again, and I gave myself to him."
Вскоре он пришел опять, и я отдалась ему (XXXI: 20, 14).

"It has turned out that I am unsuitable for a modern Soviet man".

Современному советскому мужчине я оказалась непригодна (XXXI: 21, 16).

"B. rejected me for failing to handle his body."

Б. отверг меня за то, что я не сумела обойтись с его телом (XXXI: 23, 23).

"The Archive Initiated Me into the Brotherhood of Universal Man"
Архив приобщал меня к братству мирового человека

"One could stop eating! . . ."

Ведь можно перестать есть. [. . .] Так просто, доступно! Я стала в радостном оживлении продумывать: у себя дома, на своей постели, заранее все подготовив и завершив полностью свои дела, летом [. . .] без пропуска служебной работы . . . [. . .] Я сразу повеселела, успокоилась. [. . .] Отныне я имела цель жизни: жить для смерти! Срочно готовить архив (XXVI: 75, 55–56).

"Precisely during those good days, I got an invitation from the Public Library . . ."

Как раз в эти хорошие дни я получила приглашение от Публичной библиотеки передать ей свой архив: рукописи, письма, заметки, материалы к биографии, записки и т. д. [. . .] Можно себе представить, как меня подняло и воодушевило это предложенье! (XXVI: 75, 56).

"The sense of history as an objective process has always spoken in me with great force."

Чувство истории, как объективного процесса, всегда говорило во мне с огромной силой. Здесь лежала моя уверенная вера, абсолютное мое преклонение перед объективным надчеловеческим процессом,—мой, если угодно, матерьялизм, для которого единая человеческая жизнь составляла составную часть всего сущего. Я говорю не об историографии, этой жалкой науке, а об истории как мировом процессе. Здесь ничто не бывает презрено или забыто. Это абсолютная жизнь бытия и небытия, выражающаяся в вечной изменчивости. Рай, который строили народы, бессмертие, «тот свет»—это все существует, но его зовут не небом, не парадизом, не вальгаллой, а историей. Обмануть ее невозможно, сколько бы ни фальсифицировались документы и ни искажались или

APPENDIX: THE RUSSIAN ORIGINAL OF MAJOR QUOTATIONS

утаивались факты; это можно обмануть только историографию. На раз я слышала от друзей: «Этого никто никогда не узнает! Все источники будут подделаны, все следы преступлений скрыты. Никогда не узнает история нашей жизни!» [. . .]

Идея архива была идеей истории. На меня пахнуло большим временем. Патетика над-личного и над-эпохального была для меня родной стихией. Я получала письмо, из которого я узнавала, что не одна на свете. Архив приобщал меня к братству мирового человека.

Я стала неузнаваема. Лицо стало мягким и светлым. Это была давно покинувшая меня радость (**XXVI**: 75, 56–57).

"The archive! Who is going to lug that chest? To where?"
Архив! Кто потащит этот сундук? Куда? (**XXVIII**: 19, 86).

"My Life is Over. This Is Where I End Its Manuscript"
Моя жизнь окончена. На этом я обрываю ее рукопись

"My life is over. This is where I end its manuscript."
Моя жизнь окончена. На этом я обрываю ее рукопись.

Она может длиться недолго или годы, но это не имеет значенья. Ее главный тур прошел полным круговоротом, и теперь он может либо повторяться, либо варьироваться в деталях. Ничего нового или живого уже не может быть, того, от чего душа растет (**XXVII**: 83, 6).

"In winter, I will turn yellow, heat the stove, wait for death . . ."
Зимой я буду желтеть и топить печку, ждать смерти, писать исследования и записки для архива, отсчитывать время, видеть сны. Летом я буду загорать, молодеть и рваться от оков к счастью… Я напишу о лирике, о комедии, о прозе. [. . .] Я потеряю, я переживу своих друзей. . . Будут неисчерпаемые бытовые мученья. [. . .] Будут те или иные преследования в университете. Возможно, что усилится газетная травля, которая и сейчас преследует ученых и писателей (**XXVII**: 83, 6–8).

"We live in complete cultural isolation . . ."
Мы живем в полной культурной изоляции. [. . .] Человека преследуют и медленно, беспрерывно душат. На него оказывают физическое и моральное давление. Кучка авантюристов говорит от

имени подавленной, обезличенной, измученной массы. Давление таково, что нельзя иметь друзей по свободному выбору, нельзя переписываться с близкими, нельзя говорить в своей квартире, заселенной чужими людьми. Нигде и ни в чем нет свободы. Образ мыслей вылавливается из мозга, и как Сталин хотел бы изобрести особый рентген, чтобы залезать в душу и в печенку! Сейчас период полного изъятия духовной культуры. Искусство запрещено полицией. Гуманитарных наук не печатают. Биология, химия, физика объявлены «государственной тайной, не подлежащей разглашению». Вокруг однообразие и серость. Все застыло и обезжизненно.

До возмездия я не доживу. Я не увижу Московского Нюрнберга... (XXVII: 83, 9).

"I am discontinuing these notes."
Записки я прекращаю. Сюжеты, формы, истолкования будут неизменно повторяться (XXVII: 83, 10).

"I no longer believe in freedom and humanity, without which I cannot live."
Я уже не верю в свободу и человечность, без которых жить не могу. Конечно, есть разные степени заключения. Мы живем прекрасно. Нужно сравнивать не с Европой, а с концлагерями и тюрьмами, с каторгой и фабриками смерти. Мы имеем право работать по специальности, ходить в театр, в кино, в гости, гулять свободно по улице. Мы имеем право топить печку и загорать на солнце. Наша категория—находящихся под надзором тайной полиции в большом городе-лагере (XXVII: 83, 10).

"Dovatur unexpectedly returned from 13 years in exile."
Неожиданно вернулся из 13-летней ссылки Доватур. В нем оказалось больше жизни, чем во мне. Мы стали вспоминать, сравнивать. Он рассказал мне о далеком, мрачном концлагере, где томятся и умирают от физических мук десятки тысяч людей. [...] Нет особой разницы между их и нашей жизнью. Нет разницы по существу. Только степень разная. У нас свободнее режим (XXVII, Послесловие 2, 21).

"This strange, alien person coming to me! From the realm of death."
Этот чужой, враждебный человек—ко мне! из царства смерти (XXXII: I, 45).

APPENDIX: THE RUSSIAN ORIGINAL OF MAJOR QUOTATIONS

"How happy she is to be back in Leningrad!"
Как она счастлива, что опять в Ленинграде! Как она смеется, как клокочет в ней жизнь! [. . .] Как я была мертва по сравнению с Мусей. Лагерь, где я нахожусь, больше гнетет ростки жизни, чем тот, ее. Нет, не так: она видела перед собой цель и надежду и это держало ее; а я ничего не вижу впереди (XXXII: II, 49–50).

"Life, life! Everything in it is possible, any paradox."
Жизнь, жизнь! Все в ней возможно, любой парадокс. За моим столом сидел чекист, и я питала к нему теплое братское чувство. Я мысленно благословляла его за то, что он взял к себе Мусю, что любит ее, что служит ей поддержкой (XXXII: II, 50).

"—No, no one, no one can understand my happiness in being here . . ."
—Нет, никто, никто не может понять моего счастья, что я здесь, что я жива, что я все, все преодолела . . . только тот, кто пережил то самое, что я! Тот понял бы! (XXXII: II, 50).

"Both of them were from a special, otherworldly place . . ."
Оба они были из потустороннего особого мира, мира советской реальности и советского подполья, из Колымы, из легендарного рабства и каторги. Я ни одного вопроса не задавала страдалице. Страшные вещи сами вставали леденящим пугалом с ее сапог и пальто, из ее невольных рассказов. [. . .] Когда они ушли, я еле доплела ноги до кровати. Они, мои ноги, не могли вынести груза моих мыслей и ужаса (XXXII: II, 51).

"B. used to say to me: 'Don't judge people. Especially Soviet people.'"
Мне Б. говаривал: «Не осуждайте людей. Особенно советских». Он хотел сказать, что они поставлены в такое положение, в котором им, для спасенья жизни, приходится прибегать к любым средствам (XXVII: 83, 10).

"They are guided by vanity, ego, honors, money . . ."
Они руководствуются тщеславием, самолюбием, почестями, деньгами. . . (XXVII: 83, 12).

"Apparently, I Cannot Do Without These Notes"
По-видимому, без этих записок я обойтись не могу

"It's been a month and a half. I am ill . . ."
Прошло полтора месяца. Я болею сердцем и не лечусь, чтоб ускорить смерть. Очистила железный сундук и в этот гроб укладываю свои работы и свой внутренний мир. Это будет мой архив (XXVII: Послесловие, 15).

"It's no longer a regime. It's confinement."
Это уже не режим. Это заключение (XXVII: Afterword, 18).

"Finally, into the iron chest."
Итак, в железный сундук! (XXVII, Afterword, 19).

"Apparently, I cannot do without these notes. "
По-видимому, без этих записок я обойтись не могу (XXVII, Afterword, 19).

"As I look back over the three years in which I did not die . . ."
Окидывая взором три года, в которые я не умерла, тщетно я ищу их смысла. Что они мне дали? Ни одной радости. За эти годы я создала паллиату и Сафо,—родила двух детей в заточеньи. Горькое материнство! (XXVIII: 19, 86).

"And suddenly the image of siege."
И вдруг образ осады. [. . .] Я видела, как лоб умирающего отца становился покатым, точно у кретина. Я видела самое себя, когда, дрожа от жадности, я укрывалась от мамы и в кухне, одна, в полутьме, трепетно жевала и запивала бурдой. Я видела, как мы с матерью, глубоко тая, внутренне соревновались, у кого останется, чья из нас, недоеденная доля. Я видела, как рыли яму для матери и как ее гроб опускали в зеленое болото (XXVIII: 5, 36).

"to make it to the grave somehow . . ."
Как-нибудь добрести до могилы. [. . .] Да искуплю я свою душу, видевшую Сталина и Гитлера, этими страданьями своих последних лет! (XXVIII: 5, 36).

"A heavy task still awaits me, one that I instinctively shy away from."
Еще ждет меня тяжелая задача, от которой я инстинктивно уклоняюсь. Мне необходимо вызвать из могилы свое прошлое,

APPENDIX: THE RUSSIAN ORIGINAL OF MAJOR QUOTATIONS

чтобы заполнить в записках лакуны от поступления в Университет до блокады (XXVIII: 20, 90).

"there is no louder impulse in me than this self-evaluation of my life . . ."
и нет во мне громче импульса, чем этот жизненный самоотчет, чем этот тет-а-тет со вселенной, именуемой тетрадью (XXVIII: 20, 90).

"I cannot live any longer . . . I lie here and wonder . . ."
Я дольше жить не могу. [. . .] я лежу и думаю, куда девать это оставшееся непогребенное тело. Увезти его и бросить? Свалить в воду? Выкинуть из окна? Набить его микробами? Отравить? (XXVIII: 21, 91).

"The University Has Been Ravaged"
Университет разгромлен

"Stalin's claws reached the representatives of academia."
когти Сталина добрались до академических представителей (XXIX: 7, 29).

"The university is Russia in miniature."
Университет—это Россия в миниатюре (XXIX: 5, 19).

"Finally, a meeting was scheduled to "discuss" the harassment at our Philological Faculty."
Наконец, было назначено заседание, посвященное «обсуждению» травли, на нашем филологическом факультете. Накануне прошло такое же «заседание» в Академии, в Институте литературы. Позорили всех профессоров литературы. Их принуждали, под давлением политической кары, отрекаться от собственных взглядов и поносить самих себя. Одни, как Жирмунский, делали это «изящно» и лихо. Другие, как Эйхенбаум, старались уберечь себя от моральной наготы, и мужественно прикрывали стыд. Впрочем, он был в одиночестве. Пропп, которого безжалостно мучили за то, что он немец, уже терял чувство достоинства, которое долго отстаивал. Прочие делали, что от них требовалось.
Профессоров пытали самым страшным инструментом пытки—научной честью (XXIX: 7, 30).

APPENDIX: THE RUSSIAN ORIGINAL OF MAJOR QUOTATIONS

"All those present at this moral flogging were in a state of severe mental nausea."
Все присутствовавшие на моральной этой экзекуции находились в состоянии тяжелой душевной тошноты. «Этого заседания, кто его пережил (говорили мне), забыть уже нельзя на всю жизнь» (XXIX: 7, 32).

"What will remain of them in the history of scholarship?"
Что же останется от них в истории науки? (XXIX: 7, 35).

"He was a confessor of a special kind, a priest of the political police."
Это был особого рода духовник, священник политической полиции (XXX: 9, 45).

"Now everything—semantics, theory, genesis, metaphor, image . . ."
Теперь все быстро получало качество криминала, и притом политического, направленного на подрыв советской науки— семантика, теория, генезис, метафора, образ (XXX: 12, 56).

"We worked in a modern, improved prison—a concentration camp."
Мы работали за проволочным ограждением, кто какую профессию имел, под надзором жестоких надсмотрщиков. Мы работали в современной усовершенствованной тюрьме—в концлагере. Везде обстановка, отношения, характер работы были совершенно одинаковы, и то, что происходило в университете или консерватории, ничем не отличалось от любого советского учреждения (XXX: 12, 57).

"A man goes to the toilet and drops his pants."
Человек ходит в уборную и сбрасывает брюки. Без этого он обойтись не может. Но на людях он брюк не снимает. Жизнь имеет два плана (XXX: 14, 65).

"[I]f you allow yourself to say anything about my research topics . . ."
«. . . если вы позволите себе сказать что-нибудь о моих семинарских темах, то я тоже позволю себе сказать, что вы, заведующая кафедрой, не были с ними знакомы и не интересовались ими . . .» [. . .] Дерзость, академическое тщеславие, неуважение к учителю— накануне политического процесса! (XXX: 14, 67).

"So that's the bomb!"
Так вот она, бомба! (XXX: 14, 69).

APPENDIX: THE RUSSIAN ORIGINAL OF MAJOR QUOTATIONS

"I would have to perform self-criticism and then expose Tronsky and Vulikh..."
Я должна была выступить с самокритикой, а затем разоблачить Тронского и Вулих... (**XXX: 14, 69–70**).

"I did not allow this meeting to touch my inner self and was not present at it, as it were..."
Я не допускала к своему "я" этого заседания, и как бы не присутствовала на нем... (**XXX: 15, 79**).

"I wanted to keep my hands clean..."
Я хотела сохранить чистые руки, никого не трогая и пронося свой крест на собственных плечах (**XXX: 15, 73**).

"He maneuvers so as not to say anything bad about me..."
Он лавирует, чтоб ничего дурного не сказать обо мне, но не сказать и ничего хорошего (**XXX: 15, 78**).

"He takes the formidable tone of a religious authority."
Он берет грозный тон ортодоксального авторитета. Ни звука о себе. [...] он громит генезис и осуждает мое выдвижение молодежи... (**XXX: 15, 78**).

"This is the moment of God's judgment..."
Это момент суда божия... (**XXX: 15, 78**).

"Dementiev delivers a guilty verdict."
Дементьев выносит мне приговор обвинительный. Он причисляет меня к последователям Веселовского. Хотя, говорит он, мне и казалось, что я отхожу от его позиций, но на самом деле я их утверждала. Доказательства: и я изучала литературные формы (значит, я формалист), и я изучала генезис. Дальше Дементьев повторяет то, что ему нашептала Вулих со слов Тронского. Не читая моих работ и не имея образования, Дементьев свободно дает ответственные научные оценки. Несколько раз он подчеркивает правильность «установок» Тронского и любовно кивает в его сторону (**XXX: 15, 78–79**).

"I stand up for my final word."
Встаю для последнего слова. Вынимаю из портфеля учебник Тронского. Соня, умолявшая меня не портить с Тронским отношений, замирает. У моих друзей перехватывает дыхание.

Теперь я сбрасываю маску и стою грудь с грудью к собранию. Никакая пружина не может сравниться с упругостью моего святого возмущения.

Я выхожу на средину зала, выпрямляюсь, руки держу за спиной. Я стою перед ними, грудь и лицо подняты к ним. В позе бесстрашия, с гневными глазами, я бросаю в этих палачей свою волю и свою правду. Сурово, грозово, изнемогая от внутренней страсти, я им твердо говорю: да, я принимаю и подчиняюсь партийной линии, но вы не можете меня заставить под видом партийности принять и то, с чем я всю жизнь боролась, с чем буду бороться и впредь. Какое право имеет Тронский делать мне диктаты? Кто он? Как он попал в мои учители? (XXX: 15, 79–80).

"This document, invisible to history, shows . . ."
Этот невидимый истории документ показывает обстановку, вернее—систему внутреннего террора, в которой жил университет. Полное подавление человеческой личности, инициативы, удручающая невозможность маневрированья живой человеческой мысли (XXX: 17, 96).

"Every member of the department watches all the others . . ."
Каждый член кафедры следит за другим и имеет право вето над ним (XXX: 17, 96–XXXI: 17, 1).

"in the concentration-camp university all good things fatally degenerate into bad things."
в университете концлагеря все доброе фатально перерождается в дурное (XXIX: 1, 2).

"All these disturbances, great and small . . ." (XXXI: 19, 8).
Все эти, большие и малые, волненья, вызванные общей системой перевернутой морали, сильно на меня действовали (XXXI: 19, 8).

"I was in a quagmire that no number of buckets could dry up."
Я находилась в трясине, исчерпать которую было невозможно никакими ведрами (XXXII: I, 28).

"Something stinking flowed at my feet, amorphous and irrepressible . . ."
Что-то вонючее текло у моих ног, аморфное и неуемное, и нагнеталось с каждый часом (XXXII: I, 29).

APPENDIX: THE RUSSIAN ORIGINAL OF MAJOR QUOTATIONS

"behind Tronsky was Vulikh . . ."
за Тронским стояла Вулих, а за Вулих—он, за ним Дементьев, за Дементьевым—горком партии, за горкомом—ЦК, за ЦК—Сталин (**XXXII: I, 39**).

"That was the whole point."
В этом-то и была вся суть. Интриги всегда были и будут. Но тут дело не в интригах, а в государственной системе, которая везде, во всех учреждениях, насаждала и грозно проводила наускиванье, друг на друга, стравливанье, разложение всякого дела, «психические атаки» и удары по человеческим нервам и мозгу (**XXXII: I, 39**).

"The Berdnikovs and Dementievs, the Vulikhs and Sharovs were symbolic figures . . ."
Бердниковы и Дементьевы, Вулихи и Шаровы были символическими фигурами, отражавшими сталинскую систему. Везде и всюду обстановка работы была одна и та же (**XXXII: I, 44**).

"How to break out of this system? There is no way."
Как вырваться из этой системы? Никак (**XXXII: I, 40**).

"I do not impose my opinions on anyone."
Своих воззрений я никому не навязываю. Наши расхождение во взглядах—естественное и здоровое явление науки. [. . .] Мое личное отношенье к плосткостной эволюционной методологии Тронского осталось бы при мне, если б он не взял на себя весной роли моего научного судьи и цензора. При столкновении, в острый политический момент, наших личных взглядов, в обстановке нападения на меня, я считала возможным высказать мое несогласие с проф. Тронским. Тогда я сделала это в резкой форме, назвав метод учебника порочным, а нападки проф. Тронского—диктатом, которому я не желаю подчиняться. Он тогда допек меня (*смех*). Сегодня я могу сказать то же самое в корректной и товарищеской форме (**XXXII: 3, 64–65**).

"I have met with complete moral failure."
Я потерпела полное моральное пораженье. Дементьев рассчитался со мной. Учебник Тронского оказывался замечательным, ошибок у Тронского никаких не было. [. . .] Тем самым представитель

горкома партии был прав, дискредитируя меня и поднимая Тронского. Дементьев полностью восстановил свой престиж (**XXXII**: 3, 66).

"Fools! They did not suspect that I had won."
Глупцы! Они не подозревали, что я выиграла... (**XXXII**: 3, 66).

"How many nights I did not sleep, trying to find a means that would relieve me..."
Сколько я ночей не спала, стараясь найти средство, которое избавило бы меня от гнусной роли его «прорабатывателя» (**XXXII**: 3, 66).

"But could the Party members, the bandits..."
Но могли ли это понять партийцы, бандиты, вся эта диверсионная сволочь? (**XXXII**: 3, 66).

"In big international politics the same things are going on as in my department."
В большой международной политике делается то же, что у меня на кафедре. Сталин создал особый аппарат подрывателей, шпионов, особую систему подпольной диверсии, которую нельзя ни охватить, ни определить, ни поймать с поличными. Я не потому описываю ее, что она подтачивает мою жизнь, а потому, что она, так сказать, сверх меня, и есть факт университетский, государственный, исторический.

Полная безыдейность и беспринципность сталинизма наглядно показывает себя в последних событиях на кафедре (**XXXII**: II, 52).

"Will the historian understand the deadness of our existence?"
Поймет ли историк мертвенность нашего существования? Мертвая страна. Мертвые схемы. Люди с выкорчеванной душой мертво работают и мертво живут (**XXXII**: II, 48).

"The historian will not understand how the population could endure..."
Историк не поймет, как население могло выносить подобную систему подавлений и насилий. Так вот, я ему отвечаю: населенье и не выносит этой системы. Оно все сплошь—больное (**XXXII**: IV, 77).

APPENDIX: THE RUSSIAN ORIGINAL OF MAJOR QUOTATIONS

"Even Zhirmunsky had a heart attack. Eikhenbaum was laid up with a myocardial infarction."

Даже у Жирмунского сделался сердечный припадок. Эйхенбаум лежал с инфарктом сердца» (XXXII: I, 42–43). [. . .] Я подавлена вторым инфарктом сердца у Эйхенбаума. Этого здорового и мужественного ученого затравили (XXXII: IV, 80). [. . .] У Азадовского сделался сердечный инфаркт. Лурье в тяжелом состоянии отправлен в больницу: инфаркт миокарда (XXXII: IV, 81).

"Jewish pogroms are going on in the country, but in a 'cultured' form . . ."

По стране идут еврейские погромы, но в "культурной" форме: кровь тела заменяется кровью сердца. Подвергают опозориванию деятелей культуры, у которых еврейские фамилии (XXXII: IV, 84).

"For two days, more ordeals, this time with 'organizational consequences.'"

Через два дня—снова ордалии, но уже с «оргвыводами» (XXXII: IV, 81).

"thousands of students . . . stormed the doors in pursuit of the spectacle of moral execution."

тысячи студентов [. . .] ломились в погоне за зрелищем моральной казни. [. . .] То, что я потом узнала, было ужасно. [. . .] Жирмунскому разворотили всю его семейную жизнь (XXXII: IV, 85).

"Oh, could it be that history will tolerate these Naumovs, Makogonenkos, Lapitskys! . . ."

О, неужели история вынесет этих Наумовых, Макогоненок, Лапицких! (XXXII: IV, 85).

"Not wishing to take part in the harassment of this scholar . . ."

Не желая принимать участия в травле ученого, я выступила с защитой его, как преподавателя, а затем подала заявление с просьбой освободить меня от всякой работы в университете (XXXIII, 90).

"such things have long ceased to bother people . . ."

Впрочем, такие вещи давно перестали беспокоить людей: принудительность развязывала руки честным и нечестным (XXXIII, 91).

"With disgust, with distaste, I thought of my work and my functions."
    С отвращением, с омерзением я думала о своей работе и своих функциях. Я глубоко оплакивала кафедру, дело своей жизни, которому я отдала 17 лет помыслов, трудов и дарованья (XXXIII, 94).

"There are arrests."
    Идут аресты. Увольняют с работы или бросают на 10 лет в заточенье за "разговоры", "неправильную" точку зрения... (XXXIII, 97).

"Throw the body out the window? Drown? I can't."
    Выбросить тело из окна? Утонуть? Я не в состоянье (XXXIII, 98).

"My mind is circling back to the starting point."
    Мысль по кругу возвращается к исходной точке. Я утомлена и обессилена. Выхода нет. Нужно жить из-за невозможности умереть (XXXIII, 98).

"Barely dragging my feet, empty, I stand before eternal Space..."
    Еле волоча ноги, пустая, стою перед извечным Пространством и смотрюсь в него, ни о чем не думая (XXXIII, 98).

"I should write about him, put him in the history of technology."
    Надо написать о нем, внести в историю техники. Ведь я— последняя. На мне обрывается род. [...] Где-то, помнится, лежал ненужный сверток патентов... (XXXIII, 99).

"I will no longer describe Soviet life..."
    Больше я не буду описывать советскую жизнь, условия изнурительного и насильственного труда, возмутительнейшего быта и системы торжества оскорбителей над оскорбленными (XXXIII, 102).

"No, it is neither a prison nor a concentration camp."
    Нет, это не тюрьма и не концлагерь. В тюрьмах и концлагерях есть чувство срока и сознание, что это карательные институты; они не выдают себя за консерватории и университет (XXXIII, 102).

"1950. March. I spent several months in an agonizing internal struggle..."
    1950 г. Март. Несколько месяцев я провела в мучительной внутренней борьбе: уходить на пенсию или нет? И то гибельно, и другое (XXXIII, 107).

APPENDIX: THE RUSSIAN ORIGINAL OF MAJOR QUOTATIONS

"She, a Party leader, fiercely demands the worship of bourgeois authorities."
Она, будучи парторгом, ожесточенно требует преклоненья перед буржуазными авторитетами. Она ненавидит Марра. Она отменяет научную литературу, которую я даю руководимой мной дипломантке, и рекомендует фашистские, гитлеровские книги (XXXIII, 119).

"Alas. The time of villains and vices has passed."
Увы. Прошло время злодеев и пороков. Катастрофа заключалась в том, что люди не видели граней между дозволенным и недозволенным. Катастрофа заключалась в том, что такие люди вовсе не были злодеями. Передо мной, запивая бутерброды чаем, сидели за моим столом мои милые, любящие меня, самые близкие мне ученицы, которые откровенно делились со мной своим предательством. В их глазах это была удачная хитрость (XXXIII, 121).

"There is complete and cynical decay in the department."
На кафедре полное и циничное разложение (XXXIII, 123).

"Stalin crushed Marr, whom he himself had created and nurtured . . ."
Сталин громил созданного и взлелеянного им самим Марра (XXXIV, 134).

"It is a whole cunningly designed system of blockade, impossible to break through."
Это целая хитро продуманная система блокады, прорвать которую невозможно (XXXIV, 136).

Chapter 4. "To Fill in the Lacuna": From the University to the Last War (1918–1941)

"I Entered Petersburg University"
Я поступила в Петербургский университет

"the world of images overpowered me . . ."
Но вскоре мир образов осилил меня и искоренил мое в нем присутствие. Мной овладело сладостное ощущение повторной жизни с мамой и с наукой, сновиденье истории (XXXII: I, 27).

"*I entered Petersburg University...*"
Я поступила в Петербургский университет. [...] Стояла осень 1917–18 учебного года. Университет еще имел старый вид. Знаменитые старые профессора читали открытые публичные лекции. [...] Революция породила вольность. Интеллигентная публика свободно слушала, кого хотела. Никакого бюрократизма еще не было: ведь я пишу при Сталине... (III: 1, 1).

"*My love grew, and my studies, like my love, kept growing.*"
Моя любовь росла, мои занятия, как любовь, разрастались (III: 4, 35).

"*now, when I write this, in 1948...*"
И сейчас, когда я это пишу в 1948 году, под старость, я с трудом преодолеваю эту потребность покинуть кафедру (III: 8, 61).

"*So, from the seed that went into the ground, began my new birth.*"
Так началось мое новое рожденье из зерна, ушедшего в землю (IV: 13, 105).

Petrograd under Siege
Петроград в блокаде

"*It was a time of the greatest everyday hardship.*"
Это было время величайших житейских бедствий (IV: 9, 68).

"*Revolution is a terrible thing! It replaces one form of violence with another...*"
Страшная вещь революция! Она заменяет одну форму насилия другой, и процесс стаскиванья за ноги одного класса эксплоататоров и водворения другого ужасен (IV: 9, 68).

"*Stalin showed the true face of the revolution.*"
Сталин показал истинное лицо революции.

The past shows its true face only in the future, retrospectively.
прошлое показывает свое истинное лицо только в будущем, ретроспективно (IV: 9, 69).

"*His interests were focused on how many grams of grain there were in the soup that day.*"
Его интересы были сосредоточены вокруг того, сколько грамм крупы сегодня в супе (IV: 9, 71).

APPENDIX: THE RUSSIAN ORIGINAL OF MAJOR QUOTATIONS

"Oh, life! What horrors you have not put me through!"
О, жизнь! Через какие ужасы ты меня не проводила! Это еще не был тот несказанный голод осажденного города, когда . . . Но на этом невозможно остановиться (IV: 9, 72).

"Terrible days! Life was emptying out. Professors were dying."
Страшные дни! Жизнь пустела. Профессора умирали. Живых арестовывали. Университет покрывался пылью и тлением. [. . .] Семья распадалась (IV: 9,72).

"Having made our mortal journey in the finite, we will merge in the infinite."
Свершив смертный путь в конечном, мы сольемся в бесконечности (IV: 11, 96).

"In those terrible revolutionary years, when everything was disintegrating . . ."
В те страшные революционные годы, когда все распадалось и тлело, когда целая страна жила только одним государственным процессом—разрушеньем, в те годы учитель и ученик, как пружина, были упруги великой взаимосвязью. . . (V: 16, 2).

"Entry into Scholarship"
Вход в науку

"I saw that difference is a form of identity, and sameness carries in itself heterogeneity . . ."
Тут я увидела, что различия являются формой тождества, а одинаковость несет в себе разнородность,—мысль, уже не покидавшая меня» (V: 19, 39).

"The Acts began with Thecla listening, mesmerized, to her teacher Paul."
Деяния начинались с того, как Фекла завороженно внемлет своему учителю, Павлу. Апокриф говорил мне. [. . .] Бороздин, Жебелев, Толстой, Буш. [. . .] Мои учителя. Все привело меня к Фекле и поставило у ее окна (IV: 10, 84).

"While working on the Greek novel, I was writing my biography."
Работая над греческим романом, я писала свою биографию. Не в женских стихах, а в научной работе я находила, наконец, выход своей лирической стихии—ту настоящую форму жизнеописания своего «я», по которой с детства тосковала (V: 19, 33).

"I found in myself not myself, but a great generalization, an embryo . . ."
я находила в себе не себя, а великое обобщение, того эмбриона, который похож на всех предков и лишен индивидуальных черт [. . .] и это объясняло мне тайны форм и сущего, единство разного, своеобразие, порожденное общим (V: 19, 32–33).

"Ecstasy, rather, ekstasis? Stepping outside oneself?"
Процессы самопокиданья. Но как их понять? Экстаз, вернее экстазис? Выход из себя? (V: 19, 32).

"There are things that you cannot narrate without being an artist."
Есть вещи, о которых нельзя, не будучи художником, повествовать. Любовь к матери, близость с учителем, чувство поэзии—как это передать? Сказать «жизнь», «я», «автобиография»—мало (V: 23, 72).

"Entry into Academia"
Мое вхождение в академическую среду

"A new life began for my mother and me—a life in Marr."
Новая жизнь пошла у нас с мамой—жизнь в Марре (VI: 26, 98).

"When I started reading Marr, I began to enter a world of concepts . . ."
Начав читать Марра, я тем самым начинала входить в глубоко близкий мне мир понятий, и моему пониманью, восхищенью, счастью не было никаких границ. [. . .] Каждая его работа давала мне нечто родственное, и то, что я делала, подтверждало его, а то, что он делал, подтверждало меня (VI: 26, 98).

"Please, don't worry: it's clear that your interpretation is too new and fresh. N. M".
Пожалуйста, не волнуйтесь: ясно, что ваша трактовка чересчур нова и свежа. Н. М. (VI: 26, 102).

"On that day I was born as a polemicist and fighter."
В этот день я рождаюсь как полемист и борец (VI: 26, 102).

"Who could I appeal to? . . ."
К кому я могла взывать? Марра человек не интересовал. Он жил своей теорией. . . (VI: 28, 118).

APPENDIX: THE RUSSIAN ORIGINAL OF MAJOR QUOTATIONS

"All of this is part of the life program: we have to scold each other..."
Все это входит в программу жизни: нужно, чтобы мы бранили друг друга, падали в глазах один другого, вели недостойную переписку. Потом это покроется временем, и останется только то, с чего мы начали,—с родственного рождения,—да томики книг, на разные темы и в разных формах (VI: 28, 124).

"Its arena is abroad, not in Russia."
Ее арена заграница, не Россия (VI: 30, 138).

"A study like mine had appeared in France and was met with such honors that..."
Во Франции появилась такая же работа, как моя, и была она встречена с таким почетом, что о ней с похвалой написали немцы, и немецкая рецензия пришла к нам... (VI: 31, 145–148).

"It would be beneath my scholarly dignity to ask anything of you..."
Было бы ниже научного достоинства просить мне о чем-нибудь Вас, как лица, стоящего у власти просвещения. Мне лично не нужно ничего... (VI: 31, 148).

"Now, when I write about 1925, it is 1949..."
Сейчас, когда я пишу о 1925 годе, стоит 1949, и все выражения из моего письма к Луначарскому кажутся взятыми из модного политического словаря: русская наука, западная наука, русские достижения, русский приоритет. Какая чепуха! (VI: 31, 148).

"When a novelist writes the first chapters, he does not know..."
Романист, создавая первые главы, не знает еще, чем окончится последняя. А я, увы, знаю: мои плюсы обратятся в мои минусы. Я знаю, потому что сперва написала свои последние главы, а потом начала писать первые (VI: 31, 148).

"Big events usually pass unrecognized, like the heroes of an epic."
Большие события проходят обычно неузнанными—как герои эпоса. Мы придаем огромное значение тому, что бесследно проваливается, и не видим того, что со временем оказывается важным для всей нашей биографии (VI: 32, 151).

He has only to say 'imprimatur,' and all the journals will open their doors.
Ему стоит только сказать imprimatur, и все журналы откроют свои двери. Ибо у немцев, да и везде, пожалуй, Гарнак Jupiter Optimus Maximus» (VII: 38, 5).

"I understood perfectly well that . . ."
Я прекрасно понимала, что в России были выдающиеся ученые, но науки не было (VII: 38, 7).

"The Housing Question"
Квартирный вопрос

"Oh, if I had known what a terrible fate awaited my brother and this idle, healthy woman . . ."
О, если б я знала, какая страшная судьба ожидает моего брата и эту праздную, здоровую женщину, корчившую из себя неземное создание, как она будет чернорабочей, грузчицей, каторжанкой,—я, наверное, мыла бы ей ноги и целовала под нею пол (VII: 38, 2).

"One simply cannot, one cannot fail to interpret the unceasing content of days . . ."
Нельзя же, нельзя не осмыслить такого непрекращающегося содержания дней; оно есть, оно дано; как данность, пусть и состоящая из малого и мелкого. [. . .] [усматривает в квартирном вопросе] единый знак [. . .] этап работы, подготовлений духа, встречи с бытом и его ступенчатости (VII: 39, 8).

"The whole year 1929, all three hundred and sixty-something days of it . . ."
Весь 1929 год, все триста шестьдесят с чем-то его дней, прошел у нас под знаком неслыханного квартирного процесса (VII: 53, 186).

"the whole family of a violent, alcoholic laborer moved in . . ."
к нам въехала целая семья пьяницы и убийцы рабочего, с любовницей и двумя детьми (VII: 53, 187).

"Very urgent. To the Head of the Economics Department of the GPU."
Весьма срочно
Начальнику Экономического отдела ГПУ
Уважаемый товарищ.
  К Вам обращается научный работник-марксист, сотрудник 1 разряда Научно-исследовательского института литературы

APPENDIX: THE RUSSIAN ORIGINAL OF MAJOR QUOTATIONS

и языков при ЛГУ, Института марксизма и Яфетического института с горячей просьбой освободить меня от шантажа, в борьбе с которым я надрываю силы вот уже 9 месяцев и вот-вот потону окончательно. Разрешите ознакомить Вас со всем делом, чтоб восстановить всю картину.

В прошлом году советская власть предоставила гражданам право раздела квартир с тем, чтобы они предоставлялись трудящимся. Этим правом воспользовалась и я (VII: 53, 199).

"Comrade. My life is nothing but nightmarish torture . . ."
Товарищ. Моя жизнь—сплошная кошмарная пытка: Я во власти шантажа и произвола. [. . .] Нужна сильная и смелая власть органов дознания, которая охватила бы всю картину в целом, а не ее отдельные отрывки. Моя единственная надежда на Вашу смелую помощь. Я отдаю все силы государству и прошу защитить меня перед тремя хищниками. . . (VII: 53, 207).

"Comrades! I am a Marxist . . . I am an ordinary worker . . ." (VII: 53, 209).
Товарищи! Я—марксист. . . Я—маленький работник. . . (VII: 53, 209).

"But this Sukhovo-Kobylin document did not help one iota either."
Но не помог ни на иоту и этот Сухово-Кобылинский документ (VII: 53, 209).

"I Lived through Khona"
Я жила Хоной

"My scholarship was inextricably connected with love. I lived through Khona . . ."
Моя наука была неразрывна с любовью. Я жила Хоной. . . (IX: 69, 157).

"intimacy . . . such that the individuality of one was lost in the other."
и близость здесь была такова, что индивидуальность одного терялась в другом. Природа создала из нас, чужих двух и далеких людей, близнецов (VI: 37, 204).

"we were wedded by the commonality of lives and loves. Our destinies merged".
мы были обвенчаны общностью жизней и любовей. Наши судьбы слились (VII: 44, 70).

"O, where have we not whispered, hugged, and cried? . . . In entryways . . ."
о, где мы не шептались, не прижимались, не плакали! [. . .] подворотни, темные углы парадных, своды церквей—(IX: 69, 166).

"I told you [Vy] this "morning" (by telephone) that after yesterday's conversation . . ."
Я сказал Вам сегодня «утром» (по телефону), что после вчерашнего разговора у меня в душе осталась большая сумятица, но когда вы ответили, что тут надо многое прояснить, то у меня мелькнуло сомнение в самой возможности подобного прояснения (VII: 45, 80).

"Today, when you [Vy] told me on the telephone that you had a letter for me . . ."
Сегодня, когда Вы сказали мне по телефону, что имеете для меня письмо [. . .]—вдруг такая большая радость охватила меня, воздушная, легкая,—что я поняла природу своей души, для которой дороже всего в свете язык от сердца к сердцу, с полным отходом от жизни, от мира звуков, от (в философском значении!) всего чувственного (VII: 45, 83).

"He meant the ordinary denouement of love . . ."
Он имел в виду обычную развязку любви, а я поняла, что речь идет о судьбе, о предопределенности нашей жизненной встречи (VII: 45, 79).

"Strong passions shook me precisely when I did not love."
Сильная природа потрясала меня именно тогда, когда я не любила (VII: 51, 169).

"Could it be that the passion that was given to me by nature . . ."
Не сублимируется ли та страсть, что в такой мере была дана мне природой, в научное творчество? (VII: 51, 170).

"I thought about her always, worried about her every hour . . ."
Я думала о ней всегда, тревожилась за каждый час. . . (X: 80, 116).

"We both, hiding from each other, thought our terrible thought about the same thing."
Мы обе, скрывая друг от друга, думали об одном и том же нашу страшную думу. [. . .] Наша жизнь тех лет, исполненная великим

счастьем близости и величайшим взаимным проникновением, одновременно была молчаливой умопомрачающей драмой (X: 80, 116–117).

Tristan and Isolde
Тристан и Исольда

"Without moving across the water..."
без поездки по воде была бы нарушена вся структура сюжета (VIII: 58, 43).

"Olya, I think about you every day, of course, not about you alone, but about the two of us."
Оля, я думаю о тебе каждый день, конечно, не о тебе одной, а об нас двоих. Положение принимает просто трагический характер. Я не договариваю, но ты поймешь. Конечно, я не боюсь самого страшного: я верю в тебя, в твою стойкость не менее чем в мое чувство. Но все-таки так дальше нельзя, а как быть не знаю. Думаю, жизнь сама принесет разрешение—больше ждать неоткуда (VIII: 58, 45).

"He spoke about death—he always spoke about death..."
Он говорил о смерти,—он всегда говорил о смерти... (VII: 44, 72).

"You [Vy] upset me a lot on Saturday..."
Вы очень огорчили меня в субботу и положили тяжелый гнет на мое сердце. Это было в те минуты, когда Вы говорили о смерти (VII: 44, 72).

"If someday, at the end of my life, death does not take me by surprise..."
Если когда-нибудь, в конце жизни, смерть не застанет меня врасплох и будет момент, когда я в один миг окину взором всю свою жизнь,—все пережитое, вся жизнь с ее так наз. «смыслом» и то неведомое, что именуется «небытием», разве все это не будет окрашено для меня в другой цвет оттого, что судьба послала, наконец, ту встречу, в которой счастье,—и радость и «боль и примирение»... (VII: 46, 102).

"My Department"
Моя кафедра

"And so I reach the year 1932, the beginning of my university activity."
И вот я дохожу до 1932 года, до начала моей университетской деятельности (VIII: 57, 20).

"There was an order to open a department of classical philology..."
Приказано открыть кафедру классической филологии, и вот просят меня организовать ее.... Я стала еще и еще отказываться... (VIII: 60, 57).

"Looking Back, You See"
Оглядываясь назад, видишь

"These were the years of the first five-year plan, the emergence of socialist competition..."
Это были годы первой пятилетки, возникновенья соц. соревнованья, «шести условий товарища Сталина»... (VII: 56, 247).

"In 1931, I was already a Soviet person who wanted to explore, understand, respect..."
В 1931 г. я была уже человеком советским, желавшим вникнуть, понять, уважать и строить новое. [...] Но с воцареньем Сталина пошла система, сути которой никто не понимал, но о которую ударялся головой (VII: 56, 247).

"Looking back, you see how simple it was: the strangulation of the country..."
Оглядываясь назад, видишь, как это было просто: удушенье страны средствами голода и тщательно поддерживаемой разрухи; полное подавленье личности, мысли, идеи, человеческого «я». Эта система осуществлялась при помощи неслыханных размеров доноса, преследований политических и «идеологических», а также публичных оскорблений. Я помню всеобщую растерянность при первом появлении печатной брани с называньем имен и окатываньем грязью. Я помню первые кампании подрыва всех авторитетов, служебных, политических, моральных. Разгром, как самоцель политики, только начинался (VII: 56, 247).

"And so, came the year 1934."
And so, came the year 1934 (VIII: 62, 79).

APPENDIX: THE RUSSIAN ORIGINAL OF MAJOR QUOTATIONS

"Of course, I was very naïve then . . ."
Конечно я была очень наивна. . . (VIII: 64, 107).

"Now begins what ended in my just written words."
Сейчас начнется то, что кончилось в моих только что написанных словах (VIII: 63, 92).

"Life has become easier, comrades; life has become more fun . . ."
Жить стало легче, жить стало веселей»: таков был официальный лозунг (VIII: 63, 92).

"Dancing, wine, flowers, banquets were created by the directive of the secret police . . ."
Танцы, вино, цветы, банкеты создавались по директиве тайной полиции. . . Юбилеи, вечера, тосты, балы шли по всем учреждениям (VIII: 63, 93).

"the university was a barometer of politics . . ."
Университет был барометром политики. Кафедры то расширялись, то сокращались; факультеты и институты переименовывались. . . (VIII: 63, 95).

"The year 1936 was approaching. We all thought that the repressions . . ."
Подходил 1936 год. Мы все думали, что репрессии, которые составляли ту политическую систему, в которой мы жили, и есть ответ на убийство Кирова. Мы не знали, что нас ждет (IX: 70, 170).

"Your Book Has Been Confiscated"
Ваша книга конфискована

"In May 1936, my Poetics was published. It was a big day in my life . . ."
В мае 1936 г. моя Поэтика вышла в свет. Это был большой день моей жизни (IX: 71, 184).

"Your book has been confiscated."
Ваша книга конфискована (IX: 71, 186).

"A huge article in the official press was in itself a harbinger of political persecution."
Огромная статья в официальном органе предвещала сама по себе политическое преследование. Но еще убийственней

было примечание жирным шрифтом от редакции, это уже представляло собой некий сигнал травли. Вопрос шел не шуточный (X: 73, 24).

"I felt a terrible longing for my arrested book."
Я испытывала страшную тоску по своей арестованной книге. Теперь, когда я пишу, у меня нет слов, чтобы передать эту тоску, это алканье, страсть увидеть книгу живой (X: 73, 28).

"All powerful people could do anything: kill, distort, pervert . . ."
"Все могли сделать всемогущие люди: убить, исказить, извратить . . . Воздействовать на историю они не имели средств, как ни были всемогущи (X: 73, 29).

"I Don't Know How Historians Will Describe 1937"
Не знаю, как историки будут описывать 1937 год

"When you write retrospectively, you are forced to see only the main lines of your life."
Когда пишешь ретроспективно, поневоле видишь одни крупные линии своей жизни. Письма, документы, дневники—это увеличительные стекла, очки для дальнозоркой истории (X: 78, 69).

"Conversation with Khona: . . ."
Разговор с Хоной:
— Что с тобой? Что ты испытываешь? . . .
— Я испытываю страх.
— Страх? Но кого, чего ты боишься?
— Не знаю. Это вне меня.
И он добавлял, прижимая меня к себе, тихо:
— Страх (X: 79, 110).

"On the 31st, near the Institute of Language and Thought, a motor vehicle . . ."
31-го, на повороте от ИЯМ'а [Институт языка и мышления], на Хону наехала машина,—по-видимому, он шел, как все последнее время, самоуглубленно, подавленно (X: 83, 139).

"Still in Khona's lifetime, Stalin launched the extermination machine . . ."
Еще при жизни Хоны Сталиным была запущена истребительная машина, известная под именем Ежовщины. [. . .] Начались ужасные политические процессы, аресты и ссылки. . . (X: 84, 142).

APPENDIX: THE RUSSIAN ORIGINAL OF MAJOR QUOTATIONS

"So this is what it looks like after I die!"
Так вот как оно выглядит после моей смерти! Так оно и будет выглядеть (X: 84, 144).

"What devil but Stalin could have devised such torture for a man?"
Какой дьявол, кроме Сталина мог придумать для человека такую пытку? (XI: 85, 157).

"for 12 years now, I've seen him every night in my dreams."
. . . вот уже 12 лет, как я его вижу каждую ночь во сне. Он приходит домой, и я плачу, кидаюсь, кричу: «это сон, это мне снится!»—и убеждаюсь, что это явь. Потрясенная, я просыпаюсь (XI: 85, 158).

"The year 1937 will go down in Russian history as . . .
1937 год войдет в историю России той главой Апокалипсиса, которая знаменует собой социальный и моральный конец страны. [. . .] Не знаю, как историки будут описывать 1937 год (XI: 86, 158–159).

"They arrested everybody, all around . . ."
Арестовывали всех, сплошь. . . (XI: 86, 159).

"Betrayal burst from the womb of black Russia . . ."
Предательство вырвалось из чрева черной России как великая народная стихия (XI: 86, 160).

"Every person waited at night for a search and arrest."
Каждый человек ждал ночью обыска и ареста. Подавляющее большинство людей не ложились спать или ложились одетыми. У меня, как и у других, на ночь приносилась к постели шуба и маленький чемоданчик для тюрьмы. . . (XI: 86, 161).

"From that time the Russian nation lost its honor and its will to live."
С тех пор народ утратил честь и волю к жизни (XI: 86, 168).

"my mind wandered in the distant future, and I wanted to tell posterity . . ."
моя мысль блуждала в далеком будущем, и я хотела сказать потомкам, которые найдут эту бумагу в архиве, что я не доносы писала, а давала показания в качестве свидетеля. Я обливала их слезами отчаянья и стыда. . . (XII: 95, 235).

"*I Wrote My Autobiography for Him*"
Я писала для него свою автобиографию

"*Life is a strange creature.*"
Но жизнь—странное существо (XI: 88, 178).

"*I read myself: "The second semester, 1940. It's cold, cold . . ."*"
Читаю у себя: «Второй семестр, 1940 год. Холод, холод». . . (XI: 92, 208).

"*He said he read it at once, read it all night till morning . . .*"
Сказал, что прочел сразу, читал всю ночь до утра. . .

"*The denouement. There's nothing to connect us anymore. Dead despair.*"
Развязка. Больше нас ничего не связывает. Мертвое отчаянье. Нечем жить (XI: 92, 209).

"*It's shameful to count oneself as a Russian.*"
Позорно числиться русским (XI: 91, 203).

"*Stalin untied Hitler's hands and thus let the war begin.*"
Сталин развязал руки Гитлеру и дал начало войне (XII: 93, 220).

Chapter 5. The Mythopolitical Theory of Olga Freidenberg in the Context of the Political Thought of Her Time

"*Hitler and Stalin, two tyrants, created a new form of government . . .*"
Гитлер и Сталин, два тирана, создали новую форму правления, о которой Аристотель не мог знать (XXVIII: 7, 47).

"*Until now, political and religious terror had been known.*"
До сих пор был известен политический и религиозный террор. Сталин ввел и террор бытовой (XXVIII: 19, 84).

"*At work, he is thrown into a 'collective' . . .*"
Он брошен в "коллектив" на службе, где за ним следят и на него доносят, в собственной квартире, в собственной комнате и даже в собственной семье (XXXIV, 144).

APPENDIX: THE RUSSIAN ORIGINAL OF MAJOR QUOTATIONS

"I am not even talking about the surveillance . . ."

Я уже не говорю о слежке, регулярных доносах, о надзоре спецотдела, парткома, парторга, студентов и аспирантов, дворников, управхоза, соседей, всяких подслушивателей, осведомителей, агентов тайных и явных из знакомых. Я не говорю о «засекреченных» служащих, которые кишат вокруг каждого отдельного человека, о машинистках, уведомляющих советское гестапо насчет частных рукописей, о телефонном шпионаже, о вскрытии частной переписки. Все это—привычное, неотъемлемое условие советского быта. Я имею в виду другое (XXXIV, 144).

"they lock the doors, trapping employees . . ."

Во многих учреждениях запирают двери, не выпуская служащих, которые бегут с насильственных лекций и собраний после рабского трудового и голодного дня (XXXIV, 144).

"Another column on the same form indicates . . ."

в другой графе указывается, кто твой "консультант" (т. е. надсмотрщик), когда ты был у него, какую оценку он тебе дал, когда назначил вновь явиться. . . (XXXIV, 145).

"Marxism in being developed and elaborated in our country."

у нас развивают и разрабатывают марксизм. [. . .] Марксизм в стране Сталина не мировоззрение и не метод, а плетка. Это полицейско-карательная категория (XXXIV, 146).

"The year 1937 will go down in Russian history as the chapter of the Apocalypse . . ."

1937 год войдет в историю России той главой Апокалипсиса, которая знаменует социальный и моральный конец страны. Для России здесь должна начаться пелопонесская [sic] война, за которой идет падение—и гибель. Я не верю, что народу может быть все позволено. Его еще ждет моральный Нюрнберг. Не знаю, как историки будут описывать 1937 год. . . (XI: 86, 158–159).

"People crushed each other, smothered each other."

Давили, душили друг друга. Доносы достигали беспредельности (XI: 86, 160).

"Political plague roamed the whole of Russia."
Политическая чума гуляла по всей России (XI: 86, 160).

"Betrayal burst from the womb of black Russia as an elemental force . . ."
Предательство вырвалось из чрева черной России как великая народная стихия... Предавали друг друга, один друг другого своего друга. Предавали соседи по квартире, члены семьи, товарищи по работе, жильцы дома, прохожие, дворники (XI: 86, 160).

"Stalin created an entirely new concept and a new term . . ."
Сталин породил совершенно новое понятие и новый термин, не переводимый ни на один культурный язык: склока. Всюду, во всех учреждениях, во всех квартирах чадит склока. Трудно объяснить, что это такое. Это низкая, мелкая вражда, злобная групповщина одних против других, это ультрабессовестное злопыхательство, разводящее мелочные интриги. Это доносы, клевета, слежка, подсиживанье, тайные кляузы, разжиганье низменных страстишек одних против других. Напряженные до крайности нервы и моральное одичание приводят группу людей в остервененье против другой группы людей или одного человека против другого. Склока—это естественное состоянье натравливаемых друг на друга людей, беспомощно озверевших, загнанных в сталинский застенок. Склока—это руль «кормчего коммунизма» Сталина. Склока—альфа и омега его политики. Склока—его методология. Международная его политика, его дипломатия построены на склоке (XXXIV, 150–151).

"[Stalin] was carrying out a process of ruthless massacre of the population . . ."
[Сталин] совершал процесс беспощадной расправы над населением и отрубаньем [sic] у народа головы; отныне оставалось в живых одно туловище. Такой версии мифа человечество никогда не придумывало, даже самое дикое. Ходили мифы о гидре, о голове Руслана, но никому не приходила на ум ужасающая картина отрубленных и функционирующих туловищ—даже самому Иоанну Богослову (XI: 86, 159).

"'The organized foundation of Hitler's party—said the Nuremberg prosecutor . . .'"
"Организационной основой гитлеровской партии,—говорил нюрнбергский обвинитель,—был принцип 'фюрерства', на котором было построено все руководство германским

государством сверху донизу. [. . .] Носитель власти обязан был наблюдать за всем, что происходило в его области" (XXV: 72, 47).

"I don't know whether there was anything comparable in history!"
Не знаю, было ли когда-либо в истории что-либо подобное! Такое официальное государственное признание, что все люди—идиоты, слепцы, «уклонисты». [. . .] У диких народов, там известно: только шаманы владеют истиной. У нас ни Академии, ни Университеты истиной не владеют. Один pontifex maximus, Сталин (XXV: 63, 13).

"If a soccer or chess player . . . or musician won . . ."
Если побеждал футболист, шахматист [. . .] музыкант, то это был не он, а сила Сталина, стоящий за ним «народ», чьим он был лишь орудием. Все победы, успехи, все достижения на войне и в труде шли в карман Сталина. Это отражалось в языке (XXV: 63, 13).

"A stable epithet appeared: "stalinist" (stalinskii)."
Появился стоячий эпитет «сталинский». Он прилагался ко всему положительному, к людям, событиям, временам года, вещам, местностям. Слово «хорошо» исчезло, потому что его как понятия не стало. Говорили: «неплохо», «не плохо». [. . .] Такие слова, как «родной», «любимый», «друг», «отец», «учитель», прилагаемые ежеминутно к Сталину, стерлись и стали почти юмористическими (или «мудрый»). Таковы были значенья слов «подъем», «воодушевленье», «энтузиазм», рыночные сталинские слова («собрание с большим подъемом приняло обращение к товарищу Сталину» и другие клише). Язык стал содержать куски общих мест, полицейский эпический язык (XXV: 64, 13–14).

"Stalin's seventieth anniversary has clearly shown that . . ."
Семидесятилетие Сталина показало воочию, что наш советский «социализм»—старая, как мир, религия, что это все та же религия воинствующей католической церкви, но религия XX века, религия не Бога, а человека, религия политическая (XXXIII, 111).

"All of individual life, up to the minutest detail . . ."
Вся личная жизнь до мельчайших деталей втянута в микроскоп, сделана «чистым сосудом», наполняемым божеством-Сталиным. [. . .] Идеальный тип партийца—богонаполненный,

сталинонаполненный человек, без воли и разума, верующий в конечное царство божие вопреки всему, что подсказывает ему логика и показывают глаза (XXXIII, 112).

They are creating another new Rome from Moscow (the third one? the fourth?).
Из Москвы создают вселенский Рим (который по счету?). Большевистская теократия правит страной, разливаясь по всему свету и вербует обездоленных с мечом и кошельком в руках. [. . .] Партийцы—духовенство. Партийный билет—это благодать (XXXIII, 112).

"All of Stalinist messianism, its flower-strewn idols resembling the Catholic Virgin Mary . . ."
Все сталинское мессианство, его кумиры с цветами наподобие католической богородицы, модуляции голоса при произнесении его имени [. . .] ритуал вставания, невидимое председательствование («почетное») на всех собраниях, молитвы-обращения к нему всем собранием верующих—все это старо, как мир. [. . .] Опять Август, «отец» и «отец отечества», эсхатологический Фридрих Барбаросса и «праведный царь», создатель мирового плодородия («счастливого материнства») и «сталинских урожаев»! [. . .] Снова перед нами карающий и благостный «вельтгеррьер» или, как его недавно назвали, «командир двадцатого столетья» (XXXIII, 113).

"History has known sieges and catastrophes."
История знала осады и катастрофы. Но еще никогда человеческие бедствия не бывали задуманы в виде нормативного бытового явления (XVIII: 138, 10).

"I will not live to see the retribution."
До возмездия я не доживу. Я не увижу московского Нюрнберга. . . (XXVII: 83, 9).

"Stalinism, without a doubt, introduced many new things."
Сталинизм, несомненно, внес много нового. Он забросил на чердак устаревшего и наивного Макиавелли. . . (XXXIV, 148).

"With us, the secret police is not an organ of the government, but a regime . . ."
Секретная полиция у нас не орган, а режим, охватывающий весь объем государственной и частной, весь объем личной жизни (XXXIV, 149).

"Stuffed like herrings in a tightly corked barrel..."
Набитые, как сельди в бочку, наглухо закупоренные, все больные, там копошатся и давят друг друга омертвелые человеческие существа (XXXIV, 150).

"also introduced a new system, unheard of until then..."
[Сталинизму] принадлежит введенье и нового строя, до той поры неслыханного,—состоянье войны с каждым в отдельности человеком, входящим в состав населенья России (XXXIV, 148).

"mystification of nations, death in prison cells..."
мистификация народов, смерть в застенках, удушенье каждого в отдельности человека и универсальная склока—вот методы Сталина (XXXIV, 151).

Chapter 6. "Conclusion" (1950)

"Notes, these notes! I was afraid of a search, not for my own sake..."
Записки, эти записки! Я боялась обыска не за себя, но за них—что их уничтожат. Сколько раз моей души касалось колебание: записки—или свобода? Уничтожить их, но стать свободной и ничего не бояться, ни обыска, ни смерти! Но даже свободу я не могла поставить выше этих записей. Я не желала умереть безгласной. Это значило бы, что я принимаю то худшее, что когда-либо знал мир—мистификацию добра, идейный цинизм, обесчеловеченье. Я вспоминала идеалы, которыми маскировали убиение человека, совесть, свою собственную совесть, лежавшую на анатомическом столе,—когда тиран заставлял нас носом ткнуться в свою биологическую физиологию, и мы жили полуумершие, завидовавшие куску, съеденному нашими любимыми близкими, тайно от самих себя мечтавшие отнять их кусок себе. О, эти муки совести, то, что никогда не проходит и лишает жизнь прав на существованье! Чего не сделал Сталин с человеком, чего не убил, сквозь что не провел? Над чем в истории не насмеялся? (XXXIII, 110–111).

"That is really all about my life."
Вот, собственно, и все о моей жизни. Какой может быть эпилог и в чем его значенье? Проживу ли я долго или мало, это уже асемантично. Природа дала мне изобилье моральных сил и

способностей, но я их утрачивала в непрестанной борьбе, где я тщилась противостоять государственной машине насилия и убийству заживо (XXXIV, 153).

"My husband, given to me by life, as grace is given by god, was crushed..."
Мой муж, данный мне от жизни, как дается благодать от бога, был раздавлен пьяной машиной... (XXXIV, 153).

"My brother died amid the most horrible tortures of the Stalinist dungeon."
Мой брат умер среди самых ужасных мучений сталинского застенка (XXXIV, 153).

"My father and my mother died of starvation and shock."
Мой отец и моя мать погибли от голода и потрясения (XXXIV, 153).

"My scholarship was strangled by Stalin's fingers."
Моя наука была задушена пальцами Сталина (XXXIV, 153).

"my love was debased, as was my honor."
Моя любовь поругана, как и моя честь (XXXIV, 153).

"My students moved away from me, scared by the Stalinist state."
Мои ученики отошли от меня, испуганные сталинским государством. Я должна была отказаться от последнего, чем дорожила,—от кафедры (XXXIV, 153).

"The most terrible thing was the siege..."
Самое ужасное—осада, которую я увидела воочью, то скальпирование живого человека, перенести которое не может ничья душа (XXXIV, 153).

"Inwardly, of course, I will continue not to give up."
Я, конечно, внутренне не сдамся и дальше. Записки, написанные среди обысков, арестов и казней, есть мой человеческий протест против артиллерии антихриста. Я буду дальше рыться в земле в поисках целебного корня и выступать против штаб-квартиры Марьи Лазаревны и кретинизма Боровского, буду бунтовать, делать усилия, чтоб написать последнюю книгу; я буду верить в науку и в историю (XXXIV, 154).

APPENDIX: THE RUSSIAN ORIGINAL OF MAJOR QUOTATIONS

"I don't know when and of what I'll die."

Не знаю, когда и от чего я умру. Но одно знаю: если я буду умирать в сознанье, в моих глазах будут стоять два образа: моей матери—и московского Нюрнберга.

10 декабря 1950 г.   О. Фрейденберг

(XXXIV, 154)

Chronology of Olga Freidenberg's Life and Times

1890
March 15 (March 28 Old Style): Olga Mikhailovna Freidenberg is born in Odessa to Anna Osipovna Freidenberg, née Pasternak (1860–1944) and Mikhail Filippovich Freidenberg (1858–1920). Brothers: Alexander Mikhailovich Freidenberg (he later changed his surname to Mikhailov) (1884–1938) and Evgeny Mikhailovich Freidenberg (1887–1901). Uncle: the painter Leonid Osipovich Pasternak (1862–1945), Anna Osipovna's brother, with whose family the Freidenberg family maintains close ties.

1889
Leonid Pasternak's family moves to Moscow.

1903 (?)
The Freidenberg family moves to St. Petersburg.

1908
Olga Freidenberg graduates from the private gymnasium of E. M. Gedda in St. Petersburg.

1910
Summer: Olga Freidenberg begins correspondence with her cousin Boris Pasternak (1890–1960), the son of Leonid Pasternak, which will continue until her death.

1911–1914
Olga Freidenberg travels to and lives in Switzerland, Germany, Italy, and Sweden.

1914–1918
World War I.

At the start of the war, in August 1914, Olga Freidenberg returns to Russia from Sweden.

Performs volunteer work with wounded soldiers in Petrograd hospitals in 1914–1917.

1917
The Russian Revolution, followed by the Russian Civil War (1918–1921).

1917–1918
Olga Freidenberg begins studying classical philology at Petrograd University.

1919
Commences work on a scholarly study of the Greek apocryphal text "The Acts of Paul and Thecla."

1920

August 1: Olga Freidenberg's father dies during the blockade of Petrograd in the Civil War.

1921

Spring: Olga Freidenberg's uncle Leonid Pasternak leaves Soviet Russia with his wife and daughters, settling in Berlin.

1923

Olga Freidenberg graduates from Petrograd University.

1924

November 14: Defense of Olga Freidenberg's dissertation "The Origins of the Greek Novel" (or "The Greek Novel as Acts and Passions"), based on her study of "The Acts of Paul and Thecla."

Beginning of Freidenberg's association with the influential Soviet scholar Nikolai Marr.

1925

After several years of unemployment, Olga Freidenberg takes a part-time position, at a nominal salary, at the Institute of Comparative Study of Literatures and Languages of the West and East [Institut sravnitel'nogo izucheniia literatur i iazykov Zapada i Vostoka], or ILIaZ, later renamed the State Institute of Speech Culture [Gosudarstvennyi institut rechevoi kul'tury], or GIRK).

1926

Begins working in the mythology section of the Japhetic Institute [Iafeticheskii institut] headed by Marr (in 1931, renamed the Institute of Language and Thought [Institut iazyka i myshleniia]).

Beginning of Olga Freidenberg's collaboration with Israel ("Khona") Frank-Kamenetsky, biblical scholar and student of mythology.

1927

Olga Freidenberg publishes her first scholarly work.

1928

Beginning of her romantic correspondence with Khona Frank-Kamenetsky.

1929

The Freidenberg family's year-long struggle with the authorities over their right to remain in their apartment (called by Freidenberg the "housing question").

Late April–May: Olga Freidenberg makes a short trip to Moscow.

1929–1931

The collective study *Tristan and Isolde: From the Love Heroine of Feudal Europe to the Matriarchal Goddess of Afroeurasia*, on which Freidenberg worked with Frank-Kamenetsky and colleagues from the mythology section, appears in print.

1930

Olga Freidenberg publishes an article in the journal *Atheist* (no. 59), "The Gospel as One of the Types of the Greek Novel," featuring some materials from her (otherwise unpublished) study of the origins of the Greek novel.

CHRONOLOGY OF OLGA FREIDENBERG'S LIFE AND TIMES

1930–1932
Actively involved in research and administrative tasks, mostly at the State Institute of Speech Culture (GIRK). Publishes several articles.

1932
Olga Freidenberg is appointed chair of Leningrad University's Department of Classical Philology and tasked with organizing it upon its reopening after a hiatus.

1933–1940
Works on a major study (that will remain unpublished) of Hesiod's poem *Works and Days*.

1934
The assassination of Sergei Kirov, which marks the beginning of the Stalinist Great Terror.

1935
June 9: Olga Freidenberg defends her second dissertation, "The Poetics of Plot and Genre: The Period of Classical Literature."

1936
The publication and then suppression ("arrest") of Freidenberg's book *The Poetics of Plot and Genre*, based on her second dissertation, the only book-length study published in her lifetime.

November: Freidenberg travels to Moscow to appeal the ruling against her book, and the ban is lifted. This is the last time she would leave Leningrad and the last time she would see Boris Pasternak in person.

1937–1938
The worst phase of the Great Terror, known as the Yezhovshchina (so called for the head of state security, Nikolai Yezhov).

1937
June 4: Frank-Kamenetsky dies in a traffic accident in Leningrad.

June 9: Final letter to Leonid Pasternak in Berlin (informing him of Frank-Kamenetsky's death). After that, the political situation in the Soviet Union makes international correspondence difficult and dangerous.

Winter: Arrest of Musya (last name unclear), the wife of Freidenberg's brother Alexander.

August 3: Arrest of Freidenberg's brother Alexander Mikhailov.

1938
January: Unbeknownst to Olga Freidenberg and her mother, Alexander Mikhailov is sentenced to death (January 3) and executed (January 9) in Leningrad.

Leonid Pasternak and his daughters move from Berlin to Oxford.

1939
Winter: Beginning of Olga Freidenberg's love for B. (her colleague at Leningrad University).

The Molotov–Ribbentrop Pact, also known as the Hitler–Stalin Pact or (officially) the Treaty of Non-Aggression between Germany and the Soviet Union. It included a secret protocol establishing Soviet and German spheres of influence in Eastern Europe.

September 1: Germany invades Poland, beginning World War II.

1939–1940
Soviet annexation of Eastern Poland and other border areas. Annexation of Latvia, Lithuania, Estonia, and parts of Romania (Bessarabia, Northern Bukovina). In 1940, the Soviet Union annexes parts of Finland following the Winter War.

November 1939–February 1940: Olga Freidenberg writes her first autobiography covering the years 1890 to 1917, which later becomes notebooks I and II of her "notes" (*zapiski*).

1941–1945
The Nazi–Soviet War (known as the Great Patriotic War in the Soviet Union).

Olga Freidenberg remains in Leningrad, surviving its siege (1941–1944). Works intermittently on major scholarly studies, including "Introductory Lectures on the Theory of Folklore of Classical Antiquity" and "Homeric Etudes" (all these works would remain unpublished in her lifetime). Her employment at Leningrad University is interrupted when she declines to evacuate with it to Saratov.

1942
May 3: Olga Freidenberg begins writing her notes on the siege (blockade) of Leningrad, taking events retroactively to June 22, 1941, the first day of the war.

1943–1944
Temporary teaching at the Herzen Pedagogical Institute.

November 25, 1943: Freidenberg's mother suffers a stroke in besieged Leningrad.

1944
April 9: Freidenberg's mother dies.

May 1: Freidenberg halts work on her notes upon completing the account of her mother's death.

After Leningrad University's return from evacuation, Freidenberg resumes her position as chair of its Department of Classical Philology.

1945
May 8: End of World War II in Europe. (May 9 is Victory Day in the Soviet Union.)

May 31: Leonid Pasternak dies in Oxford. Olga Freidenberg is informed of his death in a letter from Boris Pasternak of June 21 and sends a telegram of condolence to the family in England.

June 26: Freidenberg resumes her notes, bringing them up to the end of the war, but soon halts work once more.

1947
June 19: Takes up work on her notes again.

CHRONOLOGY OF OLGA FREIDENBERG'S LIFE AND TIMES

Fall: Organizes her notebooks into a single expanded text with a table of contents (including sections projected to be written in the future) and gives the notes a title: *The Race of Life* (*Probeg zhizni*). Continues to write.

1944–1947
Works on two major studies, one on Roman comedy ("Palliata") and the other on Sappho and the origins of Greek lyric poetry, which remain unpublished. She was able to publish an abstract of the study on Sappho in 1949.

1946–1950
Soviet ideological campaigns and political repressions, starting in Leningrad.

August 14, 1946: "Resolution of the Central Committee on the Journals Zvezda and Leningrad," signaling a crackdown in the sphere of art and culture.

1947–1948
Intensification of campaigns to counter "the pernicious influence of the West." Public purges and administrative repressions at Leningrad University.

1948–1949
Winter: Freidenberg works on two sets of notes: her continuing chronicle of current events, focused on the repression, and an autobiographical account covering the period from 1918 to 1941 (until now, a lacuna in her autobiographical chronicle).

Beginning of 1949: The unleashing, across the country, of the blatantly antisemitic "anti-cosmopolitan" campaign. Arrests of faculty and students at Leningrad University.

February: Beginning of the so-called Leningrad affair, a campaign of terror against Communist Party and administrative authorities in Leningrad. Arrests of major party and municipal officials, including administrators of Leningrad University who led the repressions, are followed by trials and executions in September–October 1950.

Freidenberg steps down from her position as chair of the Department of Classical Philology.

1950
May–June: In the course of the ideological campaigns, the ideas of Nikolai Marr come under attack.

December 10: Freidenberg concludes her notes.

1951
Freidenberg retires and leaves Leningrad University.

1953
March 4: Stalin dies.

1953 or 1954
Freidenberg completes the monograph *Image and Concept* (published many years later).

1955
July 6: Freidenberg dies of cancer in Leningrad.

1956
Beginning of de-Stalinization in the Soviet Union.

1973 or 1974
Freidenberg's personal archive is discovered in an iron chest in the home of her heir, Rusudan Orbeli. Publication of her unpublished scholarship begins in 1973. Over one hundred publications would appear in subsequent decades, including translations into other languages, mostly English, Polish, and Serbo-Croatian. In the mid-1970s, Freidenberg's notes are typed and smuggled abroad at the initiative of Boris Pasternak's son, Evgeny Pasternak, and his wife, Elena Pasternak. The notes are deposited in the Pasternak family archive in Oxford, established by Leonid Pasternak.

1981–1982
Correspondence between Olga Freidenberg and Boris Pasternak, with short excerpts from her notes interspersed between letters, is published in New York in Russian (1981), then in English (1982) by Harcourt Brace Jovanovich, followed by translations into German, French, Italian, Dutch, and Hebrew.

1986–1987
Beginning of the policy of openness (*glasnost*) and reconstruction (*perestroika*) in the Soviet Union.

Two excerpts from Freidenberg's notes are published in Paris in émigré editions (in Russian).

1988
First publications of the Pasternak–Freidenberg correspondence in Russia.

1991
December: Dissolution of the Soviet Union.

2015
Freidenberg's notes, with other documents from the Pasternak family archive in Oxford, are deposited in the archives of the Hoover Institute on War, Revolution, and Peace.

Notes

Introduction

1. Parenthetical citations from Freidenberg's notes are explained in the acknowledgments.

2. The detailed analysis and description of the structure and composition of Freidenberg's notes (*zapiski*) was made by N. Iu. Kostenko (Glazyrina), "Problemy publikatsii memuarnogo i epistoliarnogo nalediia uchenykh: Po materialam lichnogo arhiva prof. O.M. Freidenberg" (MA thesis, Ros. gos. gumanitarnyi universitet [RGGU], Moscow, 1994), http://freidenberg.ru/Issledovanija/Diplom. See also her later study: N. Iu. Kostenko, "Ia ne nuzhdaius' ni v sovremennikakh, ni v istoriografakh: Istoriia arkhiva Ol'gi Freidenberg," *Ol'ga Mikhailovna Freidenberg v nauke, literature, istorii. Materialy XXIII Lotmanovskikh chtenii. Vestnik RGGU. Seriia "Istoriia. Filologiia. Kul'turologiia. Vostokovedenie"* 4, no. 25 (2017): 117–127. In another publication, Kostenko also reflected on the meaning of the title, *Probeg zhizni*: N. Iu. Kostenko, "'Probeg zhizni': K interpretatsii zaglaviia vospominanii O. M. Freidenberg," in *Mif, ritual, literatura* (Moscow: Izdatel'skii dom Vysshei shkoly ekonomiki, 2023), 43–50. I have benefitted from, and largely followed, Kostenko's description (a few exceptions, when my own analysis of the manuscripts differs from Kostenko's, are marked in footnotes).

3. Hannah Arendt, "Dilthey as Philosopher and Historian" [1945], in *Essays in Understanding* (New York: Schocken Books, 1994), 137.

4. Brief overviews of Freidenberg's life and her contributions to scholarship include: Nina Braginskaya [Braginskaia], "Olga Freidenberg: A Creative Mind Incarcerated," in *Women Classical Scholars: Unsealing the Fountain from the Renaissance to Jacqueline de Romilly*, eds. Rosie Wyles and Edith Hall (New York: Oxford University Press, 2016), 286–312; N. V. Braginskaia, "'U menia ne zhizn', a biografiia," *Ol'ga Mikhailovna Freidenberg v nauke, literature, istorii*, 11–38. There is a comprehensive book-length study: Nina Perlina, *Ol'ga Freidenberg's Works and Days* (Bloomington, IN: Slavica, 2002). There is a published dissertation in German: Annette Kabanov, *Ol'ga Michajlovna Frejdenberg (1890–1955): Eine sowjetische Wissenschaftlerin zwischen Kanon und Freiheit* (Wiesbaden, Germany: Harrassowitz Verlag, 2002). A bibliography of Freidenberg's works and studies about her can be found at the site Elektronnyi arkhiv Ol'gi Mikhailovny Freidenberg (the Freidenberg Electronic Archive website curated by N. V. Braginskaia and N. Iu. Kostenko): http://freidenberg/ru/Vxod.

5. Hostility toward Freidenberg has long reigned in the Department of Classical Philology at Leningrad University (after 1992, St. Petersburg University). The brief sketch of the history of the department, which she headed from 1932 to 1949, was posted on the official website of the Philological Faculty (Filologicheskii fakul'tet;

see under Kafedra klassicheskoi filologii), but, as of 2025, while displaying the names of her senior colleagues, did not mention Freidenberg's name. Viewed at http://phil.spbu.ru/o-fakultete/#!/tab/652619846-2 (last accessed June 6, 2025).

6. The paradoxes of Freidenberg's reputation are discussed in: N. V. Braginskaia, *Mirovaia bezvestnost': Olga Freidenberg ob antichnom romane* (Moscow: GU-VShE, 2009), 15, 21–27; Nina V. Braginskaia, "From the Marginals to the Center: Olga Freidenberg's Works on the Greek Novel," *Ancient Narrative* 2 (2002): 64–85; Nina Braginskaya, "Olga Freidenberg: A Creative Mind Incarcerated," 305–307, 311 N. V. Braginskaia, "U menia ne zhizn', a biografiia," 14–15, 31–32. Braginskaia speculates on the reasons why Freidenberg's work has been largely ignored by Russian scholarship both under and after Stalin, as well as by scholarship on classical antiquity in the West. Writing from a different position, Galin Tihanov comments on Freidenberg's reputation in: Galin Tihanov, "*Image and Concept: Mythopoetic Roots of Literature* by Olga Freidenberg, eds. Nina Braginskaia and Kevin Moss" [book review], *Slavonic and East European Review* 77, no. 1 (1999): 160–162. He also comments on Braginskaia's efforts "almost to canonize Freidenberg" (162). Both Braginskaia and Tihanov address a difficult issue of how Freidenberg's association in the 1920s and 1930s with the controversial Soviet scholar Nikolai Marr, promoted by Stalin, may have influenced the tendency to ignore her work in the post-Stalinist era. For comments on both methodological and ideological criticism of Freidenberg, see Katerina Clark and Galin Tihanov, "Soviet Literary Theory in the 1930s," in *A History of Russian Literary Theory and Criticism: The Soviet Age and Beyond*, eds. Evgeny Dobrenko and Galin Tihanov (Pittsburgh: University of Pittsburgh Press, 2011), 140–143, 354n100.

7. In her scholarship, Freidenberg advanced a coherent method, "genetic semantics," or the "genetic method." In brief, this implied tracing the genesis and transformation of meaning carried by symbolic forms of culture, from archaic myths to folklore to literary plots, and she ascribed a special role in the formation of symbolic forms to metaphors. On Freidenberg's methodology, see S. A. Troitskii, "Geneticheskii metod O. M. Freidenberg v issledovanii kul'tury," *Ol'ga Mikhailovna Freidenberg v nauke, literature, istorii*, 39–60. A short introduction to her method can be found in: Nina Perlina, "Ol'ga Freidenberg on Myth, Folklore and Literature," *Slavic Review* 50, no 2. (1991): 371–384. In another brief article, Perlina comments on how Freidenberg used her scholarly methodology in her autobiographical writings, applying mythological patterns to her own life: Nina Perlina, "Primeval and Modern Mythologies in the Life of Ol'ga Mikhailovna Freidenberg," *Russian Review* 51 (1992): 188–197.

8. Hannah Arendt, *The Origins of Totalitarianism* (New York: Harcourt Brace Jovanovich, 1973), 460.

9. Stefan-Ludwig Hoffmann wrote about Arendt's "anthropology of historical experience" or "political-historical anthropology," comparing it to Reinhart Koselleck's, in his "Koselleck, Arendt, and the Anthropology of Historical Experience," *History and Theory* 49, no. 2 (2010): 212–236.

10. In presenting Koselleck's and Arendt's work on the historical experience of Hitler's subjects, Hoffmann notes that both scholars put their trust in the analysis of "non-participatory observers." As he puts it, "Certainly both agree that histories can be analyzed conceptually or depicted narratively only after the fact, so we learn to

deal with the meaninglessness of an event or to attribute meaning to it" (Hoffmann, 230). Freidenberg's case is different: she writes as a participant-observer.

11. While Freidenberg wrote without a draft, she used notes made earlier on loose pieces of paper (occasionally, she cites these notes, done in real time). And the handwritten notebooks contain some crossed-out words, insertions, and occasional blacked-out and cut-out text.

12. Hannah Arendt, *The Human Condition*, 2nd ed. (Chicago: University of Chicago Press, 1998), 50.

13. Providing this information about the archive, I follow Kostenko as well as my own research. See Kostenko, "Ia ne nuzhdaius' ni v sovremennikakh, ni v istoriografakh."

14. On Lotman and other early visitors to the chest, S. Iu. Nekliudov and S. S. Averintsev, see an interview with Nina Braginskaia: "Iazyk nauki: Beseda s doktorom istoricheskikh nauk, rukovoditelem Nauchno-uchebnogo tsentra antikovedeniia IVKA RGGU Ninoi Braginskoi," February 10, 2010, https://polit.ru/articles/nauka/yazyk-nauki-beseda-s-doktorom-istoricheskikh-nauk-rukovoditelem-nauchno-uchebnogo-tsentra-antikovede-2010-02-10/.

15. Iurii Lotman, "O. M. Freidenberg kak issledovatel' kul'tury," *Trudy po znakovym sistemam* 6 (1973): 482–514. English translation: Yuri Lotman, "O. M. Freidenberg as a Student of Culture," *Soviet Studies in Literature: A Journal of Translations* 12, no. 2 (1976): 3–11.

16. Braginskaia told the story of her discovery of the archive several times, dating it, from memory, as taking place in 1972, 1973, or 1974; for the latest versions, see Braginskaia, "A Creative Mind Incarcerated," 306, and "U menia ne zhizn', a biografiia," 13–14.

17. Boris Pasternak's father, the painter Leonid Pasternak (Olga Freidenberg's mother was his sister), had moved from Soviet Russia to Berlin in 1921 with his wife and their daughters; in 1938, they moved to Oxford.

18. Editions of the correspondence include: Boris Pasternak, *Perepiska s Ol'goi Freidenberg*, ed. and commented by Elliott Mossman (New York: Harcourt Brace Jovanovich, 1981); English translation: *The Correspondence of Boris Pasternak and Olga Freidenberg, 1910–1954*, ed. Elliott Mossman, trans. Elliott Mossman and Margaret Wettlin (New York: Harcourt Brace Jovanovich, 1982). The first Russian edition: "Boris Pasternak—Ol'ga Freidenberg: Pis'ma i vospominaniia," eds. E. V. Pasternak, E. B. Pasternak, and N. V. Braginskaia, *Druzhba narodov*, no. 7 (1988): 201–224; no. 8 (1988): 237–261; no. 9 (1988): 235–256; no. 10 (1988): 232–242. Among subsequent Russian editions, the following is the most thorough: Boris Pasternak, *Pozhiznennaia priviazannost': Perepiska s O. M. Freidenberg*, eds. E. B. Pasternak and E. V. Pasternak (Moscow: Art-Fleks, 2000). In all editions, extracts from Freidenberg's notes contain unmarked omissions and adjustments.

19. O. M. Freidenberg, "Osada cheloveka," in *Minuvshee: Istoricheskii al'manah*, vol. 3 (Paris: Atheneum, 1987), 9–44. Olga Freidenberg, "Budet li moskovskii Nurnberg? (iz zapisok 1946–1948)," *Sintaksis*, no. 16 (1986), 149–163.

20. P. A. Druzhinin, *Ideologiia i filologiia. Leningrad. 1940-e gody*. Vol. 1 (Moscow: Novoe literaturnoe obozrenie, 2012).

21. Irina Levinskaia, "O filologii bez ideologii: Replika po povodu dvukhtomnika P. A. Druzhinina 'Ideologiia i filologiia,'" *Zvezda*, no. 8 (2013), 173–186. Braginskaia's

retort appeared in the online journal *Gefter* on August 16, 2013, http://gefter.ru /archive/9736?fb_action_ids=10200098293535121&fb_action_types=og.likes&fb _source=other_multiline&action_object_map=[518906881510960]&action_type _map=[%22og.likes%22]&action_ref_map=[].

Both comments were then reposted, on August 20, 2013, at the site of Novoe literarturnoe obozrenie: "Irina Levinskaia vs Nina Braginskaia: Polemika po povodu knigi Petra Druzhinina 'Ideologiia i filologiia,'" http://www.nlobooks.ru /node/3659. At present, Braginskaia's comment is no longer available online. Druzhinin also responded to criticism: P. A. Druzhinin, "Ol'ga Freĭdenberg kak memuarist: Nabliudeniia istorika," *Ol'ga Mikhailovna Freidenberg v nauke, literature, istorii,* 128–140. A sharp retort followed from Levinskaia, posted at: https://independent.academia .edu/IrinaLevinkaya.

22. Here I name some studies that can guide the reader through the large corpus of personal documents of the Soviet experience. For an overview, see Irina Paperno, *Stories of the Soviet Experience: Memoirs, Diaries, Dreams* (Ithaca, NY: Cornell University Press, 2009). Diverse diaries from the 1930s are presented in the anthology: *Intimacy and Terror: Soviet Diaries of the 1930s*, eds. Veronique Garros, Natalia Korenevskaya, and Thomas Lahusen (New York: New Press, 1997). There is a book-length study that deals with the diaries in which the writer attempts to create a Soviet self: Jochen Hellbeck, *Revolution on My Mind: Writing a Diary under Stalin* (Cambridge, MA: Harvard University Press, 2006). A collection of diverse diaries from the Leningrad blockade can be found in: *"V etikh krupinkakh—zhizn'": Fenomen blokadnogo dnevnika*, eds. A. Iu. Pavlovskaia and N. A. Lomagin (St. Peterburg: Izdatel'stvo Evropeiskogo universiteta v Sankt Peterburge, 2021), with introductory articles by N. A. Lomagin, M. Mel'nichenko, and P. Barskova. This collection draws on a large and growing online database of diaries from different periods of Soviet history, Prozhito, at https://prozhito.org/. There is a selection from the siege diaries in English (which include some excerpts from Freidenberg's notes): *Writing the Siege of Leningrad*, eds. Cynthia Simmons and Nina Perlina (Pittsburgh: University of Pittsburgh Press, 2005). Specific diaries from the Leningrad blockade are discussed in: Alexis Peri, *The War Within: Diaries from the Siege of Leningrad* (Cambridge, MA: Harvard University Press, 2020). See also the collection of articles on diverse aspects of the siege diaries: *Blokadnye narrativy: Sbornik statei*, eds. P. Barskova and R. Nicolosi (Moscow: Novoe literaturnoe obozrenie, 2017).

23. Originally published in selections in Germany in 1995 by Aufbau Verlag in Berlin, Victor Klemperer's lifelong diaries have later appeared in a fuller version in several editions made up of many volumes. The autobiography of his early years, *Curriculum Vitae: Erinnerungen 1881–1918*, has also been published. There is an abridged English translation of his diaries for the years spanning the Nazi regime and the years of the German Democratic Republic, in three volumes, translated and commented by Martin Chalmers: Victor Klemperer, *I Shall Bear Witness: The Diaries of Victor Klemperer, 1933–41* (London: Weidenfeld & Nicolson, 1998); *To the Bitter End: The Diaries of Victor Klemperer, 1942–1945* (London: Weidenfeld & Nicolson, 1999); *The Lesser Evil: The Diaries of Victor Klemperer, 1945–1959* (London: Weidenfeld & Nicolson, 2003).

24. The political ideas in Lidiia Ginzburg's *Zapiski blokadnogo cheloveka* (literally, "notes of a blockade man") and other siege writings have been analyzed in: Irina

Sandomirskaia, "A Politeia in Besiegement: Lidiia Ginzburg on the Siege of Leningrad as a Political Paradigm," *Slavic Review* 69, no. 2 (2010): 306–326; I. Sandomirskaia, *Blokada v slove: Ocherki kriticheskoi teorii i biopolitiki iazyka* (Moscow: Novoe literaturnoe obozrenie, 2013), 173–265. Sandomirskaia briefly commented on the similarity between Ginzburg's ideas and Freidenberg's (based on published excerpts): "A Politeia in Besiegement," 307n2, 317–318n38 and 40; *Blokada v slove*, 55n187. Sandomirskaia's analysis of Ginzburg helped me in analyzing Freidenberg's political theory.

25. As far as I know, the two philologists, Olga Freidenberg and Lidiia Ginzburg, both born to assimilated Jewish families in Odessa, must have known about each other, but they did not socialize even though they had common friends and enemies, among them B. M. Eikhenbaum, V. V. Propp, V. M. Zhirmunsky, G. A. Gukovsky, and M. L. Tronskaia. In 1989 Ginzburg wrote a brief introduction to the publication of Pasternak's correspondence that included the Pasternak–Freidenberg letters: *Perepiska Borisa Pasternaka*, eds. E. V. Pasternak and E. B. Pasternak, introductory article by L. Ia. Ginzburg (Moscow: Khudozhestvennaia literatura, 1990). She commented on the intelligence, wit, and style of Freidenberg's "remarkable" letters (10).

26. Arendt, *The Origins of Totalitarianism*, 478.

27. Several prominent historical studies focused on the Stalinist everyday. The historian Sheila Fitzpatrick, in her book *Everyday Stalinism: Ordinary Life in Extraordinary Times: Soviet Russia in the 1930s* (Oxford: Oxford University Press, 1999), describes "the practices of everyday life in Stalin's Russia" (227), focusing on the formative period of the 1930s. Fitzpatrick speaks about the economy of shortages, the housing, surveillance, family problems, and much more but (in her formulation) "largely excludes topics like friendship, love, and some aspects of leisure and private sociability." For the purposes of her book, she defined the "everyday" as "everyday interactions that in some ways involved the state" (3). An earlier study is based on a field project conducted in 1950–1951 by a team of Harvard social scientists and psychologists who interviewed more than three thousand postwar Soviet refugees in Europe and the United States with a goal to create a "working model" of the Stalinist society: Alex Inkeles and Raymond Bauer, *The Soviet Citizen: Daily Life in a Totalitarian Society* (Cambridge, MA: Harvard University Press, 1959). Needless to say, these professional efforts are hardly compatible with Freidenberg's private project. And Freidenberg believed that all everyday interactions involved the Stalinist state.

28. Comparing Stalinism and Nazism has long been a subject of controversy among social scientists, historians, and public intellectuals, challenged on both intellectual and political grounds. It suffices to mention a comprehensive and discriminating guide to this controversy: Michael Geyer with assistance from Sheila Fitzpatrick, "Introduction: After Totalitarianism—Stalinism and Nazism Compared," in *Beyond Totalitarianism: Stalinism and Nazism Compared*, eds. Michael Geyer and Sheila Fitzpatrick (New York: Cambridge University Press, 2009), 1–38.

29. Biographical information can also be found in: Braginskaia, "A Creative Mind Incarcerated," and "'U menia ne zhizn', a biografiia." See also the biographical outline in Kostenko, "Problemy publikatsii memuarnogo i epistoliarnogo naslediia uchenykh," at http://freidenberg.ru/Issledovanija/Diplom/Glava1/1. I used these sources as well as my own research.

1. "Overture" (1890–1917)

1. Notebook I–II (two notebooks sewn into one) has the subtitle "The Most Important" (*Samoe glavnoe*) on its first page. The text is divided into four chapters with headings; the chapters are further divided into numbered sections: 1. "The First Chapter" (*Pervaia glava*); subtitle illegible in the manuscript, possibly "Jubilee on Paper" (*Iubilei na bumage*). In typescript, this chapter remains untitled. The first chapter is composed of sections 1–24; numbering begins with the second section. 2. "The New Chapter" (*Novaia glava*), sections 1–16. 3. "The Third Chapter" (*Tret'ia glava*), sections 1–38. 4. "The War" (*Voina*), sections 1–25. Page numbering in the typescript is consistent over both notebooks. When citing notebook I–II, I give page numbers, but not chapter numbers. N. Iu. Kostenko, who was the first to explore and describe the structure and composition of the notes, suggested that only chapter 1 was written in 1939–1940. See N. Iu. Kostenko (Glazyrina), "Problemy publikatsii memuarnogo i epistoliarnogo naslediia uchenykh: Po materialam lichnogo arhiva prof. O.M. Freidenberg" (MA thesis, Ros. gos. gumanitarnyi universitet [RGGU], Moscow, 1994), http://freidenberg.ru/Issledovanija/Diplom. In a later publication, Kostenko did not question the dating of the first two notebooks: N. Iu. Kostenko, "Ia ne nuzhdaius' ni v sovremennikakh, ni v istoriografakh: Istoriia arkhiva Ol'gi Freidenberg," in *Ol'ga Mikhailovna Freidenberg v nauke, literature, istorii. Materialy XXIII Lotmanovskikh chtenii. Vestnik RGGU. Seriia "Istoriia. Filologiia. Kul'turologiia. Vostokovedenie"* 4, no. 25 (2017): 117–127. Having examined the notebooks, I see no reason to doubt the dating and therefore follow Freidenberg's own version: the main text was written from November 1939 (one of the fragments of the first notebook is dated November 11, 1939) to February 11, 1940 (the date on the last page).

2. Nina Braginskaia analyzed the mythological meanings of the concept of twinship, which Freidenberg applied to her relationship with Lifshits, Boris Pasternak, and other people in her life (including Frank-Kamenetsky). See Braginskaia's afterword to her publication of Freidenberg's short memoir devoted to Elena Lifshits, "'Lifshits-tsar': Elena Lifshits—Ol'ga Freidenberg, ili travestiia bliznechnogo mifa," *Novoe literaturnoe obozrenie*, no. 6 (1993–1994): 107–115.

3. Similarities between Freidenberg's notes and Pasternak's early autobiographical prose have been noted by scholars: Boris Gasparov, "Poetika Pasternaka v kul'turno-istoricheskom izmerenii (B. L. Pasternak i O. M. Frejdenberg)," in *Sbornik statei k 70-letiiu prof. Iu. M. Lotmana* (Tartu: Tartuskii universitet, 1992), 366–384; Nina Perlina, *Ol'ga Freidenberg's Works and Days* (Bloomington, IN: Slavica, 2002), 17–27. Perlina also traced affinities with Pasternak in the later parts of the notes and in Freidenberg's other works; see 27–41. On Pasternak's autobiographical prose, I also used Alfred Bem's article, "'Okhrannaia gramota' Borisa Pasternaka," *Rul'*, no. 33048 (October 1931).

4. On Dilthey's views on autobiography and the further developments of these ideas, I used, among other sources: Dieter Thomä, Ulrich Schmid, and Vincent Kaufmann, *Der Einfall des Lebens: Theorie als geheime Autobiographie* (Munich: Carl Hanser Verlag, 2015). These authors examine the interaction between theory and autobiographical practices in a range of twentieth-century cultural theorists, including Georg Lukacs, Hannah Arendt, Claude Levi-Strauss, Mikhail Bakhtin, Victor Shklovsky, Roland Barthes, Yuri Lotman, and others, and they trace the tension between theory

and "life." Thomä, Schmid, and Kaufmann interpret Dilthey's hermeneutics (his view of "life" as an object of understanding and interpretation in the categories of humanistic knowledge) precisely as an attempt to apply theory to life: "Wilhelm Dilthey made a remarkable attempt . . . to reconcile theory and autobiography. He argued that we are actually engaged in the same thing, whether we are theorizing or writing autobiography" (11). (English translation mine.) And while Freidenberg, to my knowledge, did not mention Dilthey as one of her sources, I believe that some of her formulations are close to his ideas, which were well known to the scholars of her generation.

5. Roland Barthes, *A Lover's Discourse: Fragments*, trans. Richard Howard (New York: Hill and Wang, 1978), 6, 67 (translation adjusted).

2. Blockade (1941–1945)

1. I follow Mark Edele and Michael Geyer, "States of Exception: The Nazi-Soviet War as a System of Violence," in *Beyond Totalitarianism: Stalinism and Nazism Compared*, eds. Michael Geyer and Sheila Fitzpatrick (New York: Cambridge University Press, 2009).

2. There is a vast scholarship on the siege of Leningrad. The following source has been often cited by many scholars: *The Leningrad Blockade, 1941–1944: A New Documentary History from the Soviet Archives*, eds. Richard Bidlack and Nikita Lomagin, trans. Marian Schwartz (New Haven, CT: Yale University Press, 2012). Listed here (in chronological order) are selected studies from recent decades that offer diverse approaches to the siege by Western and Russian scholars: David M. Glantz, *The Siege of Leningrad, 1941–1944: 900 Days of Terror* (Staplehurst, UK: Spellmount, 2001); N. A. Lomagin, *Neizvestnaia blokada* (St. Petersburg: Neva, 2004); John Barber and Andrei Dzeniskevich, eds., *Life and Death in Besieged Leningrad, 1941–44* (New York: Palgrave Macmillan, 2005); Jörg Ganzenmüller, *Das belagerte Leningrad 1941–1944: Die Stadt in den Strategien von Angreifern und Verteidigern* (Paderborn: Brill Schoningh, 2005); Sergei Iarov, *Blokadnaia etika: Predstavleniia o morali v Leningrade 1941–1942 gg.* (Moscow: Tsentrpoligraf, 2013) (English translation: Sergey Yarov, *Leningrad 1941–42: Morality in the City under Siege*, trans. Arch Tait [Cambridge: Polity Press, 2017]); Polina Barskova, *Besieged Leningrad: Aesthetic Responses to Urban Disaster* (DeKalb: Northern Illinois University Press, 2017); Sergei Iarov, *Povsednevnaia zhizn' blokadnogo Leningrada* (St. Petersburg: Izdatel'stvo Evropeiskogo universiteta v Sankt Peterburge, 2018).

3. For references to the main editions of the blockade diaries, see note 22 to the Introduction.

4. An important issue in the intense and painful discussions surrounding the Leningrad siege is the conflict between two modes of remembering the blockade: accounts focused on the heroic, self-sacrificing endurance of the besieged civilians and accounts that emphasize the citizens' suffering and degradation. An issue that is unacceptable to many is the assignment of responsibility for the humanitarian catastrophe to both Nazi Germany and Stalinist Russia. Of all the personal accounts known to us, Freidenberg's notes may be the most radical in her depiction of degrading, dehumanizing suffering, without any reference to patriotic heroism, and in her readiness to blame both Hitler and Stalin. So far, Freidenberg's blockade notes, because they are practically unknown, have not been implicated in the debates. Listed here are some of the sources on the decade-long controversies around the memory

of the blockade: Lisa A. Kirschenbaum, *The Legacy of the Siege of Leningrad, 1941–1995: Myth, Memories, and Monuments* (Cambridge: Cambridge University Press, 2009); Andrea Zemskov-Züge, *Zwischen politischen Strukturen und Zeitzeugenschaft: Geschichtsbilder zur Belagerung Leningrads in der Sowjetunion 1943–1953* (Göttingen, Germany: V&R unipress, 2012); Tat'iana Voronina, *Pomnit' po-nashemu: Sotsrealisticheskii istorizm i blokada Leningrada* (Moscow: Novoe literaturnoe obozrenie, 2018). The debates of the last decade have been surveyed in the journal forum: "Pamiat' o blokade—blokada pamiati. Forum NZ," *Neprikosnovennyi zapas* 127 (2019). Some aspects of the recent debates have been described in: Tatiana Voronina, "Between Memory and Policy: How Societies of Leningrad Siege Survivors Remember the War," in *Authenticity and Victimhood After the Second World War: Narratives from Europe and East Asia*, eds. Randall Hansen, Achim Saupe, Andreas Wirsching, and Daqing Yang (Toronto: University of Toronto Press, 2021). The memory of the blockade in Germany has been discussed in: Jörg Ganzenmüller, "Memory as a Secondary Theatre of War: The Leningrad Blockade in German Memory," *Osteuropa* 61, nos. 8–9 (2011): 7–22.

5. The blockade records occupy notebooks numbered XII-bis through XX. (Freidenberg assigned the number XII to two different notebooks, most likely by mistake, and she later called the second notebook XII-bis.) In the blockade part of the notes, the chapter numbering is continuous in both the handwritten notebooks and typescript, running from chapters 1 to 181. In the handwritten notebooks, the pages are not numbered. In the typescript, in notebooks XII-bis–XIV, the pages are numbered within each notebook. In notebooks XV–XVII, the pages are not numbered, so I assigned my own page numbers. Although the page numbering is inconsistent in notebooks XIX and XX, I cite the page numbers as indicated in the typescript.

6. "Retrospective diary" is Nina Perlina's phrase. See *Ol'ga Freidenberg's Works and Days* (Bloomington, IN: Slavica, 2002), 64. More on this concept in the following.

7. The paradoxical position of participant-observer, described in several of Malinowski's publications, shows itself with particular clarity in the personal diary that Malinowski kept in New Guinea and the Trobriand Islands during World War I. Published under the title *Diary in the Strict Sense of the Term*, in 1967, it was not known to Freidenberg, who was familiar with Malinowski's earlier work. Describing this document as a "retrospective diary," Malinowski explained that it was a "history" of events (i.e., a retrospective narrative) that were "fully accessible to the observer." He recognized that even in a field diary, we can hardly speak of objective facts because history depends on theory: "History is observation of facts in keeping with a certain theory; an application of this theory to the facts as time gives birth to them." Bronislaw Malinowski, *Diary in the Strict Sense of the Term* (Stanford, CA: Stanford University Press, 1989), 114. More on the parallel between Freidenberg and Malinowski later.

8. Clifford Geertz, "From the Native's Point of View: On the Nature of Anthropological Understanding," in *Meaning in Anthropology*, eds. K. H. Basso and H. A. Selby (Albuquerque: University of New Mexico Press, 1976), 222.

9. This is how Ernst Cassirer, whose work on metaphor and on mythical thinking influenced Freidenberg, analyzes the image of Tiamat in volume 2 of his *Philosophy of Symbolic Form* (published in 1925).

10. The image of the threatening Tiamat was also used by Anna Akhmatova. In 1942, evacuated from besieged Leningrad to Tashkent, she began working on a

tragedy about war and terror (entitled "Enuma Elish"), focused on the mythological image of Tiamat. Akhmatova's husband, the orientalist Vladimir Shileiko, translated the Babylonian epic "Enuma Elish" into Russian during the terrible winter in besieged Petrograd in 1919–1920.

11. Bronislaw Malinowski, *Myth in Primitive Psychology* (London: K. Paul, Trench, Trubner, 1926), 21.

12. In her scholarship, Freidenberg devoted much attention to myth and mythological metaphors. Scholars suggested that her sources in the scholarship of her time included Ernst Cassirer, Lucien Lévy-Bruhl, and her coworker Israel Frank-Kamenetsky. I would like to add the name of Malinowski to this list. Malinowski, whom Cassirer used as well, may have been a direct inspiration for Freidenberg's use of myth in her blockade notes.

13. Freidenberg wrote about this topic in her book *Poetics of Plot and Genre*: O. M. Freidenberg, *Poetika siuzheta i zhanra* (Moscow: Labirint, 1997), 306–307n116. Some scholars think that Mikhail Bakhtin, who analyzed the symbolic connotations of the rear end (*zad*) in his now famous book on Rabelais, written in the 1940s, used Freidenberg's ideas. It is known that Bakhtin read her book and took notes on it. Opinions on the overlap between Bakhtin and Freidenberg vary. For the latest survey of different views, see Richard P. Martin, "Against Ornament: O. M. Freidenberg's Concept of Metaphor in Ancient and Modern Contexts," in *Persistent Forms: Explorations in Historical Poetics*, eds. Ilya Kliger and Boris Maslov (New York: Fordham University Press, 2015), 310–311 and 310n47. Strong claims about Bakhtin's use of Freidenberg have been made by Perlina, *Ol'ga Freidenberg's Works and Days*, 249–262, and by Katerina Clark and Galin Tihanov, "Soviet Literary Theory in the 1930s," in *A History of Russian Literary Theory and Criticism: The Soviet Age and Beyond*, eds. Evgeny Dobrenko and Galin Tihanov (Pittsburgh: University of Pittsburgh Press, 2011), 142. Bakhtin's reading of Freidenberg's *Poetics of Plot and Genre* has been documented and discussed in: O. E. Osovskii, "M. M. Bakhtin chitaet Ol'gu Freidenberg: O kharaktere i smysle bakhtinskikh marginalii na stranittsakh 'Poetiki siuzheta i zhanra,'" in *Bakhtin v Saranske: Materialy, dokumenty, issledovaniia*, ed. O. E. Osovskii (Saransk: Krasnyi oktiabr', 2002), 1:24–35, and (a neglected work) Nina Perlina, "Eshche raz o tom, kak po khodu raboty nad knigoi o Rable, Mikhail Bakhtin chital 'Poetiku siuzheta i zhanra' Olgi Freidenberg," in *Khronotop i okrestnosti: Iubileinyi sbornik v chest' Nikolaia Pan'kova*, ed. B. V. Orekhov (Ufa: Vagant, 2011), 209–227.

14. O. M. Freidenberg, *Mif i literatura drevnosti*, 3rd ed. (Yekaterinburg, Russia: U-Faktoriia, 2008), 37.

15. For a list of Freidenberg's scholarship written during the blockade, see N. V. Braginskaia, "U menia ne zhizn', a biografiia," *Ol'ga Mikhailovna Freidenberg v nauke, literature, istorii. Materialy XXIII Lotmanovskikh chtenii. Vestnik RGGU. Seriia "Istoriia. Filologiia. Kul'turologiia. Vostokovedenie"* 4, no. 25 (2017): 29.

16. Freidenberg, *Poetika siuzheta i zhanra*. Page numbers are indicated in the text.

3. After the War (1945–1950)

1. N. Iu. Kostenko reconstructed the time of writing for the postwar notebooks. See: N. Iu. Kostenko (Glazyrina), "Problemy publikatsii memuarnogo i epistoliarnogo

naslediia uchenykh: Po materialam lichnogo arhiva prof. O. M. Freidenberg" (MA thesis, Ros. gos. gumanitarnyi universitet [RGGU], Moscow, 1994), http://freidenberg.ru/Issledovanija/Diplom; N. Iu. Kostenko, "Ia ne nuzhdaius' ni v sovremennikakh, ni v istoriografakh: istoriia arkhiva Ol'gi Freidenberg," *Ol'ga Mikhailovna Freidenberg v nauke, literature, istorii. Materialy XXIII Lotmanovskikh chtenii, Vestnik RGGU. Seriia "Istoriia. Filologiia. Kul'turologiia. Vostokovedenie"* 4, no. 25 (2017): 117–127.

2. The historian A. M. Skvortsov, who researched the history of the Department of Classical Philology at Leningrad University, challenged some of Freidenberg's statements about these dissertation defenses. He believed that the difficulties faced by Freidenberg's students were primarily caused by professional disagreements among colleagues on the methodology of classical philology. He also claims that the dissertations (specifically Galerkina's), written under difficult postwar conditions, had obvious deficiencies, of which Friedenberg was aware. A. M. Skvortsov, "Kafedra klassicheskikh iazykov i literatur LIFLI: Istoriia sozdaniia i organizatsiia uchebnogo protsessa," *Philologia Classica* 15, no. 2 (2020): 394–410, and "Kafedra klassicheskoi filologii LGU v dovoennoe i poslevoennoe vremia," *Philologia Classica* 17, no. 1 (2022): 159–172 (on dissertation defenses, see 168–170).

3. To explain the numbering of chapters in these notebooks: beginning in notebook XXXII, the numbering of parts, or chapters, in the typescript is inconsistent. Notebook XXXII is divided into three parts: the first is unnumbered, the second is numbered II, the third is numbered 3 [sic], and the fourth is numbered IV. I follow this numbering (marking the first, unnumbered part as I). In notebooks XXXIII and XXXIV, I indicate only the number of the notebook and page.

4. When she wrote her memoirs (finished in the mid-1990s), Galerkina was able to consult Freidenberg's notes. Describing her dissertation defense, she provides long quotes from the "Reminiscences" (as she calls them) of her "Teacher" (she capitalizes this word). Citing Freidenberg's words about the historical significance of this proceeding, Galerkina emphasizes the word *"history,"* noting "italics mine." While she does not explicitly comment on this, it appears that Galerkina shared her teacher's sense of the historical and political significance of these academic trials and persecutions. She also shared Freidenberg's belief that her own difficulties were connected with the animosity toward her adviser, Freidenberg, at the university. B. L. Galerkina, "Minuvshee—segodnia," *Russian Studies: Ezhekvartal'nik russkoi filologii i kul'tury* 2, no. 4 (1996): 385–394.

5. The attack on B. M. Eikhenbaum in the fall of 1946, after the "Resolution," is documented in: P. A. Druzhinin, *Ideologiia i filologiia. Leningrad. 1940-e gody* (Moscow: Novoe literaturnoe obozrenie, 2012), 1:448–487.

6. This interpretation of the ideological campaigns is advanced in the introduction to the collection of documents: *Stalin i kosmopolitizm: Dokumenty Agitpropa TsK KPSS 1945–1953*, eds. D. G. Nadzafov and Z. S. Belousova (Moscow: Materik, 2005), 9–10. The campaigns at Leningrad University are discussed in: K. Azadovskii and B. Egorov, "Kosmopolity," *Novoe literaturnoe obozrenie* 36 (1999): 83–135 (for attacks on Veselovsky, see 89–98), first published as: K. Azadovskii and B. Egorov, "O nizkopoklonstve i kosmopolitizme: 1948–1949," *Zvezda*, no. 6 (1989): 157–176. Not much is available on these campaigns in English. See Evgeny Dobrenko, "Literary Criticism and the Institution of Literature in the Era of War and Late Stalinism, 1941–1953," in *A History of Russian Literary Theory and Criticism: The Soviet Age and Beyond*, eds. Evg-

eny Dobrenko and Galin Tihanov (Pittsburgh: University of Pittsburgh Press, 2011), 169–177. Some aspects (mostly the antisemitic angle) are described in: Konstantin Azadovskii and Boris Egorov, "From Anti-Westernism to Anti-Semitism: Stalin and the Impact of the 'Anti-Cosmopolitan' Campaigns on Soviet Culture," *Journal of Cold War Studies* 4, no. 1 (2002): 66–80.

7. Attacks on A. N. Veselovsky (beginning in August 1946) are discussed in: Druzhinin, *Ideologiia i filologiia*, 1:345–364; Azadovskii and Egorov, "Kosmopolity," 89–98.

8. I. I. Meshchaninov succeeded Nikolai Marr in the role of an officially recognized leading authority in Soviet linguistics, which marred his reputation in the eyes of many. V. M. Zhirmunsky has mostly enjoyed a reputation as a prominent philologist in both official and unofficial quarters of Soviet academia, both then and now.

9. According to one study, the Soviet press started reporting on McCarthyism (in a highly critical mode) only in November of 1950. M. D. Novikov, "Makkartizm i sovetskaia periodicheskaia pechat': opyt vospriiatiia i vliianiia na otechestvennuiu istoriografiiu," *Vestnik Nizhegorodskogo universiteta im. N. I. Lobochevskogo*, no. 4 (2018): 72–78.

10. This episode was described in one of her blockade notebooks (XII: 26, 69).

11. Contrary to Freidenberg's story, Perlina insisted that "Freidenberg never shared her bed with the men she loved." Nina Perlina, *Ol'ga Freidenberg's Works and Days* (Bloomington, IN: Slavica, 2002), 4. Braginskaia reiterated this claim in Nina Braginskaya [Braginskaia], "Olga Freidenberg: A Creative Mind Incarcerated," in *Women Classical Scholars: Unsealing the Fountain from the Renaissance to Jacqueline de Romilly*, eds. Rosie Wyles and Edith Hall (New York: Oxford University Press, 2016), 291.

12. To explain the numbering of pages: in notebook XXVII, after page 15, in the part called "Afterword" (*Posleslovie*), Freidenberg started to number chapters anew. The numbered parts (or chapters) start with "2" (on page 21 of the typescript). The first part of the "Afterword," from page 15 to the middle of page 21, does not have a chapter number.

13. From my own examination of the notebooks, the list of contents (*oglavlenie*) for the whole notes is found toward the end of notebook XXVII, after the date "August 5, 1947" (which Freidenberg then thought to be the date of completion). Part 1 (one notebook) is called "The Most Important Things" (*Samoe glavnoe*). Part 2 is subtitled "A Wreath of Dill" (*Venok iz ukropa*), and this seems to relate to the yet unwritten story of Freidenberg's life from her entry into university until the war. Part 3 is called "The Siege of the Human Being" (*Osada cheloveka*); this is the chronicle of the blockade. Part 4 is entitled "Memoirs about My Own Self" (*Vospominaniia o samoi sebe*); this is the story of her life after the war. This list of contents ends with "afterword" (*posleslovie*). As Freidenberg continued to write, the part that was originally conceived as an afterword expanded, from the end of notebook XXVII to notebook XXXIV. For more detail, see Kostenko, "Ia ne nuzhdaius' ni v sovremennikakh, ni v istoriografakh."

14. Between 1946 and 1947, Freidenberg worked on a study of Sappho's lyric, begun during the blockade, and on a study of Roman comedy, under the provisional title "Palliata." In 1949, she succeeded in publishing an abstract of "Sappho." "Palliata" was partially published posthumously in: Olga Freidenberg, *Mif i teatr* (Moscow: GITIS, 1988).

15. This punitive meeting, on April 1, 1948, was noted and described in Azadovskii and Egorov, "Kosmopolity," 95–97.

16. Vulikh's speech criticizing Freidenberg was quoted based on a report in the newspaper *Leningradskii universit* on April 7, 1948. It was described in Azadovskii and Egorov's article on these repressive campaigns published in the journal *Zvezda* in 1989 (at the end of the Soviet regime): Azadovskii and Egorov, "O nizkopoklonstve i kosmopolitizme," 163. In a letter to the editorial board of *Zvezda*, N. V. Vulikh (née Moreva, 1915–2012) presented another version of events: according to her, she was asked to speak not against Freidenberg but against her teacher Tronsky, but she refused. In a revised version of this article published in 1999, Azadovskii and Egorov removed the mention of Vulikh's criticism of Freidenberg and added a footnote quoting Vulikh's letter to the editors. At the same time, they noted that the story Vulikh told in her 1989 letter referred to a different meeting, not in the spring of 1948 but in the spring of 1949 (Azadovskii and Egorov, "Kosmopolity," 129–130n51). On this matter, see also Druzhinin, *Ideologiia i filologiia*, 2:109. Freidenberg once commented in her notes that Vulikh, whose family hated the Bolsheviks, and who (Freidenberg writes) "herself was deeply anti-Soviet," was an enigma to her (X: 73, 28 and XXX: 13, 64). I would add that she remains an enigma to this day.

17. As dean of the Philological Faculty, G. P. Berdnikov took an active part in the attacks. So did A. G. Dementiev. Another person mentioned here, Sharova (her first name is not listed), was a fourth-year student who, according to Freidenberg, was active during the public shaming of professors (XXX: XV, 76–77; XXXII: I, 43).

18. The campaign against theatrical critics, who were all Jewish, began with an editorial in *Pravda* on January 28, 1949, "About One Anti-Patriotic Group of Theater Critics" (*Ob odnoi antipatrioticheskoi gruppe teatral'nykh kritikov*), and similar articles in the newspapers *Kultura i zhizn* and *Literaturnaia gazeta*. The word "cosmopolitan" entered into wide use at this time as an accusation implying a betrayal of national interests. Beginning with this "antipatriotic," "anticosmopolitan" turn, these campaigns, which started as anti-Western, took on an antisemitic character.

19. Rather enigmatically, Freidenberg comments here, "How naive I was when I thought that I would convert back to Jewishness [*pereidu obratno v evreistvo*]! We have pure fascist antisemitism" (XXXII: I, 68). What does she mean by "convert back to Jewishness"? There are some indications that in the early years of Soviet power, Freidenberg registered her "ethnic origin"—a required category in the internal Soviet passport—as "Russian" rather than "Jewish." Scholars' opinions differ. I believe this comment indicates that this may have been the case. Olga's brother Alexander Mikhailovich Freidenberg, who, in pursuit of education, was baptized before the 1917 revolution and changed his last name to Mikhailov, is believed to have done so. On this issue, see Lazar Fleishman's commentaries to "Iz semeinoi perepiski Pasternakov: Pis'ma O. M. and A. O. Freidenberg k rodnym v Germanii," eds. L. Fleishman and N. Kostenko, in *Novoe o Pasternakakh. Materialy Pasternakovskoi konferentsii 2015 goda v Stanforde*, ed. L. Fleishman (Moscow: Azbukovnik, 2017), 27n23; Braginskaya, "Olga Freidenberg: A Creative Mind Incarcerated," 288; N. V. Braginskaia, "'U menia ne zhizn', a biografiia," *Ol'ga Mikhailovna Freidenberg v nauke, literature, istorii. Materialy XXIII Lotmanovskikh chtenii. Vestnik RGGU. Seriia "Istoriia. Filologiia. Kul'turologiia. Vostokovedenie"* 4, no. 25 (2017): 18.

20. The open meeting of the Academic Council (*Uchenyi sovet*) of Leningrad University on April 4–5, 1949, is described (with excerpts from the minutes) in: Druzhinin, *Ideologiia i filologiia*, 2: 363–398.

21. Information about the speeches of E. I. Naumov and I. P. Lapitskii can be found in: Azadovskii and Egorov, "Kosmopolity," 108–111; Druzhinin, *Ideologiia i filologiia*, 2: 313–316, 535–541, 368–370. These sources confirm Freidenberg's account. About the speech of G. P. Makogonenko at the meeting of April 4–5, 1949, Azadovskii and Egorov write differently: they see it as "courageous" (111); Druzhinin notes that Makogonenko's negative comments on colleagues "were reduced to a minimum" (2: 383–383).

22. In 1932, when she became the chair of the Department of Classical Philology, Freidenberg decided against hiring Solomon Lurie (S. Ia. Lur'e), but by the late 1940s, she had obviously changed her mind, and she sheltered him in her department. After the meeting in which she did not participate, he was fired.

23. In her memoirs written many years later, Berta Galerkina (1914–2000) spoke about her advisor, Freidenberg, with warm sympathy (B. I. Galerkina, "Minushchee-segodnia," 353–433). The attitude of Sofia Poliakova (1914–1994) was more complicated. She left no memoirs. In an article devoted to Freidenberg's scholarship, Poliakova, while paying tribute to her as a scholar, also sharply criticizes some of Freidenberg's views. See S. V. Poliakova, "Iz istorii geneticheskogo metoda," *Novoe literaturnoe obozrenie*, no. 7/8 (1994): 13–20.

24. The relationship between Freidenberg and Nikolai Marr is discussed in chapter 4.

4. "To Fill in the Lacuna": From the University to the Last War (1918–1941)

1. The process of writing has been reconstructed by Natal'ia Kostenko in: N. Iu. Kostenko (Glazyrina), "Problemy publikatsii memuarnogo i epistoliarnogo naslediia uchenykh: po materialam lichnogo arhiva prof. O.M. Freidenberg" (MA thesis, Ros. gos. gumanitarnyi universitet [RGGU], Moscow, 1994), http://freidenberg.ru/Issledovanija/Diplom. According to Kostenko, notebooks III–XII were written concurrently with notebook XXXII–XXXIII in the winter of 1948–1949 (notebooks III–V in the fall and winter of 1948; notebook VI at the end of 1948 and the beginning of 1949; notebooks VII–XII in the winter of 1949).

2. Freidenberg once explained the meaning she attached to the phrase "A Wreath of Dill," which also appears on the covers of notebooks XIII and XV, written during the blockade: "The benevolent hand of the epoch crowned me with a wreath of dill. . . . And the dill changes its semantics. The Greeks planted it on graves. In the Soviet pantheon, the chapters of Zhirmunsky's and Tolstoy's monographs were crowned with laurel, but life crowned Khona and me only with dill. My title bears the bitterness of sarcasm" (XIII: 60, 97).

3. Selections from the part of Freidenberg's notes that deal with her university years have been published (with her introduction and commentary) by N. V. Braginskaia: "O. M. Freidenberg, Universitetskie gody," *Chelovek*, no. 3 (1991): 145–156.

4. It should be noted that the experience of the 1941–1944 blockade may not have been the only source of inspiration. There was a literary precedent for such descriptions of the first blockade—Victor Shklovsky's essay entitled "Petersburg under the Blockade" (*Peterburg v blokade*), published in 1920. He wrote, "Hunger and boiling

water in the morning. A quarrel at dinner in the family over food. Hunger at night. We starved obediently. The hungry talked to the hungry about hunger." Viktor Shklovskii, *Sobranie sochinenii* (Moscow: Novoe literaturnoe obozrenie, 2019), 1: 294–301.

5. Freidenberg's reading list has been discussed in: Nina Braginskaya [Braginskaia], "Olga Freidenberg: A Creative Mind Incarcerated," in *Women Classical Scholars: Unsealing the Fountain from the Renaissance to Jacqueline de Romilly*, eds. Rosie Wyles and Edith Hall (New York: Oxford University Press, 2016), 293n17. See also: N. V. Braginskaia, "'U menia ne zhizn', a biografiia," *Vestnik RGGU. Seriia "Istoriia. Filologiia. Kul'turologiia. Vostokovedenie"* 4, no. 25 (2017): 22. Nina Perlina discussed Freidenberg's sources in her "Ol'ga Freidenberg on Myth, Folklore and Literature," *Slavic Review* 50, no 2 (1991): 372–373.

6. Nina Braginskaia, who discussed the significance of Freidenberg's work on the Greek novel and contextualized it within the international field of classical philology, confirms this self-assessment. See: Braginskaya, "Olga Freidenberg. A Creative Mind Incarcerated," 293–295; Nina Braginskaia, *Mirovaia bezvestnost': Ol'ga Freidenberg ob antichnom romane* (Moscow: NIU VShE, 2009), 14–16. For more detailed discussion, see: Nina Braginskaia, "From the Marginals to the Center: Olga Freidenberg Works on the Greek Novel," *Ancient Narrative* 2 (2002): 64–85; Nina Perlina, *Ol'ga Freidenberg's Works and Days* (Bloomington, IN: Slavica, 2002), 47–67.

7. The biographical projection of Freidenberg's study of Paul and Thecla, as well as the parallels between Freidenberg's (scholar's) and Pasternak's (poet's) creative methods, were first noted and discussed in: B. Gasparov, "Poetika Pasternaka v kul'turno-istoricheskom izmerenii (B. L. Pasternak i O. M. Freidenberg)," in *Sbornik statei k 70-letiiu prof. Iu. M. Lotmana* (Tartu: Tartuskii gosudarstvennyi universitet, 1992), 366–384. Freidenberg's words about listening to Pasternak are cited in chapter 1.

8. For discussions of Marr's teaching in the context of the early Soviet ideology, see Katerina Clark, "Promethean Linguistics," in her *Petersburg, Crucible of Cultural Revolution* (Cambridge, MA: Harvard University Press, 1995), 212–223; Yuri Slezkine, "N. Ia. Marr and the National Origins of Soviet Ethnogenetics," *Slavic Review* 55, no. 4 (1996): 826–862. Clark and Slezkine tend to take some of Marr's intellectual propositions (such as his ideas about genesis) seriously, not limiting their analysis to considerations of calculated political opportunism.

9. For accounts of Freidenberg's institutional and intellectual links to Marr, which is a controversial issue, see K. Moss, "Olga Freidenberg i marrizm," *Voprosy iazykoznaniia*, no 5. (1994), English version at http://community.middlebury.edu/~moss/PDFs/F&M.pdf; Kevin Moss, introduction to *Image and Concept: Mythopoetic Roots of Literature*, by Olga Freidenberg, eds. Nina Braginskaia and Kevin Moss, trans. Kevin Moss (Oxon, UK: Harwood Academic Publishers, 1997; repr., London: Routledge, 2004), 4–27; Perlina, *Ol'ga Freidenberg's Works and Days*, 69–130; N. V. Braginskaia in her commentary to *Mif i literatura drevnosti*, 3rd ed. (Yekaterinburg, Russia: U-Faktoriia, 2008), 816–822, 830–833. See also Braginskaia's commentaries to Freidenberg's memoirs about Marr: "O. M. Freidenberg, 'Vospominaniia o N. Ia. Marre,'" in *Vostok-Zapad: Issledovaniia. Perevody. Publikatsii* (Moscow: Nauka, 1988), 198–204. For opinions voiced with less sympathy to Freidenberg, see: S. V. Poliakova, "Iz istorii geneticheskogo metoda: Marrovskaia shkola," in her *"Oleinikov i ob Oleinikove" i drugie raboty o russkoi literature* (Moscow: Inapress, 1997), 363–379. Galin Tihanov is critical of Poliakova's harsh treatment of Freidenberg as well as Frank-Kamenetsky

and Marr; see his "Framing Semantic Paleontology: The 1930s and Beyond," *Russian Literature* 72, nos. 3–4 (2012): 361–384.

10. On Marr's "semantic paleontology" (rather than other aspects of his work) and its lasting influence in literary and cultural scholarship, including the "genetic semantics" of Freidenberg and Frank-Kamenetsky, as well as Mikhail Bakhtin, see Tihanov, "Framing Semantic Paleontology," 361–384; Katerina Clark and Galin Tihanov, "Soviet Literary Theory in the 1930s," in *A History of Russian Literary Theory and Criticism: The Soviet Age and Beyond*, eds. Evgeny Dobrenko and Galin Tihanov (Pittsburgh: University of Pittsburgh Press, 2011), 109–143, and Tihanov, chapter 4, "The Boundaries of Modernity: Semantic Paleontology and Its Subterranean Impact," of his book *The Birth and Death of Literary Theory: Regimes of Relevance in Russia and Beyond* (Stanford, CA: Stanford University Press, 2019), 134–151. Tihanov tends to closely associate Freidenberg and Frank-Kamenetsky with Marr's ideas and influence and "genetic semantics" (the term used by Frank-Kamenetsky and Freidenberg) with Marr's "semantic paleontology." Other scholars disagree. Perlina tends to underplay the affinity between Freidenberg's use of the method of "semantic paleontology" and Marr's, calling Freidenberg "a Cassirer scholar in Marrist garb" (Perlina, *Ol'ga Freidenberg's Works and Days*, 99–115). Braginskaia suggests that for appreciation of the theoretical significance of Freidenberg's work, it is simply not necessary to refer to Marr (*Mif i literatura drevnosti*, 831).

11. Moss, "Olga Freidenberg i marrizm," 105.

12. Different sources list the title of Freidenberg's qualification work (not formalized as a dissertation) differently.

13. The institutional history of this organization is complex: the Institut sravnitel'nogo izucheniia literatur i iazykov Zapada i Vostoka (abbreviated ILIaZV) was created in 1919, in affiliation with Petrograd University; in the first years of its existence, it was also known as the Institut imeni A. Veselovskogo (the Veselovsky Institute); in 1930, it was renamed the Gosudarstvennyi institut rechevoi kul'tury, or GIRK (the State Institute for Speech Culture, better known as the Institut rechevoi kul'tury, or IRK, the Institute for Speech Culture).

14. There is confusion in the scholarship about Freidenberg's relationship with Russian formalism as a school of literary theory. Freidenberg considered herself an opponent and critic of the formalist school, but in later years, she was sometimes associated with formalism as well as Soviet structuralism and semiotics (which followed in the footsteps of the formalist school in the 1960s–1970s). Clark and Tihanov make the distinction between Freidenberg's method and Russian formalism clear in their "Soviet Literary Theory in the 1930s," 134–135. Perlina discussed Freidenberg's methodological differences and affinities with the formalists in her *Ol'ga Freidenberg's Works and Days*, 131–147. Braginskaia suggested that Freidenberg, the formalists, and the structuralists were lumped together in the 1970s in attempts to showcase "anything valuable that has survived under Stalin." Braginskaya, "Olga Freidenberg: A Creative Mind Incarcerated," 305.

15. Letters from this period appeared in Boris Pasternak, *Pozhiznennaia priviazannost': Perepiska s O. M. Freidenberg*, eds. E. B. Pasternak and E. V. Pasternak (Moscow: Art-Fleks, 2000), 95–123. In Freidenberg's notes, this episode is described in VI: 28, 118–124. The comparison shows that Freidenberg cites their correspondence in this period very selectively.

16. The Japhetic Institute (Iafeticheskii institut), launched in 1921, served as the main platform for Marr's "new theory of language," or the "Japhetic theory"; in 1931, this organization was renamed the Institute of Language and Thought (Institut iazyka i myshleniia, or IIaM) and affiliated with the Academy of Sciences.

17. For a document-based case of a contested apartment from the late Soviet epoch, see Vladimir Voinovich's *Ivankiada*. First published in the original Russian in the United States in 1976, it also appeared in English translation: *The Ivankiad, or The Tale of the Writer Voinovich's Installation in His New Apartment* (New York: Farrar, Straus and Giroux, 1977).

18. It remains unclear to me why, along with her actual professional affiliations, Freidenberg claimed to be an employee of the Institute of Marxism. There was an Institute of Marxism-Leninism in Leningrad at the time, but she had never been a part of it. She was a member of an educational circle known as the Marxist Society (Obshchestvo marksizma).

19. *Tristan i Isol'da: Ot geroini liubvi feodal'noi Evropy do bogini matriarhal'noi Afroevrazii* [Tristan and Isolde: From the love heroine of feudal Europe to the matriarchal goddess of Afroeurasia]. Kollektivnyi trud Sektora semantiki mifa i fol'klora pod redaktsiei akademika N. Ia. Marra [Collective work by the Sector of semantics of myth and folklore edited by the academician N. Ia. Marr] (Leningrad: Izd-vo AN SSSR, 1932).

20. Information from Tihanov, "Framing Semantic Paleontology," 364. Tihanov analyzes and contextualizes this edition as a "collective manifesto" of the Marr group (361–364). See also Clark and Tihanov, "Soviet Literary Theory in the 1930s," 131–133. A different view is presented in Perlina, *Ol'ga Freidenberg's Works and Days*, 117–124.

21. Freidenberg says "to open" the Department of Classical Philology, but the department existed before, and it was closed in 1926 (some sources list another date). From 1932 to 1937, the newly opened department belonged to a separate institution, the Leningrad Institute of Philosophy, Linguistics and History, or LIFLI; in 1937, it was incorporated into Leningrad University.

22. The story of Freidenberg's appointment and chairmanship has been discussed by scholars: Perlina in *Ol'ga Freidenberg's Works and Days*, 151–156; A. M. Skvortsov, "Kafedra klassicheskikh iazykov i literatur LIFLI: Istoriia sozdaniia i organizatsiia uchebnogo protsessa," *Philologia Classica* 15, no. 2 (2020): 394–410, and "Kafedra klassicheskoi filologii LGU v dovoennoe i poslevoennoe vremia," *Philologia Classica* 17, no. 1 (2022): 159–172. Along with Freidenberg's notes, Skvortsov used archival materials to reconstruct the circumstances of her appointment, and he provides a different perspective on these events than Freidenberg.

23. On the circumstances surrounding the publication of Freidenberg's *Poetics*, see: N. V. Braginskaia, ". . . Imeiut svoiu sud'bu," in *Poetika siuzheta i zhanra*, by O. M. Freidenberg (Moscow: Labirint, 1997), 421–433; Perlina, *Ol'ga Freidenberg's Works and Days*, 156–164.

24. Actually, the confiscation came several months after the publication. On this lapse in Freidenberg's memory, see Perlina, *Ol'ga Freidenberg's Works and Days*, 156n11.

25. There is some confusion about the dating of these events. From the family correspondence, it appears that Frank-Kamenetsky was in Moscow not in early

November but early October. See commentary to "Boris Pasternak—Ol'ga Freidenberg: Pis'ma i vospominaniia," eds. E. V. Pasternak, E. B. Pasternak, and N. V. Braginskaia, *Druzhba narodov*, no. 8 (1988): 299.

26. There is conflicting information on Musya's full name, which Freidenberg does not mention. One source lists her name as "M. Shmidt" in one case and "Maria Nikolaevna Filonenko" in another. See introduction and commentary to: Boris Pasternak, *Pozhiznennaia priviazannost'*, 14 and 403 (note 1 in chapter 6).

27. Freidenberg's last known letter to Leonid Pasternak, who was still in Berlin, telling her uncle of Frank-Kamenetsky's death, was written in July 1937. The correspondence has been published: "Iz semeinoi perepiski Pasternakov: Pis'ma O. M. and A. O. Freidenberg k rodnym v Germanii," eds. N. Kostenko and L. Fleishman, in *Novoe o Pasternakakh. Materialy Pasternakovskoi konferentsii 2015 goda v Stanforde*, ed. L. Fleishman (Moscow: Azbukovnik, 2017), 21–155.

28. As an example of publications drawn from the archives of the Soviet state security, see Vitaly Shentalinsky, *Arrested Voices: Resurrecting the Disappeared Writers of the Soviet Regime*, with an introduction by Robert Conquest (New York: Free Press, 1996), first published in Russian in 1995.

5. The Mythopolitical Theory of Olga Freidenberg in the Context of the Political Thought of Her Time

1. Hannah Arendt, *The Origins of Totalitarianism*, new ed. with added prefaces (New York: Harcourt Brace Jovanovich, 1973). Here and throughout this chapter, page numbers are given in the text.

2. Scholars have noted the significance of Arendt's insistence on the novelty of totalitarianism in comparison to previously existing forms of government. For this and other interpretations of Arendt, I relied on: Margaret Canovan, *Hannah Arendt: A Reinterpretation of Her Political Thought* (Cambridge: Cambridge University Press, 1992); Margaret Canovan, "Arendt's Theory of Totalitarianism: A Reassessment," in *The Cambridge Companion to Hannah Arendt*, ed. Dana Villa (Cambridge: Cambridge University Press, 2000); Dana Villa, *Arendt* (London and New York: Routledge, 2021).

3. Canovan noted Arendt's use of Montesquieu's formulation in *Hannah Arendt*, 87.

4. Giorgio Agamben, *Homo Sacer: Sovereign Power and Bare Life* [in Italian 1995], trans. Daniel Heller-Roazen (Stanford, CA: Stanford University Press, 1998), 86. Agamben used Arendt's idea of the concentration camp as a laboratory of totalitarianism, as well as observations on the biological life she offered in her later study, *The Human Condition*. But Agamben claimed that a biopolitical perspective is absent in Arendt's postwar studies of totalitarianism (Agamben, *Homo Sacer*, 71). However, in her *Origins of Totalitarianism*, Arendt writes about the Nazi camps as a place in which, in contrast to the situation of forced labor, the inmate has no right over his own body (444), and she develops this idea by suggesting that the forms of manipulating the body used in the camps serve the purpose of destroying the human personality (453).

5. The uses of "biopolitics" in Lidiia Ginzburg's blockade notes have been analyzed by Irina Sandomirskaia (who used this term, which of course was unknown to Ginzburg). See Irina Sandomirskaia, "A Politeia in Besiegement: Lidiia Ginzburg on the Siege of Leningrad as a Political Paradigm," *Slavic Review* 69, no. 2 (2010): 317–322; Irina Sandomirskaia, *Blokada v slove: Ocherki kriticheskoi teorii i biopolitiki iazyka*

(Moscow: Novoe literaturnoe obozrenie, 2013), 249–264. Sandomirskaia draws a parallel between Giznburg's analysis and Arendt's (*Blokada v slove*, 179n10) and mentions Freidenberg's biopolitical ideas ("A Politeia in Besiegement," 318 and 318n40).

6. Arendt's essay "Ideology and Terror: A Novel Form of Government" (1953) was included in the 1958 and subsequent editions of *The Origins of Totalitarianism*.

7. In her book *Poetics of Plot and Genre*, Freidenberg mentioned Francis Macdonald Cornford's *Thucydides Mythistoricus* (1907), which focused on presenting the *History of the Peloponnesian War* as shaped by mythological and literary plots. Cornford described the method of "mytho-historia" as "the molding of a long series of events into a plan determined by an *art form*," as well as by forms borrowed from myth and theology. Francis Macdonald Cornford, *Thucydides Mythistoricus* (Philadelphia: University of Pennsylvania Press, 1971), 133–134. For this information, I am indebted to Boris Maslov.

8. L. Ia. Ginzburg, *Zapisnye knizhki. Vospominaniia. Esse* (St. Petersburg: Iskusstvo, 2002), 308. Sandomirskaia commented on the association between Ginzburg's idea about the universal betrayal and Hobbes's principle of the war of all against all (*Blokada v slove*, 246).

9. The interest in Hobbes and in the political uses of myth in the 1930–1940s has been discussed in: John P. McCormick, "Fear, Technology, and the State: Carl Schmitt, Leo Strauss, and the Revival of Hobbes in Weimar and National Socialist Germany," *Political Theory* 22, no. 4 (1994): 619–652. Another scholar linked such diverse thinkers as Walter Benjamin and Carl Schmitt on the basis of their shared interest in Hobbes: H. Bredekamp, "From Walter Benjamin to Carl Schmitt, via Thomas Hobbes," *Critical Inquiry* 25 (1999): 247–266.

10. Carl Schmitt, *The Leviathan in the State Theory of Thomas Hobbes: Meaning and Failure of a Political Symbol* [in German 1938], trans. George Schwab and Erna Hilfstein, foreword and introduction by George Schwab (Westport, CT: Greenwood, 1996), 80–81.

11. Schmitt, *The Leviathan*, 6, 19–20.

12. Leo Strauss, *The Political Philosophy of Hobbes: Its Basis and Its Genesis*, trans. Elsa M. Sinclair (Oxford: Clarendon Press, 1936).

13. Lidiia Ginzburg, *Prokhodiashchie kharaktery: Proza voennnykh let. Zapiski blokadnogo cheloveka*, eds. Emily Van Buskirk and Andrei Zorin (Moscow: Novoe izdatel'stvo, 2011); page numbers are given in the text. These quotes are from the notebooks dating to 1943–1945, mainly under the rubrik "Teoreticheskii razdel" (292–302, 569) and from notes around "Zapiski blokadnogo cheloveka" (423–433).

14. Schmitt, *The Leviathan*, 6.

15. Among German thinkers, Ernst Cassirer, Theodor Adorno, and Max Horkheimer believed that the revival of mythical thinking in the 1930s was a sign of regression in political thinking and behavior. McCormick commented on this in his "Fear," 626 and 647n19. The British political philosopher R. G. Collingwood published a book entitled *The New Leviathan, or Man, Society, Civilization, and Barbarism* (Oxford: The Clarendon Press, 1942), in which he argued that it was only in the middle of the twentieth century, with the Nazi rise to power and the war, that people were able to appreciate Hobbes's *Leviathan* for its extraordinary power (and danger), and he introduced the concept of the new "barbarism" when speaking about Hitler's Germany.

16. Ernst Cassirer, *The Myth of the State* (New Haven, CT: Yale University Press, 1946), 279, 282, 297–298. Written in 1942–1945, this work was published posthumously.

17. While Freidenberg most likely did not know Cassirer's *Myth of the State*, published at a time when foreign books did not reach the Soviet Union, she knew his earlier work, including *Language and Myth* (*Sprache und Mythos: Ein Beitrag zum Problem der Götternamen*, published in 1925) and *Philosophy of Symbolic Forms* (*Philosophie der symbolischen Formen*, 1925–1929), as did Israel Frank-Kamenetsky, who had introduced her to Cassirer. Freidenberg's scholarly debt to Cassirer has been discussed in Nina Perlina, *Ol'ga Freidenberg's Works and Days* (Bloomington, IN: Slavica, 2002), 99–115. Perlina draws a parallel between Freidenberg's treatment of myth in her notes and Cassirer's *The Myth of State*; see Perlina, 162–164.

18. Victor Klemperer, *Language of the Third Reich: LTI—Lingua Tertii Imperii: A Philologist's Notebook* [in German 1957], trans. Martin Brady (London: Bloomsbury, 2013). Perlina notes the parallel between Klemperer and Freidenberg in her *Ol'ga Freidenberg's Works and Days*, 187. As Perlina also notes, Freidenberg went further: her analysis of Stalinist language is a part of her inquiry into the semantics of cultural forms that characterized Stalin's regime (186).

19. The notion of "political religion" (formulated by historians in the nineteenth century and mostly applied to the Middle Ages) was used by Freidenberg's contemporaries (whose work she is unlikely to have known) to speak about the Third Reich; for example, Eric Voegelin, *Die politischen Religionen* (Vienna: Bermann-Fischer Verlag, 1938). The second edition appeared in Stockholm after the author escaped from Vienna. The concept has since gained prominence in discussing totalitarian regimes. Hannah Arendt did not accept the idea of a "secular religion" in application to totalitarianism.

20. The concept of *Weltlicher Herrscher*, which Freidenberg uses here, was applied to the rulers in the Holy Roman Empire, where a head of the state also fulfilled the functions of the head of the church.

21. For a list of those few memoirs and personal testimonies of the survivors of the Nazi and Soviet camps published by the late 1940s, which she consulted, see Arendt, *The Origins of Totalitarianism*, 439n120.

22. Ginzburg, *Prokhodiashchie kharaktery*, page numbers are given in the text. These are the notes from 1943–1945. Ginzburg uses the Russian word *chelovek* ("man") (referring to individuals of both sexes) in her blockade notes, entitled (in literal translation) "The Notes of a Blockade Man." By analogy, she speaks about "Soviet man," "fascist man."

23. Giorgio Agamben, *State of Exception* [in Italian 2003], trans. Kevin Attell (Chicago: The University of Chicago Press), 2005.

24. For a discussion of historical consciousness within the Russian intelligentsia, including Ginzburg's work, see Irina Paperno, *Stories of the Soviet Experience: Memoirs, Diaries, Dreams* (Ithaca, NY: Cornell University Press, 2009), 9–14, 41–43.

25. Dilthey's understanding of history in its relation to autobiography has been discussed in: Vincent Kaufmann, Ulrich Schmid, and Dieter Thomä, *Der Einfall des Lebens Theorie als geheime Autobiografie* (Munich: Carl Hanser Verlag, 2015), 12–13.

26. Karl Löwith, *Meaning in History: The Theological Implications of the Philosophy of History* (1949; repr., Chicago: University of Chicago Press, 1957), 58–59. On this

issue, see Jeffrey Andrew Barash, "The Sense of History: On the Political Implications of Karl Löwith's Concept of Secularization," *History and Theory* 37, no. 1 (1998): 69–82.

27. Hannah Arendt, *Life of the Mind* (New York: Hartcourt Brace Jovanovich, 1978), 216. Arendt also developed her critique of the idea of history as a teleological process in her famous essay "The Concept of History: Ancient and Modern," included in Hanah Arendt, *Between Past and Future* (New York: Viking Press, 1961).

28. Hannah Arendt, "Remembering Wystan H. Auden" [1975], in her *Reflections on Literature and Culture*, ed. and with an introduction by S. Young-Ah Gottlieb (Stanford, CA: Stanford University Press, 2007), 299.

29. Gary Saul Morson has called this type of thinking "semiotic totalitarianism." (The phrase upset some of his fellow Slavists, who took offense at the word "totalitarianism.") What he meant was a tendency to ascribe meaning to everything, to see every detail as a sign of an underlying order or system. It is "the assumption that everything has a meaning, relating to a seamless whole. . . . This kind of thinking is totalitarian in its assumption that it can, in principle, explain the totality of things; it is semiotic . . . in its approach to all apparent accidents as signs of an underlying order." Morson saw "semiotic totalitarianism" in the methodology of contemporary semiotics and some other theories of culture. Cited here from one of the expositions of this concept: Gary Saul Morson and Caryl Emerson, *Mikhail Bakhtin: Creation of a Prosaics* (Stanford, CA: Stanford University Press, 1990), 28.

30. Noted by Canovan, *Hannah Arendt*, 57.

6. "Conclusion" (1950)

1. In the last years of her life, after retiring, Freidenberg indeed worked on a monograph entitled *Obraz i poniatie*. Completed in 1954, it was packed in the iron chest with other unpublished manuscripts. Selections from this enormous and loosely structured book were prepared for publication by N. V. Braginskaia in *Mif i literatura drevnosti*, ed. N. V. Braginskaia (Moscow: Nauka, 1978; 2nd ed., Moscow, Vostochnaia literatura, 1998; 3rd ed., Yekaterinburg, Russia: U-Faktoriia, 2008). There is some evidence that she planned to return to her notebooks; see N. Iu. Kostenko, "Ia ne nuzhdaius' ni v sovremennikakh, ni v istoriografakh: istoriia arkhiva Ol'gi Freidenberg," *Ol'ga Mikhailovna Freidenberg v nauke, literature, istorii. Materialy XXIII Lotmanovskikh chtenii, Vestnik RGGU. Seriia "Istoriia. Filologiia. Kul'turologiia. Vostokovedenie"* 4, no. 25 (2017): 127n15.

2. Freidenberg is referring to the death of Khona Frank-Kamenetsky, who died in a traffic accident on June 4, 1937.

Index

Adorno, Theodor, 238n15
Agamben, Giorgio, 5, 13, 125, 141–44, 237n4
Akhmatova, Anna, 228n10
anticosmopolitan campaigns (campaigns against "the pernicious influence of the West"), 61–64; 85–87; 90–91, 219
anthropology, 5–6, 30–31, 33, 52, 58, 137–38, 222n9. *See also* ethnography
Apocalypse, 121, 124, 131, 136, 151. *See also* Last Judgement
archive
  the idea of, 60–61, 68–70, 73, 122, 144, 220
  Freidenberg's archive, 9–11, 20, 70, 73, 122, 149
Arendt, Hannah, 1–2, 5–8, 11, 13, 125–28, 130–31, 134–36, 138–39, 141, 143–47, 222n10, 237n4, 239n19
Aristotle, 5–6, 125–26, 128, 147
art, Freidenberg's conception of, 1–2, 18, 21–22, 38, 98–99
autobiography, Freidenberg's conception of, 2, 18, 22–23, 97–99
autoethnography, Freidenberg's use of, 4, 12, 31–32, 36
Azadovsky, Konstantin, 232n16, 233n21
Azadovsky, Mark, 62–63, 77, 86–88

B. (Freidenberg's beloved), 17–18, 23, 32, 50–51, 66–68, 72, 122–23, 217
Bachofen, J. J., 96
Bakhtin, Mikhail, 2, 10, 229n13
barbarism, 2, 25, 29, 137–38, 238n15. *See also* civilization, collapse of
Barthes, Roland, 24
Benjamin, Walter, 6, 49, 143, 238n9
Berdnikov, G. P., 84, 232n17
betrayal, 44, 83, 90, 121, 132
biopolitics, 6, 32, 128, 143, 237–38
blockade of Leningrad
  diaries of, 25
  historians on, 25
  memory of, 25–26, 227n4
  metaphor of (in Freidenberg's notes), 3, 28, 39–40, 55, 57, 91, 141–44
body politic (*corpus politicum*), 5, 11, 53–54, 121, 129, 132, 136–37, 146–47. *See also* Leviathan
Borovsky, Ia. M., 89, 151
Borozdin, A. K., 93–94, 97
Braginskaia, Nina V., 9–10, 222n6, 223n16, 234n6, 235n10, 235n14
Bukharin, Nikolai, 118
Bush, V. V., 94, 97

Cassirer, Ernst, 36, 96, 134, 137–38, 228n9, 229n12, 238n15, 239n17
civilization, collapse of, 31–32, 34, 43. *See also* barbarism
Clark, Katerina, 234n8, 235n14
Collingwood, R. G., 238n15
communal apartment, 7, 33, 52–53, 105, 129, 132–33, 142–43
concentration camp, 71–72
  Agamben on, 128, 141–44, 237n4
  Arendt on, 126, 128, 141–44, 147, 237n4
  city as, 71–72, 141–42
  as laboratory of domination, 6, 126, 141–44
  and siege, 3, 11, 27, 29, 44, 141
  as metaphor of Soviet life, 78, 89, 126
  university as, 78, 82, 89
Cornford, Francis Macdonald, 132, 228n7
cultural forms, 80, 98, 100, 102, 222n7, 239n18, 238n7
  form and content, 30. *See also* literary form

damage done to the author, 7, 10–11, 60–61, 81, 73, 82, 86
death and rebirth, 27, 36, 45–48, 64, 94, 123
defecation
  under coercion, 4, 32, 129
  in public, 33, 43, 57, 78, 142
Dementiev, A. G., 76–77, 80, 83–85, 232n17

241

INDEX

dependency, 4, 26, 36–39, 41–42
diary, Freidenberg's use of
   diary form, 13, 27, 56–58, 94, 194
   ethnographic diary, 34, 138
   retrospective diary, 3, 27, 31, 51, 228nn6–7
   diary-theory, 5, 12–13, 54, 57–58, 125, 138, 147–48
Dilthey, Wilhelm, 1–2, 22–23, 145
dishonor (loss of honor), 53, 76, 84–85, 87–88, 121, 127, 125
Dostoevsky, Fyodor, 78
Dovatur, A. I., 71, 121
Druzhinin, Petr, 10, 233n21

Egorov, Boris, 232n16, 233n21
Eikhenbaum, Boris M., 61, 65–66, 75–77, 86, 88, 225n25, 230n5
Engels, Friedrich, 130
l'état de siège, 5, 141–44
ethnography, Freidenberg's use of, 4, 8, 12, 30–31, 34, 58, 138, 140, 143. See also autoethnography
everyday, the (everyday life, byt), 5, 7–8, 11, 13, 26, 28–30, 31n, 32–33, 43–45, 51–58, 95, 106, 108–09, 126–31, 133, 143–44, 148
   Stalinist everyday, 6–7, 51, 54–55, 126–28
   everyday terror (terror bytovoi), 5, 55–58, 126–28, 148
   as deliberate system of difficulties, 4–5, 51, 54–58, 86, 127, 134
excrements (human waste), 8, 31, 33–36, 65, 82–83

Fadeev, Alexander, 62
fictitious world (official fictions), 29, 115–16, 126
Filonenko, Maria Nikolaevna (brother's wife, aka M. Schmidt), see Musya
Fitzpatrick, Sheila, 225n27
Foucault, Michel, 128
Frank-Kamenetsky, Dora, 109, 111
Frank-Kamenetsky, Israel (Khona), 16–17, 103, 109–13, 117–18, 123, 216–17, 229n12, 237n27, 239n17, 240n2
Frazer, James George, 96
Freidenberg, Alexander (brother Sashka), 14, 17, 19, 64, 95, 104–05, 107–08, 120–21, 150, 215, 217, 232n19
Freidenberg, Anna Osipovna (mother), 14, 18–19, 26–28, 38–43, 45–47, 74, 94–95, 98–99, 104–05, 109, 111–12, 150–51

Freidenberg, Evgeny (brother), 14, 19, 215
Freidenberg, Mikhail Filippovich (father), 14–15, 19, 74, 89, 95, 149–50, 215–16
Freidenberg, Olga Mikhailovna
   biographical information on, 14–17, 215–20
   as department chair, 16–17, 50, 77–79, 81, 83–84, 88–89, 100, 122, 149, 151, 217–19, 233, 236n22
   dreams of, 45, 49–50, 60, 67, 70
   as a Jew, 14, 19, 87, 116, 232n19
   reading list of, 96, 234n5
   reputation of, 2, 10, 104, 222n6
   as a woman, 32–33, 116
   works of: "The Acts of Paul and Thecla," 15, 96–98, 100–05, 215–16; *Image and Concept*, 17, 149, 219; *Lectures on Folklore of Classical Antiquity*, 46, 218; *Palliata*, 74, 219, 231n14; *Poetics of Plot and Genre*, 16, 36, 47, 79, 112, 116–19, 229n13, 238n7; *Sappho*, 74, 219, 231n14; *The Works and Days of Hesiod*, 123–24, 217
Führer principle, the (Führerprinzip), 138–41

Galerkina, Berta (Beba), 48, 50, 59–60, 76, 90, 230n4, 233n23
Geertz, Clifford, 34
genesis, 3, 16, 63, 78–80, 97, 99–100, 222, 234
genetic semantics, 3, 23, 100, 109
Ginzburg, Lidiia, 11, 19n, 31n, 42n, 47n, 125–26, 129, 132, 135, 142, 144, 224n24, 225n25, 237n5, 238n8, 239n22
Gogol, Nikolai, 19
Gukovsky, Grigory, 87–88, 225n25

Harnack, Adolf, 103–04
Hegel, Georg Wilhelm Friedrich, 69, 144–45
historical experience, 6, 13, 49
   anthropology of, 6, 222nn9–10
history, Freidenberg's conception of, 2, 6–7, 60, 69, 76, 82, 118–19, 144–46, 151
   future historian, 2, 5, 86, 118–19, 121, 131, 146
Hitler, Adolph, 11, 87, 124, 143, 145, 218. See also Stalin and Hitler
Hobbes, Thomas, 5–6, 125, 132, 134–37, 147, 238nn8–9, 238n15
Hoffmann, Stefan-Ludwig, 222n10
Horkheimer, Max, 238n15

INDEX

intelligentsia, 52–53, 93, 114, 130, 135–36

Kagan, Iudif' Matveevna (Nevel'skii), 10
Kagan, Matvei, 10
Kaufmann, Vincent, 227n4
Kerényi, Károly, 102
Khona, *see* Frank-Kamenetsky, Israel (Khona)
Kirov, Sergei, 16, 115–16, 217
Klemperer, Victor, 11, 139, 224n23, 239n18
Kostenko, N. Iu., 221n2, 223n13, 225n29, 226n1, 229n1, 233n1, 240n1

language, observations on, 139–40
Lapitskii, I. P., 88, 233n21
Last Judgment, 131, 146, 151
    Moscow Nuremberg as, 131, 144, 151
Lazurkin, M. S., 118
Leitenzen, Ts., 117
Lenin, Vladimir, 130–31
Lermontov, Mikhail, 19
Levi, Primo, 141
Leviathan, 6, 27, 42n, 134–38
    as symbol of body politic, 136
    and Tiamat, 136–38
Levinskaia, Irina, 10
Lévy-Bruhl, Lucien, 96, 229n12
Lifshits, Elena, 20, 37–38, 226n2
literary form, 3, 16, 22–23, 63–64, 71, 79–80, 98, 103. *See also* cultural forms
living dead, the (living corpse), 48, 50, 64, 86, 89, 120–21, 141–42, 147–48
Lotman, Yuri, 2, 9
love, Freidenberg's conception of, 23–24, 66–68, 110–13, 122–23
    love and death, 112–13
    love and work, 66, 83, 94, 124
Löwith, Karl, 6, 145
Lunacharsky, Anatoly, 101–04
Lurie, Solomon, 86, 88, 233n2

Machiavelli, Niccolò, 5, 125, 146–47
Makogonenko, G. P., 88, 233n21
Malinowski, Bronislaw, 31, 34, 36, 228n7, 229n12
Marr, Nikolai, 16, 87, 90–91, 99–101, 103, 112–13, 216, 219, 234n8, 235n10, 236n16
Marx, Karl, 130, 145
Marxism, 54, 107, 130–31
meaning, Freidenberg's conception of, 1–5, 13, 18–19, 22–24, 38, 68, 73–74, 98–99, 106, 110, 113, 146, 240n29

Meshchaninov, Ivan, 65, 231n8
metaphor, Freidenberg's use of, 3, 5, 8, 12, 27–29, 34–36, 39–40, 50–51, 53, 55, 78, 82–83, 89, 91, 120, 132, 134, 136, 138, 141–44, 147, 222n7, 228n8, 229nn12–13
Montesquieu, 127
Moreva, Natalia, *see* Vulikh
Morson, Gary Saul, 240n29
Moscow Nuremberg, 70–71, 122, 131, 144, 146, 151
Moss, Kevin, 234n9
Musya (brother's wife), 71–72, 104–05, 120, 217, 237n26. *See also* Filonenko, Maria Nikolaevna
myth, Freidenberg's use of, 3, 12, 27–28, 34–36, 43, 46–48, 79, 94, 96–98, 111–13, 121, 123–24, 131–32, 134–38, 222n7, 226n2, 229n12, 239n17
mythopolitical theory, Freidenberg's, 6, 12–13, 125

Naumov, E. I., 88, 233n21
Nikol'skaia, Olga Vladimirovna (Orbeli), 201
Nina (student), 28, 37
Norden, Eduard, 102
normalization, 29, 43–44, 142–44
Nourry, Émile (P. Saintyves), 102

Orbeli, Rusudan, 9, 149, 220

participant-observer, 4, 7–8, 31, 34, 58, 222–23n10, 228n7
Pasternak, Alexander, 15
Pasternak, Boris (Borya), 1–2, 9, 14–15, 19–23, 98, 101, 105, 218, 220
Pasternak, Elena Vladimirovna, 9, 220
Pasternak, Evgeny Borisovich, 9, 220
Pasternak, Leonid Osipovich (uncle), 9, 14–15, 17, 19, 101–3, 121, 215–18, 220, 223n17, 237n27
Perlina, Nina, 222n7, 226n3, 228n6, 231n11, 235n10, 235n14, 239nn17–18
Plato, 5–6, 125, 134
Poliakova, Sofia (Sonya), 48, 50, 59, 65, 76, 78–81, 90, 117, 149, 233n23
political religion (secular religion), 140–41, 239n19
political philosophy, Freidenberg's use of, 30, 143
Popkov, Pyotr Sergeevich, 32, 129
Propp, Vladimir, 62–63, 75–76, 225n25

INDEX

prorabotka, 62, 76, 85
Pushkin, Alexander, 18–19

Raisa (Shmidt, Raisa, friend), 38–39
repetition (in Freidenberg's notes), 7, 13, 27, 45, 54, 56, 70–71, 125–27
retrospective understanding, 12, 40, 95, 102–103, 112, 114, 116, 119. *See also* retrospective diary

Sandomirskaia, Irina, 42n, 225n24, 237n5, 238n8
Schmid, Ulrich, 227n4
Schmitt, Carl, 6, 134–38, 142–44, 238n9
semantic paleontology, 100, 112, 235n10, 236n20
semiotics (semiotic method), 4, 9, 106, 235n14
    semiotic totalitarianism, 240n29
Sharova (student), 84, 232
Shileiko, Vladimir, 229n10
Shishmarev, Vladimir, 62–63
Shklovsky, Victor, 233n4
Skvortsov, A. M., 230n2, 236n22
Slezkine, Yuri, 234n8
Spengler, Oswald, 96
squabble, 5, 8,10, 34, 50, 58, 61, 67, 82–83, 94, 122, 132, 146, 151
Stalin, Joseph, 5, 27, 38, 44–46, 48, 53, 55, 57, 63, 67, 70, 73, 83, 85, 87, 90, 93, 95, 99–100, 104, 112, 114–15, 117, 119–21, 126–28, 130–31, 136, 138–41, 150, 218–19
    Stalin and Hitler, 4–6, 17, 26, 29–30, 32, 74, 124, 126, 134, 138, 145
Stalinism, 2, 13, 16, 86, 125–29, 140, 142, 146–47, 150
    Nazism and Stalinism, 2, 13, 128, 225n28
Strauss, Leo, 6, 134–35
suicide, 64, 68, 74, 89
Sukhovo-Kobylin, Alexander, 107–08
surveillance, 7, 52, 127, 129–31, 133, 142–43, 146

Tamara (Petukhova, Tamara, friend), 38
teacher-student relationships, 20, 37, 48, 50, 59–60, 64, 72, 78–80, 82, 88, 90, 94–98, 101, 114, 117, 130, 133, 150, 230nn2–4
terror, 5, 17, 44, 55–58, 64, 82–83, 87, 109, 115, 117–22, 124, 126–28, 131–33, 135, 142, 145–46
Thomä, Dieter, 227n4
Thucydides, 132
Tiamat, 34–36, 134–38, 228nn9–10, 229n10
    and Leviathan, 136–38
Tihanov, Galin, 234n9, 235n10, 235n14, 236n20
time, 28–29, 49, 67, 102–103
Tolstoy, Ivan Ivanovich, 50, 80, 94, 97, 233n2
Tomashevsky, Boris, 77
Tronskaia, Maria Lazarevna, 50, 151, 225n25
Tristan and Isolde, 79, 111–13
Tronsky, Iosif Moiseevich, 50, 59, 66, 76–81, 83–85, 87, 89, 151, 232n16
twin (image/myth of), 19–20, 109, 226n2

underworld, 27, 35, 45–48, 67, 72, 136n
Usener, Hermann, 96, 102

Veselovsky, A. N., 62–63, 76–77, 79–81, 84, 96, 231n7
Voegelin, Eric, 239n19
Volin, B. M., 117
Vulikh, Natalia (née Moreva), 59, 76–81, 83–85, 90, 117, 139, 232n16

war of all against all, 6, 44, 82, 132–34, 147, 238n8

Zhdanov, A. A., 61–62
Zhebelev, S. A., 97, 104
Zhirmunsky, Victor M., 65–66, 75, 86–88, 225n25, 231n8, 233n2
Zoshchenko, Mikhail, 108

www.ingramcontent.com/pod-product-compliance
Lightning Source LLC
Chambersburg PA
CBHW031353230426
43670CB00006B/531